BRITISH COLUMBIA

from SCRATCH

RECIPES *for* EVERY SEASON

Along the Sea to Sky Highway from Vancouver to Whistler

DENISE MARCHESSAULT
&
CAROLINE WEST

BRITISH COLUMBIA
from SCRATCH

RECIPES *for* EVERY SEASON

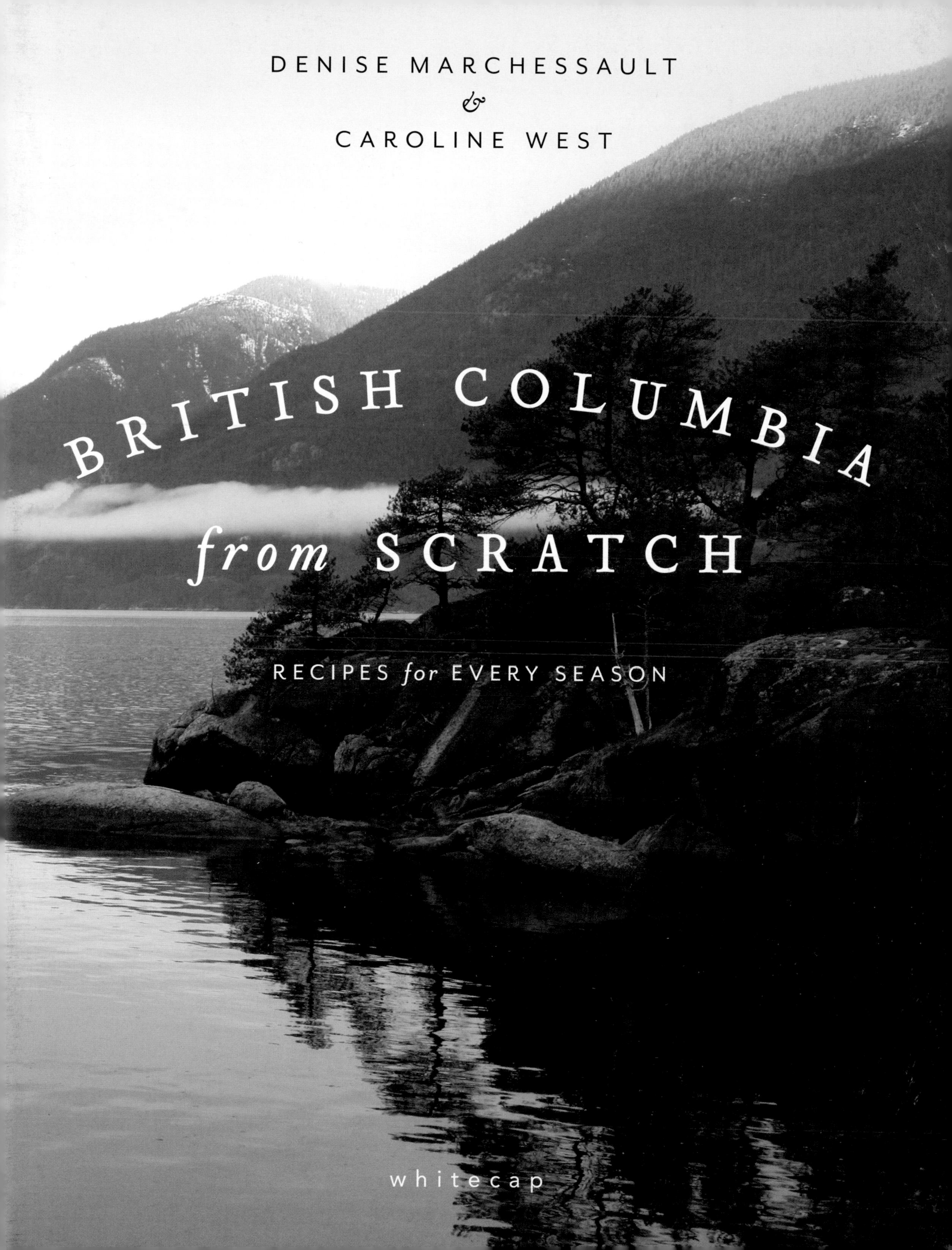

whitecap

Whitecap Books is known for its expertise in the cookbook market, and has produced some of the most innovative and familiar titles found in kitchens across North America. Visit our website at www.whitecap.ca.

EDITOR: Patrick Geraghty
DESIGN: Andrew Bagatella and Caroline West
COVER DESIGN: Andrew Bagatella
PHOTOGRAPHY: Caroline West
FOOD STYLING: Denise Marchessault
PROP STYLING: Caroline West
PROOFREADER: Jesse Marchand

Printed in China

Library and Archives Canada Cataloguing in Publication

Marchessault, Denise, 1959-, author
British Columbia from Scratch / text by Denise Marchessault; photography by Caroline West.

Includes index.
ISBN 978-1-77050-234-5 (paperback)

1. Cooking, Canadian--British Columbia style. 2. Local foods-- British Columbia. 3. Food--British Columbia. 4. Cookbooks. I. West,
Caroline, 1966-, photographer II. Title.

TX715.6.M3665 2015   641.59711   C2015-903079-X

We acknowledge the financial support of the Government of Canada, the Province of British Columbia through the Book Publishing Tax Credit.

17 18 19 5 4 3 2

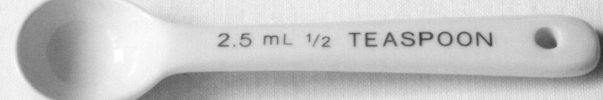

For

Claude Marchessault

and

Marco Khalil

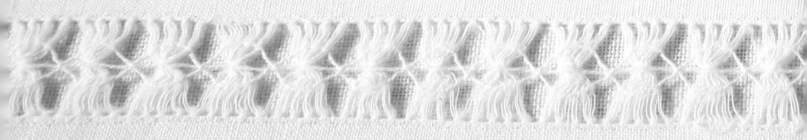

CONTENTS

PREFACE

IMAGINE A land so vast it could swallow France and Germany in a single bite. A land so wild over half of it is blanketed under dense forest, untouched by man. Picture snow-capped mountains and tumbleweed deserts, grassland cattle ranches and majestic fjords. From Arctic glaciers to the glittering towers of cosmopolitan Vancouver, British Columbia is Canada's portal to the Pacific and all its treasures.

BC's greatest blessing is its water: the countless rivers and lakes, and thousands of miles of zigzagging coastline. The salmon-rich Fraser River traverses the province from the Rocky Mountains to the ocean, nourishing countless farms and orchards along the way.

Just off the mainland are the lush and fertile expanses of Vancouver Island and Haida Gwaii, embracing a marine paradise amidst thousands of tiny coastal islands, both inhabited and wild.

Come join us at the banquet table that is British Columbia.

INTRODUCTION

....

EVERY COOKBOOK has a story. Ours began over a bowl of beef stew. At the time, I had a cooking school in Victoria (French Mint) and was hosting a Julia Child tribute. Caroline had been invited to photograph the event. When it was over, I offered her a steaming bowl of Julia's Beef Bourguignon. After she finished her stew she asked, "Have you ever considered writing a cookbook?" I smiled in response. I was familiar with Caroline's work and knew something beautiful was about to take hold. We like to think the spirit of Julia had a hand in our collaboration.

I prefer to cook food more rustic than styled and this meshes well with Caroline's design sensibility. She's one of those rare individuals who finds beauty in everyday objects and embraces life's imperfections. Whenever I'd cringe at something that didn't come out of the oven as perfectly as I'd hoped, Caroline would inevitably say, "I love it!" Indeed, she loves the charred bits, the wonky soufflés, the imprint that parchment leaves on a cake's edge. It's this authenticity that makes her images so real, so palatable you can almost taste them.

The book's theme was a natural choice for us. We were both drawn to the beauty of British Columbia and its fresh, wholesome food culture. I was born on Vancouver Island and had returned after a long absence with a renewed appreciation for the province's weather, its laid-back pace and quirky charm. Caroline had recently moved from Sydney, Australia, and was enjoying the province from a fresh new perspective, through the curious eyes of a photographer.

We set out to explore British Columbia, season by season. We harvested oysters from the shores of Mudge Island, picked peaches in the sunny Okanagan Valley, foraged for mushrooms in an ancient rain forest on Vancouver Island, gathered plump berries on Westham Island and watched farmers in the Fraser Valley flood their cranberry bogs.

The more we travelled, the more we appreciated our hardworking farmers. Once you've seen a cranberry bog flooded, it's impossible to enjoy a glass of cranberry juice without thinking of the effort that went into harvesting the berries. The mantra "Fresh, Local and Seasonal" may sound like a cliché but for farmers who depend on the sun and soil, it's their way of life. Cooking with the ebb and flow of the seasons makes good sense: food tastes better in season.

Whether you're an ambitious cook or someone who likes to putter in the kitchen now and then, we hope this book inspires you to explore our beautiful province and cook from its delicious bounty, whatever the season.

Okanagan Valley

ABOUT THIS BOOK

This book is a celebration of British Columbia through a cook's palate and a photographer's lens. It's a personal collection of recipes using local ingredients, rather than a compendium of wild, foraged or indigenous foods. Those topics have already been skillfully covered by chefs and authors I admire, whose books line my shelves.

The recipes in this book are completely biased; I included only foods I truly enjoy. Ultimately, we strove for a book as practical as it is beautiful, and to that end, we've leaned towards foods that are easily accessible.

British Columbia from Scratch is a nod to wholesome, unprocessed ingredients, simply prepared. Simple, however, is not always synonymous with quick. It's simple to make chicken stock, for example, but it takes time. Some recipes, like beef stew, require long slow braises, while others, like an omelette, can be whipped up faster than it takes to set the table.

Seafood lovers will find plenty of ideas for enjoying the Pacific's bounty: pan-fried in heaps of garlic, tossed in chowders, cured in salt, poached, breaded, baked—we love it every which way.

We've presented the pick of BC's summer fruit in pies, tarts, meringues, ice cream and sorbet. Fall and winter desserts show off local pears, apples and cranberries.

The Fraser Valley's meats appear throughout the book, as do the region's vegetables that make up vegetarian dishes like the award-winning Ratatouille Pie (page 90).

We've even included a chapter on all the essentials for getting back to basics. You'll find recipes for everything from stocks, to pasta, to honest-to-goodness real mayonnaise. We're fanatics when it comes to fresh, wholesome ingredients. Once you've tasted food cooked from scratch, we think you'll find it's worth the effort too.

A note about pantry staples used in this book: Kosher salt is used in savoury dishes (it's easier to pinch), table salt in desserts. Eggs are large and butter is unsalted. Recipes call for vegetable oil unless otherwise specified. Grapeseed oil is my go-to vegetable oil, but any mild tasting oil, such as canola or corn, are good choices too.

FOOTNOTE

By the time we were awarded the contract for this book, I was living on the Mainland in a temporary home with a kitchen that can only be described as dysfunctional. Caroline had to travel by ferry from Vancouver Island for each photo session, lugging not only her photography equipment but also her bulky collection of vintage crockery and fabric, unique to each recipe. It may reassure the reader to know that most of the food images in this book were prepared on a temperamental stove, duct-taped in place, without benefit of a door handle or oven window. In the end, I think my wonky little stove did this book a favour. I had to work a little harder to get the food just right and that resulted in solid recipes—no matter the stove.

SPRING

....

A season of growth and renewal. Food gets lighter and brighter. We celebrate the arrival of spot prawns, the first shoots of asparagus and the start of halibut season. Farmers' markets open, rhubarb is everywhere and the air is fragrant with budding flowers. Stroll under a canopy of Vancouver's cherry blossoms on a breezy day and you'll experience a pink snow flurry.

....

As soon as I put my winter jacket away, my tastes veer from hearty slow-braised meats to salads, seafood and delicate soups. I crave emerald fava beans, fresh asparagus and the season's best herbs, which I toss into anything that needs a refreshing lift.

Because BC's asparagus season is so fleeting, we covet this vegetable. Whenever possible, I show asparagus off to every advantage: puréed in creamy soups, tossed in salads and even peeled naked and draped alongside seared halibut. I have no shame.

The Creston Valley in southeastern BC has ideal conditions for growing asparagus: a fertile flood plain, rich with clay, silt and sand. It's a curious vegetable, popping leafless from the soil, but the harvesting is even more peculiar; asparagus pickers lie, belly down, on an open flatbed fitted with narrow planks, arms dangling at soil level, chins resting on pillows. A trailer pulls the prone workers through the fields as they snap off the asparagus with their fingers. Under ideal conditions, asparagus can grow anywhere from 1–3 inches (5–8 cm) per hour, obliging the pickers to cross the fields twice a day.

Although farmers' markets offer limited fare this time of year, BC's indoor gardeners, our greenhouse growers, spoil us with spring-ready bell peppers, lettuce, cucumbers and vine-ripened tomatoes. The Fraser Valley offers just the right balance of sunlight, warmth and cool ocean breezes— ideal conditions for greenhouse growers. Greenhouses do more than harness the sun, they use science and technology to grow vegetables hydroponically, on a fraction of the land. I've included recipes for stuffed bell peppers (page 34) and a Cucumber Sorbet (page 44) so refreshing you'll enjoy it all year long.

Spring brings firm-textured Pacific halibut, a clean-tasting fish with sparkling white meat, little fat and relatively few bones. I love it poached in fish stock (page 41), pan-fried as the centrepiece of a Niçoise Salad (page 30) and bundled in parchment and steamed to perfection (page 37). Don't be misled by those modest-sized fillets at the grocer, halibut are the world's largest flatfish, some of them heftier than the people who reel them in. (They're nicknamed whales and soakers for good reason.)

While I wait for summer fruit to ripen, I bake with rhubarb (see the lattice pie on page 55), and rely on simple baking staples for the season's desserts: farm fresh eggs, dairy cream and butter. You'd be surprised how many desserts you can bake with so few ingredients: jelly rolls, pastry straws, ice cream, creme brûlée and more. A sweet tooth knows no season.

Tulip fields in Agassiz

EACH SPRING, for up to three spectacular weeks, the Tulip Festival of Agassiz is in full bloom. About an hour and a half east of Vancouver, you'll find nearly 40 acres of tulips so vibrant you'll think you've landed in Holland.

The flowers generally bloom in April or May but if it's a warm spring you might see flowers in March. The tulip blooms are removed just before the petals start to drop (it's a bulb-growing operation), so be sure to check the festival's website for updates before you visit: *tulipsofthevalley.com.*

SPOT ON

SPOT PRAWNS are harvested from our coastal waters each spring, starting in May and lasting just six to eight weeks. They're wildly popular, not only because they're the sweetest, most succulent seafood imaginable, but because they're a sustainable seafood choice. Fishermen harvest prawns by placing baited traps along the ocean's floor, which is kind to the environment and all but eliminates unintended by-catch.

BC's spot prawns are the number one sashimi grade prawns in the world according to Mike McDermid, marine biologist and Ocean Wise sustainable-seafood champion. They're in heavy demand and most are exported overseas. Fortunately, organizations like the Chefs' Table Society and the Spot Prawn Festival make sure locals have a chance to enjoy them too.

When shopping for spot prawns, buy them live and kicking, otherwise select prawn tails. Prawns contain an enzyme in their carapace (head end) that causes them to deteriorate and turn mushy soon after they're dead. That's why it's important to purchase them live and cook them straightaway. Remove their heads (a swift twist does the trick) and save them for stock, unless you enjoy sucking the briny delicacy from the heads. Some aficionados swear it's the best part.

If you're purchasing prawn tails they should be translucent and firm and, as with all fish, they should not smell fishy or of ammonia. You'll have no problem identifying spot prawns by the white spots on their shells. Store prawn tails in the refrigerator nestled atop a colander filled with ice, with a larger bowl underneath to catch the melting ice.

To devein shrimp, run a sharp paring knife along the curve of a peeled shrimp, just deep enough to touch the vein (the dark thread of the digestive tract) and remove it with the tip of your knife.

Save prawn shells to make a tasty stock. Store in the freezer until you've accumulated enough to make a decent amount.

However you enjoy your prawns, in a chunky seafood soup or sautéed in butter, timing is everything—a minute or two is all you need to cook them to perfection. They'll be eaten faster than you can prepare them.

While spot prawns are BC's most celebrated crustacean, they're not the only game in town: sidestripe, pink, king (humpback) and coonstripe shrimp are excellent choices too.

Tofino, Vancouver Island

SPRING | *savoury*

....

CRAB CAKES *with* CILANTRO MINT SAUCE 14

SPOT PRAWNS *in* LEMON *&* HERB BUTTER 17

ASPARAGUS SOUP *with* LEMON CHÈVRE CUSTARD 18

BEEF CARPACCIO 21

CHICKEN BROTH *with* PORK *&* SHRIMP MEATBALLS 22

FRITTATA *with* RED ONION RELISH 25

RAVIOLI *with* PEA SHOOT PESTO 26

ASPARAGUS *&* LENTIL SALAD *with* HAZELNUT VINAIGRETTE 29

SALADE NIÇOISE 30

BEAN SALAD *with* PARSLEY DRESSING 33

SWEET BABY PEPPERS *with* GINGER *&* PORK 34

HALIBUT COOKED IN PARCHMENT *with* OLIVE *&* CAPER BUTTER 37

CREAMY TOMATO SAUCE 38

POACHED HALIBUT *in a* LIGHT BROTH 41

CRAB CAKES
with CILANTRO MINT SAUCE

makes 6 crab cakes

....

CRAB CAKES

1 cup (250 mL) finely diced Yukon
    Gold or new potato (cut into ¼-inch
    [6 mm] pieces)

½ lb (250 g) cooked crab meat
    (about 1 medium crab), picked over and
    flaked (chop larger pieces into ¼-inch
    [6 mm] pieces)

1 tsp (5 mL) freshly grated ginger

¼ tsp (1 mL) kosher salt

2 tsp (10 mL) fish sauce

2 tsp (10 mL) freshly squeezed lemon juice

1 tsp (5 mL) hot sauce

1 Tbsp (15 mL) finely minced shallot

2 Tbsp (30 mL) homemade Mayonnaise
    (page 296)

1 Tbsp (15 mL) plain yogurt

¼ cup (60 mL) fresh cilantro, chopped

BREADING

½ cup (125 mL) all-purpose flour

¼ tsp (1 mL) kosher salt

2 eggs, lightly beaten

¾ cup (185 mL) panko bread crumbs

Vegetable oil (for shallow-frying the
    crab cakes)

Cilantro Mint Sauce (recipe follows)

SPECIAL EQUIPMENT

Instant-read thermometer (optional)

I LOVE crab cakes that taste of sweet crabmeat, not the filler that binds them. These cakes include plenty of crab seasoned with fresh ginger, lemon and cilantro.

Crab can be expensive if you're not trapping your own. Feel free to substitute the crab with cooked shrimp or a combination of the two.

I've included a refreshing cilantro mint sauce that's so good you'll be slathering it on more than just crab cakes, but if you're in a hurry, a squirt of lemon or lime juice will do nicely too.

Crab cakes can be prepared and refrigerated up to 24 hours in advance before frying.

....

■ Cook potatoes just until tender. (Keep in mind that if the potatoes are not finely diced, the cakes will not hold together.) In a medium bowl, gently combine the potatoes with the rest of the crab cake ingredients. Carefully shape the mixture into 6 cakes about 2½ inches (6 cm) in diameter, without compressing them too much. Cover with plastic wrap and refrigerate for at least 30 minutes.

Place 3 shallow bowls on your work surface: place the flour and salt into the first bowl, the eggs into the second and the panko bread crumbs into the third.

Working with 1 chilled cake at a time: dredge first in the flour, then gently coat with eggs and finally with panko. If a cake starts to fall apart, reshape and recoat it in the breading mixture. Cover and refrigerate at least 1 hour, or up to 24 hours, before frying.

When ready to fry the crab cakes, pour enough oil in a heavy skillet to cover the cakes halfway. Bring the oil slowly to temperature until an instant-read thermometer reaches 350°F (175°C) or when a cube of bread dropped in the oil turns golden within a minute.

Add the chilled crab cakes, being mindful not to overcrowd the pan, which will cool the oil temperature and render the coating soggy, rather than crisp. When the cakes have browned on one side, carefully turn them over with a pair of tongs and cook on the other side until golden.

Place the cakes on a paper towel and sprinkle lightly with salt while warm.

Serve immediately with Cilantro Mint Sauce (recipe follows).

. . . recipe continued

. . . Crab Cakes with Cilantro Mint Sauce (cont.)

CILANTRO MINT SAUCE *makes 1 cup (250 mL)*

½ cup (125 mL) fresh mint, finely chopped

1 cup (250 mL) fresh cilantro,
    finely chopped

1 tsp (5 mL) shallots, finely minced

½ cup (125 mL) plain yogurt

¼ cup (60 mL) homemade Mayonnaise
    (page 296)

2 Tbsp (30 mL) freshly squeezed lime juice

1 tsp (5 mL) fish sauce

2 tsp (10 mL) fresh ginger, finely grated

1 tsp (5 mL) hot sauce (such as Sriracha)

1 tsp (5 mL) kosher salt

1½ tsp (7.5 mL) sugar

SPECIAL EQUIPMENT

Food processor (optional)

■ Combine the sauce ingredients in a small bowl and mix well. Alternatively, toss everything in a food processor and purée until smooth, scraping down the sides of the bowl with a spatula. Taste and season with additional salt, if desired. Cover and store in the refrigerator until ready to use.

....

Crabmeat contains tiny bits of cartilage and shell. Your fingers are more reliable at detecting the light-coloured fragments than your eyes, so be sure to sift through the crabmeat with your fingers, one small portion at a time.

If using live crab, plan on a yield of about 25 percent meat per pound of crab. Cook live crabs in heavily salted, rapidly boiling water, allowing 7 minutes per pound. Plunge the boiled crab into ice water to prevent it from cooking further and to cool the shell before removing the meat.

SPOT PRAWNS
in LEMON *&* HERB BUTTER
makes 4 servings

¼ cup (60 mL) Lemon and Herb Butter
    (page 290)

2 lb (900 g) spot prawns, heads removed,
    shells peeled, tails intact (freeze shells
    for fish stock)

BRITISH COLUMBIANS look forward to spot prawn season like kids anticipate Christmas. We celebrate the haul at festivals with local celebrity chefs who demonstrate recipes and spark our imaginations with a broad palate of flavours.

You'll understand what all the fuss is about once you experience spot prawns' sweet and delicate meat. It's a short season, only six to eight weeks from May to June, so be sure to get them while they're fresh.

Some purists eat them raw, right off the boat. I prefer them cooked simply and briefly in a bit of flavoured butter.

However you decide to enjoy them, just promise me you won't smother them in cocktail sauce. That's no way to treat a gift from the sea.

....

■ Melt 1–2 Tbsp (15–30 mL) of the butter in a large nonstick skillet over medium-high heat. Working in batches, so as not to crowd the pan, cook the shrimp in the butter for about 2 minutes or until the shrimp are opaque in the centre. Transfer to a plate and repeat with the remaining shrimp.

Drizzle the shrimp with the pan's buttery juices and serve immediately.

ASPARAGUS SOUP *with* LEMON CHÈVRE CUSTARD

makes 4 servings

....

CUSTARD

2 oz (60 g) chèvre cheese

3 large eggs

1 cup (250 mL) light cream

5 tsp (25 mL) freshly squeezed lemon juice

1 tsp (5 mL) kosher salt

SOUP

2 bunches asparagus (about 1½–2 lb
  [700–900 g])

1 cup (250 mL) whipping cream

Kosher salt

2 cups (500 mL) chicken stock (page 257)

2 Tbsp (30 mL) freshly squeezed
  lemon juice

½ cup (125 mL) freshly chopped parsley

½ cup (125 mL) freshly chopped chives

SPECIAL EQUIPMENT

Food processor or blender

Six 3-oz (8 cm) ramekins or ovenproof
  containers

Ovenproof pan large enough to hold the
  ramekins and deep enough for the hot
  water to come halfway up the sides of
  the containers

*You'll have more custard than needed for the
soup, but it's difficult to make a smaller batch.
Leftover custard keeps for days in the fridge. It
can be served with salad, like a quiche, or simply
smeared on toast.*

I CAN'T think of a better way to celebrate the arrival of spring than with a delicate asparagus soup garnished with a velvety lemon custard.

I developed a fondness for savoury custards from award-winning Chef David Mincey who taught at my former cooking school, French Mint. David created custards in imaginative ways that added flavour and texture to soups, salads and appetizers (nothing like the dreary custards I remember from culinary school). Suddenly custards are cool again!

This soup could be modified to suit any season by replacing the asparagus with another vegetable; think broccoli in the summer, corn in the fall, root vegetables in the winter and so on.

....

■ Bring a kettle of water to a boil and preheat the oven to 325°F (160°C).

Pour the custard ingredients into a food processor or blender and mix until smooth. Pour the mixture through a fine-mesh strainer into a spouted container.

Line the ovenproof container with a small tea towel, then position the ramekins on top, leaving about a 1-inch (2.5 cm) space between each. Pour the custard into each ramekin and add hot water to the pan until it reaches halfway up the sides of the ramekins; be careful not to splash water into the custard.

Cover the pan with foil and poke about a dozen scattered holes into the foil with a skewer. Bake for about 20 minutes or until the custard is barely set and the centre is slightly wobbly.

While the custards are baking, trim the woody ends from the asparagus about 2–3 inches (5–8 cm) from the base and discard. Reserve 2 stalks for garnish and chop the remaining spears into ¼-inch (6 mm) pieces.

Combine the asparagus slices and cream in a medium saucepan and simmer, uncovered, over medium heat for about 30–40 minutes or until the asparagus is completely tender and the cream has reduced.

Steam or blanch the 2 reserved stalks until tender. Slice very thinly and and set aside for the garnish.

Transfer the asparagus and cream to a food processor or blender; add 1¼ tsp (6 mL) salt, the chicken stock, lemon juice and herbs. Purée until smooth.

Pour the puréed soup through a fine-mesh strainer into a clean saucepan, pressing the solids against the strainer with a ladle or spoon to extract as much liquid as possible. Discard the pulp.

Reheat the soup; the texture should be thick enough to lightly coat a spoon. You may have to adjust the soup's consistency—if too thick, add additional stock; if too thin, simmer until reduced and thickened.

. . . recipe continued

. . . *Asparagus Soup with Lemon Chèvre Custard (cont.)*

Taste and season with additional salt or lemon juice if desired.

Run a knife around the edges of the ramekins to loosen the custards, then invert them into warm soup bowls. The custards need not be hot.

Pour the soup around the custards and garnish with the reserved chopped asparagus.

BEEF CARPACCIO
makes 6 – 8 appetizer-sized servings

8 oz (230 g) beef tenderloin fillet

6 cups (1.5 L) salad greens

1 Tbsp (15 mL) sliced shallots

House Dressing (recipe follows)

1 cup (250 mL) fresh Parmesan shavings

Freshly ground black pepper

Fleur de sel

EVER WONDERED how to slice raw beef so thin it practically melts on your tongue?

All you need is a sharp knife, a sheet of plastic wrap and something with weight, like the bottom of a small saucepan, to flatten the beef. Some cooks firm the meat in a freezer before slicing, but a sharp knife will do the trick without compromising the meat.

You can prepare and refrigerate individual servings of beef carpaccio in advance, covered with plastic. When you're ready to serve, simply remove the plastic and top the beef with freshly dressed salad, shaved Parmesan and fleur de sel.

■ Using a sharp knife, carefully slice the beef as thin as you can manage.

Place about 1 oz (30 g) sliced beef onto a square sheet of plastic wrap measuring about 6 × 6 inches (15 × 15 cm); cover with a second layer of plastic about the same size. Using the bottom of a small saucepan, gently pound the beef until it is paper thin. Remove the top layer of plastic and invert the beef onto a plate. Cover the beef and plate with a clean sheet of plastic, smoothing the plastic so that no air seeps in (the meat changes colour when exposed to air). Continue with remaining beef. Refrigerate for up to 24 hours.

Just before serving, remove the plastic wrap from the beef. Toss the salad with the dressing. Place a handful of salad on each portion of beef and top with sliced shallots, freshly shaved Parmesan, freshly ground black pepper and a pinch of fleur de sel. Drizzle any exposed beef with additional dressing if desired. Serve immediately.

HOUSE DRESSING *makes about ½ cup (125 ml)*

2 Tbsp (30 mL) white wine vinegar

1 tsp (5 mL) Dijon-style mustard

¼ tsp (1 mL) kosher salt

½ cup (125 mL) vegetable oil

■ To prepare the dressing, combine the vinegar, mustard and salt in a small bowl, then whisk in the oil in a slow narrow stream. Alternatively, combine the ingredients in a small lidded jar and shake well. Taste the dressing and add additional salt, if desired.

CHICKEN BROTH
with PORK & SHRIMP MEATBALLS
makes 4 servings

....

MEATBALLS (MAKES ABOUT 44)

4 oz (120 g) lean ground pork

6 oz (175 g) raw shrimp, peeled
    and finely diced

½ cup (125 mL) finely chopped bok choy
    or Napa cabbage

¼ cup (60 mL) finely chopped Shiitake
    mushrooms, stems removed

2 Tbsp (30 mL) chopped cilantro

1 tsp (5 mL) finely grated ginger

1 tsp (5 mL) finely grated garlic

½ tsp (2.5 mL) kosher salt

2 tsp (10 mL) vegetable oil

2 tsp (10 mL) sesame oil

½ tsp (2.5 mL) cornstarch

BROTH (MAKES ABOUT 5½ CUPS [1.4 L])

6 cups (1.5 L) chicken stock (page 257)

1 clove garlic, peeled and sliced in half

One 1- or 2-inch (2.5 or 5 cm) cube ginger,
    peeled and cut in half

1 stalk lemongrass, bottom third only,
    chopped into ½-inch (1 cm) slices

Kosher salt

1 spring onion, sliced thinly

SPECIAL EQUIPMENT

Meat or melon baller (optional, but nice to
    have if you're a stickler for uniformity)

....

*A small spoon is a great tool for peeling fresh
ginger: Gently scrape the ginger with the tip of
the spoon to remove the top layer of skin.*

....

*A microplane grater makes mincing ginger and
garlic easy and you'll never have to worry about
biting into a large piece of raw garlic.*

....

HOMEMADE STOCK is the foundation, the very heart and soul of this comforting soup. If you don't have the time to make your own stock, check out your local delicatessen or gourmet outlet; some retailers offer house-made stock.

The savoury pork and shrimp meatballs are a recipe from my friend, Chef Akemi Akutsu, who teaches Japanese cooking classes. Akemi uses a variation of this recipe for her gyoza dumplings and the flavours work beautifully in this Asian-inspired soup.

It's hardly worth making just a few meatballs; the recipe yields enough so that you'll have leftovers to freeze for the next time you're craving soup (unless you're my husband, who crams as many meatballs in his bowl as possible with little room for broth).

For those who don't eat pork, substitute ground turkey instead.

....

■ MEATBALLS Be sure to chop the ingredients finely, otherwise the meatballs won't hold together in your soup.

Combine the meatball ingredients in a medium bowl and stir until well mixed. Gently shape the mixture into balls with a 1-inch (2.5 cm) diameter, using your hands and being careful not to compress the mixture together too tightly.

If not serving immediately, cover with plastic and store in the fridge or freezer. (If freezing, place on a parchment-lined baking tray, leaving space between each. Freeze until firm and transfer to a freezer bag.)

BROTH Heat the stock in a medium saucepan over medium heat. Add the garlic, ginger and lemongrass, and reduce the heat to simmer for 20–30 minutes until the stock is aromatic.

To check the seasoning pour ¼ cup (60 mL) broth into a small cup and add a pinch of salt. If the flavour is lacking, continue to simmer and reduce until the stock is more concentrated. Season the broth with salt only after it has been reduced, otherwise it will become too salty.

Discard the garlic, ginger and lemongrass.

Just before serving, carefully lower the meatballs into the simmering broth, in batches so as not to crowd the pan. When the meatballs are cooked through, about 3 minutes, remove them with a slotted spoon.

Place 3–5 meatballs in each warmed soup bowl and ladle hot broth on top. Garnish with spring onions and serve immediately.

FRITTATA
with RED ONION RELISH
makes 1 frittata (2–3 servings)

....

1 Tbsp (15 mL) Clarified Butter (page 289)
  or half unsalted butter/half vegetable oil
½ cup (125 mL) chopped onion or shallots
6 eggs, lightly beaten
¼ tsp (1 mL) kosher salt
Freshly ground black pepper
½–1 cup (125–250 mL) cooked and seasoned
  filling (see Suggested Fillings below)
¼–⅓ cup (60–80 mL) cheese (such as
  crumbled feta, grated cheddar, Parmesan
  or goat cheese)
Red Onion Relish (recipe follows)

SUGGESTED FILLINGS
Roasted carrots, peppers, cauliflowers
  or potatoes
Diced potatoes, pasta or rice
Diced ham, chicken, bacon or sausage
Diced olives, cooked mushrooms or
  marinated artichokes
Handful of herbs and/or finely
  chopped spinach

I'VE BEEN serving my family frittata once as week for as long as I can remember. Sometimes it's served alongside the main dish, sometimes it is the main dish. It's a creative and tasty way to round up odds and ends in the refrigerator that might otherwise go neglected.

I love pairing eggs with leftover pasta and barely melted feta cheese, but your fridge may have a different character altogether. Whatever additions you include, make sure they are well seasoned.

Because I use whatever's available, I offer no firm recipe, only suggestions and guidelines.

All you need are eggs, a nonstick skillet and a little imagination.

Frittata is lovely served with Red Onion Relish (recipe follows).

....

■ Preheat oven to 350°F (175°C).

Heat the clarified butter (or butter/oil mixture, if using) in a nonstick skillet over medium heat and cook the shallots until softened, about 2–3 minutes. Add the eggs, salt and a bit of pepper, then add cheese and the filling of your choice, dispersing it evenly over the eggs. Cook partially covered, without disturbing, for about 3–5 minutes, or until the edges are firm. Remove the lid and transfer to a preheated oven for a few minutes until just cooked through.

Serve directly from the pan or slide the frittata onto a cutting board and cut into wedges. Serve immediately with red onion relish, if desired.

RED ONION RELISH *makes 2 cups (500 mL)*

2 Tbsp (30 mL) vegetable oil
2½ cups (625 mL) sliced red onion (about
  3 onions)
½ tsp (2.5 mL) kosher salt
½ cup (125 mL) red wine vinegar
2 Tbsp (30 mL) honey

■ Heat the oil in a large skillet over medium heat; add the onions, turning them with tongs to coat them evenly. Add the salt and cook until the onions soften, about 10–12 minutes, stirring occasionally to prevent burning.

Add the vinegar, scraping the bottom of the pan as you do so. Add the honey, reduce the heat and continue simmering until the liquid has evaporated.

Serve warm or at room temperature. Store in the refrigerator for up to 2 weeks.

RAVIOLI *with* PEA SHOOT PESTO
makes about 40 ravioli (3–4 servings)

....

1 lb (450 g) Fresh Pasta dough (page 270)
½ cup (125 mL) goat cheese
1 egg, lightly beaten
½ cup (125 mL) finely grated Parmesan
1 tsp (5 mL) freshly squeezed lemon juice
Pea Shoot Pesto (recipe follows)

SPECIAL EQUIPMENT
Ravioli stamp, mold or press, or a cookie
    cutter about 2½ inches (6 cm) diameter

IF YOU enjoy fresh pasta, you'll love these light ravioli stuffed with tangy goat cheese and topped with a vibrant pesto.

There are all sorts of gadgets for making ravioli (molds, rolling pins and presses), and I've tried most, but the best results come from my old fashioned, wooden-handled ravioli stamp.

It's helpful to have an extra pair of hands to manage the long sheets of fresh pasta. It's always more fun to make ravioli with a friend and pasta seems to taste better when shared with a cooking buddy.

....

■ You'll need to first prepare the pasta dough according to the instructions on page 270.

Roll the pasta dough into strips about 2 ft (60 cm) long and 5 inches (12 cm) wide (or wide enough to stamp out 2 ravioli, side by side). Place the strips onto a flour-dusted surface, and cover with plastic wrap or a tea towel until ready to use.

Combine the goat cheese, egg, Parmesan and lemon juice in a small bowl and mix well with a fork. Transfer the mixture to a small piping bag or fashion one with a plastic sandwich bag with a small hole snipped from a corner. This helps distribute the filling onto the dough evenly—and without a mess.

Ravioli is easy to make but it helps to first visualize the process; a strip of pasta will be dotted with the filling, at equal intervals, then covered with another strip of pasta and cut and sealed with a ravioli stamp or cookie cutter.

Place a strip of fresh pasta dough on a floured work surface. To help guide the filling onto the pasta, create a target by marking a very light impression of the ravioli stamp onto the pasta strip in equal intervals, without cutting into the dough. Squeeze a nugget of filling into the centre of each target, filling about half the impression. Cover with another sheet of pasta and stamp out the lumps of filling. (Note: If using a cookie cutter, you'll need to moisten the pasta around the filling with a damp finger or brush before enclosing the filling with the other sheet of pasta. This helps to form a seal and prevents leaking.)

Repeat with the remaining pasta, and re-roll any leftover trim.

Place the filled ravioli onto a parchment-lined surface and cover with plastic wrap. Continue with the remaining pasta and filling.

When ready to serve, bring a large pot of heavily salted water (2 Tbsp [30 mL] salt per 24 cups [6 L] water) to a gentle boil. Too rapid a boil can tear the ravioli. Working in 2–3 batches (to prevent the pasta from sticking together), boil the ravioli for about 3 minutes or until just tender (you'll need to test a ravioli at the 3 minute mark). Remove the pasta with a small strainer or a slotted spoon and transfer to a shallow bowl. Continue boiling the remaining pasta.

When ready to serve, portion the warm ravioli into bowls and top with (room-temperature) Pea Shoot Pesto.

PEA SHOOT PESTO *makes about 1 cup (250 mL)*

3 anchovies, lightly rinsed

2 Tbsp (30 mL) capers, lightly rinsed

1 clove garlic, peeled, roughly chopped

¼ tsp (1 mL) kosher salt

2 tsp (10 mL) freshly squeezed lemon juice

½ cup (125 mL) vegetable oil

½ cup (125 mL) walnuts, chopped

½ cup (125 mL) chopped pea shoots

½ cup (125 mL) chopped parsley

■ If you have a mortar and pestle, use it to pound the anchovies, capers, garlic and salt into a paste. (The salt acts as an abrasive.) Alternatively, chop the ingredients finely by hand. Scrape the mixture into a small bowl, add the lemon juice and stir to combine. Slowly add the oil and combine with a whisk. Toss in the walnuts, pea shoots and parsley. Taste and season with additional salt or lemon juice if desired. Re-mix the pesto just before serving.

ASPARAGUS & LENTIL SALAD *with* HAZELNUT VINAIGRETTE

makes 2 servings as a light lunch, 4 as a side salad

1 bunch asparagus (about 1 lb [450 g])

1¼ lb (600 g) fresh fava beans
   in pods (optional)

⅓ cup (80 mL) skinned hazelnuts, halved

1 cup (250 mL) cooked Puy lentils
   (sometimes called French green lentils)

1½ Tbsp (22.5 mL) finely sliced shallots

Hazelnut Vinaigrette (recipe follows)

2 cups (500 mL) mixed greens

1 Tbsp (15 mL) freshly chopped herbs
   (such as mint, parsley, dill, tarragon or a
   combination)

Sherry vinegar

Kosher salt

I LOVE the combination of firm lentils, delicate asparagus and toasted hazelnuts tossed with baby greens. Everything comes together with a light dressing made of sherry vinegar and mellow hazelnut oil.

If you can't find hazelnut oil at your local grocer, gourmet markets usually carry a larger selection of fine oils and vinegars. A good sherry vinegar is like wine, some are better than others. It's worth paying a little extra for quality vinegar, especially if you enjoy simple salads like this one.

I add fresh fava beans to this salad whenever I can find them at my local market—the season is brief so they're not always available. Fresh fava beans are a bit fiddly—the beans are removed from their pods (just like peas), then blanched and peeled. If you enjoy puttering in the kitchen, you'll be rewarded with the incomparable texture of these buttery emerald green beans.

Puy lentils are ideal for salads because they're firm and hold up well. Lentils cooked from their dried state are always preferable to tinned. If you've never cooked beans, see page 246 for details.

■ Trim and discard the woody ends from the asparagus, about 2–3 inches (5–8 cm) from the base. Blanch the asparagus in heavily salted boiling water until just tender, about 3–5 minutes. Retain the boiling water if using fava beans. Remove with a slotted spoon and transfer to a bowl of ice cold water. Drain the asparagus and chop finely.

If using fava beans, remove the beans from their pods then blanch the beans in the same boiling water as the asparagus for about a minute. Remove with a slotted spoon and transfer to a bowl of ice water. Peel and discard the thin outer layer from each bean.

Toast the hazelnuts in a dry skillet over medium heat until aromatic, about 2–3 minutes.

In a large bowl, combine the chopped asparagus, shelled fava beans (if using), lentils and shallots. Drizzle with enough hazelnut vinaigrette to moisten the ingredients. Taste the lentils and add additional sherry vinegar or salt, if desired.

Just before serving, toss in the mixed greens, toasted hazelnuts and chopped herbs.

Serve immediately with extra dressing on the side.

Hazelnut oil, like all nut oils, is fragile and should be stored in the fridge to prevent it from turning rancid too quickly.

HAZELNUT VINAIGRETTE *makes about ½ cup (125 ml)*

¼ cup (60 mL) sherry vinegar

½ tsp (2.5 mL) kosher salt

1½ tsp (7.5 mL) Dijon-style mustard

6 Tbsp (90 mL) hazelnut oil

■ To prepare the dressing, whisk together the vinegar, salt and mustard in a small bowl. Add the hazelnut oil in a slow, narrow stream while continuing to whisk. Alternatively, combine the ingredients in a small, lidded jar and shake well. Taste the dressing and add additional salt, if desired.

SALADE NIÇOISE
makes 4 servings

....

2 halibut fillets (about 8 oz [230 g] each)

1 bunch fresh asparagus (about 1 lb [450 g])

Kosher salt

½ lb (250 g) fresh green beans, tops trimmed

12-14 small red or new potatoes (about 1-1½ inches [2.5-4 cm] each)

4 large eggs

Caper Garlic Dressing (recipe follows)

1 Tbsp (15 mL) vegetable oil

1 cup (250 mL) ripe cherry tomatoes, halved

8 anchovy fillets, drained and rinsed

¼ cup (60 mL) caper berries

1 red onion, sliced

¼ cup (60 mL) Niçoise olives

Freshly ground black pepper

I'VE NEVER met anyone who doesn't enjoy this classic French salad. It's traditionally made with tinned tuna but I've used seared halibut instead.

This recipe calls for Niçoise olives—nutty, mellow-flavoured olives available in most speciality food shops. If you can't find them, Kalamata olives are a good substitute.

I've used capers in this recipe, as well as the larger, milder caper berries. Both are from the same bush (but rarely found in the same aisle at the store). Capers are the unopened flower buds, while caper berries are the fruit.

All but the fish can be prepared ahead of time. If you prefer your eggs slightly warm, as I do, boil them about 15 minutes before serving.

....

■ Bring the halibut to room temperature before cooking.

Peel the tough outer fibres from the asparagus with a vegetable peeler and snap off the woody ends. Reserve the trim (see sidebar). Place the peeled asparagus in a large pot of rapidly boiling, generously salted water (about 2 tsp [10 mL] kosher salt per quart of water) for about 3–5 minutes, or until just tender. Remove with a slotted spoon and plunge into a bowl of ice cold water to stop the cooking and retain the colour. Repeat with the beans, boiling for about 3–5 minutes, or just until tender. Drain the vegetables.

Place the unpeeled potatoes in a saucepan of generously salted water. Bring to a gentle simmer and cook until the tip of a knife can easily pierce a potato. Drain and rinse in cool water to prevent further cooking. Quarter or halve the potatoes.

Place the eggs in gently simmering water for 8 minutes, then plunge into cool water to prevent further cooking. Shell and quarter the eggs just before serving.

Smear 1 Tbsp (15 mL) Caper Garlic Dressing onto each side of the halibut fillets. Marinate for about 5 minutes, but not much longer or the acid in the dressing will start to "cook" or cure the fish.

Heat 1 Tbsp (15 mL) oil in a large nonstick skillet over medium-high heat. Add the fillets and cook about 3 minutes on each side, without disturbing the fish. Remove pan from the heat, loosely cover with foil and set aside. The fish will continue to cook with the residual heat.

Toss the asparagus, beans, potatoes and tomatoes, one variety at a time (to keep them looking their best), in just enough dressing to lightly coat them, about 1–2 Tbsp (30 mL).

Arrange the halibut in the centre of a large platter or portion onto individual plates. Surround with the dressed vegetables, eggs, anchovies, caper berries, onions and olives. Season with freshly ground black pepper if desired.

Drizzle the fish with additional dressing, if desired. Serve remaining dressing on the side.

....

What to do with all the asparagus trim? For a beautiful creamy green sauce, finely chop the asparagus trim and woody ends, rinse in a colander, then toss in a saucepan. Cover with cream and simmer about 40 minutes, adding additional cream as necessary to keep the asparagus trim covered. Strain the cream into a small clean saucepan (discard the trim) and season the sauce with salt and lemon juice. Thin with additional cream or chicken stock if desired. Refrigerate up to 3 days. Delicious warmed and drizzled over chicken breasts, fish or eggs.

....

CAPER GARLIC DRESSING *makes about 1¼ cups (310 mL)*

1 Tbsp (15 mL) Dijon-style mustard

¼ cup (60 mL) white wine vinegar

3 cloves fresh garlic, minced

2 Tbsp (30 mL) capers, drained and
    roughly chopped

¼ tsp (1 mL) kosher salt

¾ cup (185 mL) vegetable oil

■ Whisk together the mustard and vinegar in a small bowl. Add the garlic, capers and salt and slowly add the oil, mixing until well blended. Alternatively, combine the ingredients in a small lidded jar and shake well.

BEAN SALAD *with* PARSLEY DRESSING
makes 4–6 servings

....

1½ cups (375 mL) cooked garbanzo beans

1½ cups (375 mL) cooked black beans

1½ cups (375 mL) cooked white beans

Parsley Dressing (recipe follows)

Kosher salt

Lime juice

....

Herbs last longer if you roll them in a damp paper towel, seal them in a plastic bag and store in the fridge.

....

¾ cup (185 mL) freshly chopped flat
  leaf parsley

2 Tbsp (30 mL) freshly squeezed lime juice
  (about ½ lime)

½ tsp (2.5 mL) hot sauce (such as Sriracha)

1 tsp (5 mL) soy sauce

½ tsp (2.5 mL) kosher salt

¼ cup (60 mL) vegetable oil

1 Tbsp (15 mL) unseasoned rice vinegar

2 Tbsp (30 mL) homemade Mayonnaise
  (page 296)

SPECIAL EQUIPMENT

Food processor (optional)

THIS SIMPLE salad started off as a bean and cilantro salad, until I made it for my friend, Don, who has an aversion to cilantro. I replaced cilantro with parsley and found it so refreshing I decided to stick with it. You can, of course, use either herb.

Use canned beans if you're in a hurry, but starting with dried beans always provides more flavourful results. If you're not familiar with how to cook beans see the guidelines on page 246.

....

■ Toss the beans in a large bowl.

Pour the dressing over the beans and mix until well coated. Taste and season with additional salt or lime juice if desired.

PARSLEY DRESSING *makes about ½ cup (125 ml)*

■ Combine the dressing ingredients in a small bowl and mix well. Alternatively, toss everything in a food processor and purée until smooth, scraping down the sides of the bowl with a spatula.

SWEET BABY PEPPERS
with GINGER *&* PORK
makes about 12 mini peppers

....

12 sweet mini peppers (with a 1½ to
   2½-inch [4–6 cm] height)

½ cup (125 mL) cooked sushi rice

½ lb (250 g) lean ground pork

2 tsp (10 mL) finely grated ginger,
   preferably with a microplane

1 tsp (5 mL) finely grated garlic, preferably
   with a microplane

1 Tbsp (15 mL) vegetable oil

1 Tbsp (15 mL) sesame oil

1 tsp (5 mL) hot sauce (such as Sriracha)

1 tsp (5 mL) soy sauce

1 Tbsp (15 mL) unseasoned rice vinegar

2 green onions thinly sliced

1 tsp (5 mL) kosher salt

WHEN I first saw these sweet baby peppers at Granville Island Market in Vancouver, I knew they'd be perfect for bite-sized appetizers. Between 1½ and 2½ inches (3.8–6.3 cm) in height, these miniature peppers are ideal containers for savoury fillings.

I've combined ginger and pork with cooked sushi rice (because it's sticky and holds together nicely), but you can use any rice you have on hand.

For those who don't eat pork, substitute ground turkey instead.

....

■ Preheat oven to 350°F (175°C).

Slice off the tops of the peppers and reserve; carefully remove the seeds, being mindful not to damage the peppers. Slice just enough from the base of each pepper to keep it upright, without cutting all the way through the pepper.

Combine the remaining ingredients in a medium-sized bowl, stirring gently to combine. Stuff the raw filling into the peppers with a small spoon, being careful not to pack them too tightly or to damage the peppers.

Tuck the stuffed peppers, upright, in an ovenproof container lined with crumpled foil, adjusting the foil as necessary to prevent them from toppling over. Place the reserved pepper "tops" alongside the peppers. Pour about ½ inch (1 cm) water into the container to prevent the bottoms of the peppers from burning. Cover the pan with foil and roast in the oven just until the peppers can be easily pierced with the tip of a knife, about 25–30 minutes for mini peppers or up to 60 minutes for larger peppers.

Blot the cooked peppers dry on paper-towels before transferring to a platter. Serve warm or at room temperature.

HALIBUT COOKED *in* PARCHMENT *with* OLIVE *&* CAPER BUTTER
makes 4 servings

....

1 lb (450 g) fresh halibut, divided into
    4 equal portions, skin removed

1 cup (250 mL) cherry tomatoes,
    sliced in half

1 Tbsp (15 mL) olive oil

1 tsp (5 mL) fresh thyme leaves, finely
    chopped + 4 thyme sprigs

Kosher salt

1 sweet yellow pepper, cored and
    thinly sliced

1 sweet orange pepper, cored and
    thinly sliced

20 deli-style black olives, pitted

¼ cup (60 mL) Olive and Caper Butter
    (page 290)

1 egg white, lightly beaten

COOKING FISH in parchment is a fabulous way to keep it moist and tender. Tinfoil does the job too, if you don't mind the Girl Scout presentation. The real flavour of this dish comes from the savoury Olive and Caper Butter. If you're not a fan of olives, take a peek at the other flavoured butters on page 290.

Once the fish is in the oven call your guests to the table. You'll want to serve the packets as soon as the fish is done, otherwise they continue to cook outside the oven.

Serve the packets in shallow bowls and allow your guests to open their own and savour the fragrant steam before digging in.

This classic cooking technique works beautifully with any type of fish.

....

■ You'll need to first prepare the olive and caper butter following the instructions on page 290. Set aside.

Preheat oven to 375°F (190°C).

Bring the halibut to room temperature.

Spread the tomatoes on a parchment or foil-lined baking sheet, drizzle with oil and sprinkle with fresh thyme and a generous pinch of kosher salt. Roast in the oven for 8–10 minutes or until the tomatoes are softened and aromatic.

Cut 4 sheets of parchment measuring 16 × 12 inches (40 × 30 cm). Each sheet will be folded in half to create 4 "packets" that are 8 × 12 inches (20 × 30 cm) each, large enough to encase the fish and vegetables with room to spare.

Place a portion of halibut on the lower half of each sheet and season generously with salt. Divide and portion the sliced peppers, roasted tomatoes and olives on each fillet. Top with a 1 Tbsp (15 mL) disc of olive and caper butter and a sprig of fresh thyme.

Using a pastry brush, lightly coat the edges of the parchment with the beaten egg white. Fold the parchment in half to enclose the fish and press the edges together to form a seal. Crimp the edges to reinforce each packet then transfer to a baking sheet.

If not cooking immediately, refrigerate. Bring the fish to room temperature before placing in the oven.

Bake for about 7–8 minutes or until the packets puff up. Open 1 package to test for doneness (yours, naturally). Insert the tip of a knife into the fish; all but the centre should be opaque.

Serve unopened in shallow bowls and allow your guests the pleasure of opening the packets themselves.

CREAMY TOMATO SAUCE

makes about 2 cups (500 mL)

1 Tbsp (15 mL) vegetable oil

1 onion, diced

¼ tsp (1 mL) kosher salt

2 cloves garlic, finely chopped

One 14½-oz (411 g) can good quality
    tomatoes, whole, diced or crushed

1 cup (250 mL) chicken stock (page 257)

½ cup (125 mL) whipping cream

½ cup (125 mL) freshly grated Parmesan
    cheese, divided (half for the sauce, half
    as garnish)

Freshly cracked black pepper

1 tsp (5 mL) fresh thyme leaves

SPECIAL EQUIPMENT
Food processor or blender

THIS SUMPTUOUS tomato sauce is one of my favourite weekend indulgences. The sauce is enriched with chicken stock and cream, which impart a luxurious mellow flavour.

If you wish to double the recipe and freeze half the sauce for later use, do so before the addition of cream and Parmesan.

I ladle the sauce over fresh pasta (page 270) for a splendid appetizer or comforting lunch. It's also terrific on homemade gnocchi or drizzled over seared halibut.

You'll need ⅓–½ cup (80–125 mL) of sauce for each 4 oz (120 g) serving of fresh (uncooked) pasta.

Heat the oil in a medium skillet over medium heat; add the onion and salt. Stirring frequently, cook the onion for about 5 minutes or until it begins to brown. Add the garlic and stir until aromatic, about half a minute. Scrape the onions and garlic into a food processor or blender.

Add the tomatoes and their liquid to the onion and garlic mixture and purée until smooth. Place a fine-mesh strainer over a saucepan and pour the purée through it, pressing the solids against the strainer with a ladle or spoon to extract as much liquid as possible. Discard the solids (or freeze them for vegetable stock).

Add the chicken stock to the saucepan of strained tomatoes, bring to a boil, then reduce the heat to a simmer, over medium heat, stirring occasionally until the mixture has reduced and thickened, about 20–30 minutes.

Remove the saucepan from the heat and add the cream and ¼ cup (60 mL) Parmesan cheese. The sauce should be thick enough to just lightly coat the back of a spoon.

Taste and season with additional salt if desired.

Serve over fresh pasta and top each serving with the remaining Parmesan cheese, cracked black pepper and fresh thyme leaves.

POACHED HALIBUT *in a* LIGHT BROTH

makes 4 servings

....

2 lb (900 g) fresh halibut

¼ cup (60 mL) unsalted butter, divided

3 shallots, diced

1 small fennel bulb, finely diced, core
   included, fronds reserved for garnish

Kosher salt

½ cup (125 mL) dry white wine

6 cups (1.5 L) Halibut Stock (page 261)

1 sprig fresh thyme

1 Thai chili pepper or 2 Serrano peppers,
   halved and seeds removed

12 oz (360 g) green beans, washed
   and tops trimmed

¾ cup (185 mL) peas, fresh or frozen

POACHING FRESH halibut in a light broth is a fantastic way to enjoy this fish without masking its fine, delicate flavour. The success of this dish, not surprisingly, lies with the broth, made with halibut stock.

Fish stock is one of the quickest and least complicated stocks, but tends to be overlooked by home cooks, perhaps because fish bones are not openly sold (like soup bones for stock). They may be out of sight but they're available anywhere fresh fish is sold, just ask the shop manager.

When serving fish, I always call everyone to the table before the fish is ready. Fish takes only minutes to poach and continues to cook as it lingers in its broth. I remove the fish while it's slightly undercooked in the centre, so that by the time it reaches the table, it's cooked to perfection.

....

■ Bring the halibut to room temperature. Remove the skin and portion the fish into 4 servings.

In a wide saucepan deep enough to poach the halibut, melt 2 Tbsp (30 mL) butter over medium heat. Add the shallots, fennel and ¼ tsp (1 mL) salt and cook, stirring occasionally, until soft. Increase the heat and add the wine, scraping the bottom of the pan to loosen any bits stuck to the bottom; cook until almost no liquid remains. Add the stock, thyme and chili pepper and simmer until the stock has reduced to about 4½ cups (1.12 L). Strain and discard the solids, then return the stock to the saucepan and keep warm.

Drop the beans in a large pot of generously salted boiling water and cook until just tender, about 3–5 minutes. If the peas are fresh, cook them with the beans; if frozen, simply thaw. Drain the vegetables and toss them in a skillet with 1 Tbsp (15 mL) butter and a generous pinch of salt; stir to coat and keep warm.

Generously season the halibut with salt. Bring the stock to a very gentle simmer 160–180°F (71–82°C) and poach the fish in batches if necessary, to avoid crowding. The fish should be completely submerged in the liquid. Poach until the fish is slightly undercooked, about 5–7 minutes. Insert a knife into the thickest part of the fillet; all but the centre should be opaque.

Remove the fish with a slotted spoon and transfer to warmed serving bowls. Swirl the remaining butter into the fish broth. Taste and season with additional salt, if desired.

Pour the broth around the fish and top with beans and peas. Garnish with fennel fronds serve immediately.

SPRING | *sweet*
....

CUCUMBER SORBET 44

JELLY ROLL 47

PASTRY STRAWS 48

COFFEE ICE CREAM 51

SWEET WAFERS 52

RHUBARB PIE *with* APPLE & GINGER 55

CARAMEL CRÈME BRÛLÉE 56

HAZELNUT HONEYCOMB 59

CUCUMBER SORBET

makes about 2 cups (500 mL)

....

2 large English cucumbers
½ cup (125 mL) water
7 Tbsp (105 mL) sugar
Zest and juice from 1 lime
½ cup (125 mL) mint leaves, torn

SPECIAL EQUIPMENT
Electric ice cream maker
Food processor or blender

WHEN I first started making this refreshing sorbet, I served it in containers fashioned from hollowed cucumbers. I later moved to delicate sherry glasses with ridiculously small spoons. These days, I serve it by the jugful, often laced with gin. Whatever the container, cucumber sorbet is always a hit.

You'll need an ice cream maker for a fine-textured sorbet. If you don't have one, you can make a granita instead using a shallow container and a fork (instructions below). Sorbets are smooth and granitas are granular—both refresh.

You'll want to plan ahead. If using an electric ice cream maker, you'll need to freeze the machine's canister insert 24 hours before using.

....

■ Peel the cucumbers and cut in half lengthwise. With a small spoon, scoop out the seeds and discard. Chop the cucumber; you should have about 4 cups (1 L).

In a blender or food processor, purée the cucumber until smooth and pour the liquid and pulp through a fine-mesh strainer placed over a bowl. Extract as much liquid as possible by pressing on the cucumber pulp with the back of a large spoon or ladle. Discard the pulp. You should have about 1⅔ cups (410 mL) of cucumber juice. Refrigerate until well chilled.

In a small saucepan, combine the water and sugar and heat until the sugar has dissolved. Remove from heat and add the lime zest, lime juice and mint. When the syrup has cooled to room temperature, cover and refrigerate until well chilled.

Strain the mint from the syrup. Combine the cucumber juice with the syrup and mix well. Pour the mixture into a frozen ice cream canister and turn according to the manufacturer's instructions.

If you don't have an ice cream maker, pour the mixture into a wide shallow container and place it in the freezer. When it starts to form ice crystals, drag a fork along the bottom of the container to agitate and turn the mixture. Repeat this every half hour or so until the mixture is icy and fairly uniform.

JELLY ROLL
makes 1 jelly roll (10–12 servings)

6 eggs, room temperature, whites and
yolks separated

Pinch of cream of tartar

¾ cup (185 mL) sugar, divided

1 cup (250 mL) all-purpose flour, sifted
through a fine-mesh strainer

¼ cup (60 mL) powdered sugar + extra
for serving

1½ cups (375 mL) fruit jam or jelly

1½ cups (375 mL) whipped cream,
sweetened to taste (optional)

SPECIAL EQUIPMENT

12- × 16-inch (30 × 40 cm) rimmed baking
sheet lined with parchment paper

Electric mixer

*To bring eggs to room temperature quickly,
immerse them (in their shells) in a bowl of warm
tap water for about 5 minutes.*

FEW THINGS are as reassuring as a slice of cake and a cup of tea with an old friend.

This jelly roll is light, moist and simple to prepare.

The recipe came about after several attempts at buttery cakes that rolled beautifully but were too dense. I had read somewhere that butter was the secret to successful rolling, but with each version I reduced the butter until I eliminated it all together, producing a cake that is both delicate and supple. You'll want to splurge on the very best preserves—I especially love cherry and raspberry jam.

■ Preheat oven to 350°F (175°C) and prepare the baking sheet.

Whisk the egg whites with the cream of tartar in a meticulously clean bowl at medium speed until a network of tiny bubbles have formed, about 1 full minute. Gradually add ¼ cup (60 mL) sugar then increase the speed to high and whip until the whites have expanded and formed billowy, firm and glossy peaks. Be mindful not to over-whip, otherwise the whites will turn grainy and lose their shape.

In another bowl, whisk together the yolks and the balance of sugar until light and pale, about 3 minutes.

Working in 3 to 4 batches, fold the whipped egg whites into the whipped yolks with a large spatula, scraping the bottom of the bowl as you mix.

Gently fold in the sifted flour in 3 batches until well combined.

Pour the batter onto the prepared baking sheet and spread it evenly with a spatula. Here's a little chef's tip to help release the cake from the pan, and to prevent it from sticking to the pan's edges: create a little trench border in the batter by dragging a finger around the perimeter of the pan.

Bake for about 15 minutes, rotating the pan once during baking, until the top is golden and a skewer inserted into the centre comes out clean.

While the cake is still warm, run a knife along the edges and carefully transfer the cake from the tray onto a flat work surface, with the parchment facing down. Dust with sifted powdered sugar then place a tea towel or sheet of parchment on the surface of the entire cake.

Working from a short end, gently roll the cake around the towel or parchment, peeling away the baked parchment as you roll.

Leave the cake seam-side down for about 15 minutes.

Slowly unfurl the cake and discard the parchment or towel. Spread the cake with an even layer of jam, leaving a 1½-inch (3.5 cm) border at the end of the roll. Re-roll the cake, trim the edges and cover until ready to serve.

Just before serving, dust with sifted powdered sugar. Slice the cake and serve with lightly sweetened whipping cream.

PASTRY STRAWS

makes about 24 straws

....

1½ lb (700 g) chilled Handcrafted Puff
  Pastry (page 266)
2 Tbsp (30 mL) sugar
⅓ cup (80 mL) raspberry or strawberry jam

THESE LIGHT, crisp pastry straws are absolutely addictive. I've made these with jam, but they're delicious dusted with sugar and cinnamon too.

Pastry straws are a perfect finger dessert for parties. If you want to be a little showy, you can display them in a vase like a bouquet of flowers.

They can be made into a savoury appetizer too, sprinkled with Parmesan or spread with a garlicky pesto or tapenade.

Sweet or savoury, they're best when prepared with homemade puff pastry.

....

◼ You'll need to first prepare the puff pastry according to the instructions on page 266.

Preheat oven to 385°F (195°C).

Place a sheet of parchment on your work surface and sprinkle it with the sugar. Roll the puff pastry dough onto the sugar-dusted parchment and into a square, about 14 × 14 inches (35 × 35 cm) and ⅛ inch (3 mm) thick.

Spread the jam onto the puff pastry. Using a sharp knife, cut the pastry into long, ½-inch (1 cm) wide strips. If the pastry is too warm to cut easily, place it in the fridge for 20 minutes to firm the dough.

Grasping 1 strip of pastry from opposing ends, gently twist the strip of dough in opposite directions, to fashion a spiral, and transfer to the lined baking sheet. Continue with the remaining strips, leaving about ¾ inch (2 cm) between each spiral.

Cover the dough with plastic wrap and refrigerate until ready to bake.

Bake the chilled dough in a preheated oven for 10–15 minutes, or until golden, turning the spirals over once during baking.

COFFEE ICE CREAM

makes 4 cups (1 L)

....

¼ cup (60 mL) good quality instant
 coffee (some coffee shops sell
 individual portions)
1½ cups (375 mL) whole milk
1½ cups (375 mL) whipping cream
8 egg yolks
¾ cup (185 mL) sugar

SPECIAL EQUIPMENT
Ice cream maker

BOLD, SWEET and creamy, this homemade coffee ice cream is the perfect ending to just about every meal. And it's easy to make with an ice cream maker.

I've tried this recipe with all sorts of potent espressos but found, to my surprise, instant coffee crystals, made into a strong syrup, flavour the ice cream best.

You'll need to plan in advance. An ice cream machine's canister insert must be frozen at least 24 hours before using. The custard, too, must be prepared and thoroughly chilled before it's churned in the ice cream machine.

If you don't have an ice cream maker and are considering purchasing one, it's not likely to gather dust if you're an ice cream lover. Check out our summer dessert section for more inspired sorbets and ice cream recipes.

....

■ Place the instant coffee into a small bowl and moisten with 1 Tbsp (15 mL) hot tap water, adding more water as necessary to create a syrup. Strain, if not completely smooth, and set aside.

Heat the milk and cream in a medium saucepan over medium heat, until the mixture just begins to boil. Remove from the heat.

Whisk together the egg yolks and sugar in a medium bowl. Add about 1 cup (250 mL) of the warm milk and cream to the egg yolks and whisk until the mixture is loosened and well combined. Slowly pour this mixture into the saucepan of milk and cream and bring to a bare simmer, whisking constantly until the custard thickens and lightly coats the back of a spoon.

Flavour the custard with about 2½ tsp (12.5 mL) coffee syrup and mix well. Add additional coffee syrup to taste, by the teaspoon, until the custard is richly flavoured and the colour of a latte.

Pour the custard through a strainer into a bowl. Cool the custard quickly by placing the bowl into a larger bowl filled with ice. Cover and refrigerate until well chilled.

Pour the chilled custard into a frozen ice cream canister and churn according to the manufacturer's instructions.

Transfer to a freezer-safe container and freeze until ready to serve.

Leftover coffee syrup keeps well in the refrigerator until you're ready to make your next batch.

If you are wondering what to do with leftover egg whites, they can be frozen for up to 3 months in ice cube trays and used later with little compromise to their leavening properties.

SWEET WAFERS

makes about 20–22 wafers

....

½ cup (125 mL) unsalted butter,
    room temperature
¾ cup (185 mL) powdered sugar, sifted
3 large egg whites, room temperature
¾ cup (185 mL) all-purpose flour

THESE BEAUTIFUL French wafers, traditionally called *tuiles* for their resemblance to curved roof tiles, make a sweet crisp companion to custards and ice cream.

These ingenious little cookies are made by smearing thin circles of batter onto a parchment-lined baking sheet and cooking them until their edges turn golden. While the cookies are still warm and pliable, they're peeled off the parchment and shaped around a rolling pin or bottle until they've cooled and crisped into a lovely curve.

Sweet wafers can also be shaped around wooden spoon handles for cylinder-shaped cookies or pressed into empty muffin tins for sweet edible containers, provided they're molded while still warm.

The first batch is always a little tricky, but by the second you'll have figured out how to make them without burning your fingers.

....

■ Preheat the oven to 350°F (175°C).

If you're fussy about evenly sized wafers, draw a template of circles on the back of a sheet of parchment to guide you. If you are using a baking mat, draw the circles with a black marker and slip the parchment template beneath the mat so that the circles show through.

In a medium bowl, whisk together the butter and sugar until smooth. Add the egg whites, a bit at a time, mixing after each addition. Sometimes the butter and egg whites will separate and create lumpy curds, but the batter will smooth with additional mixing. Finally, add the flour and mix until smooth.

Cover and refrigerate for an hour or up to 24 hours.

Using an offset spatula, or the back of a spoon, smear about 1 Tbsp (15 mL) batter onto the parchment or baking liner to form a fine circle about 4–4½ inches (10–11 cm) in diameter. Repeat for a total of 4–6 circles, depending on the size of your tray, leaving space between each.

Bake until the wafers are golden-edged, about 6–10 minutes. Using a spatula or knife, carefully and swiftly peel the hot wafers off the baking sheet and drape onto a rolling pin (a wine bottle works too).

Gently press and shape the hot wafer around the rolling pin, using a clean tea towel as a protective barrier between your fingers and the hot wafer.

When the wafer has firmed, carefully slide it off your rolling pin. If the wafers become too firm before you've had a chance to shape them, return them to the oven briefly to soften them. Repeat with the remaining batter.

Cooled wafers can be stored in an airtight container for up to 4 days. If the wafers lose their crisp edge, place them on a baking sheet in a 350°F (175°C) oven for about 3 minutes.

....

Sweet wafers can be flavoured by adding vanilla, lemon zest, cinnamon, or cocoa power to the batter. You can also sprinkle the unbaked wafers with finely chopped nuts or sliced almonds.

....

RHUBARB PIE *with* APPLE *&* GINGER
makes 1 lattice pie

....

Flaky Pastry Dough (page 262)

5 cups (1.25 L) cubed rhubarb, pieces
    should be about ½ inch (1 cm) thick

2 Granny Smith apples, peeled, cored and
    diced into ½-inch (1 cm) thick pieces

1 tsp (5 mL) finely grated fresh ginger

⅓ cup (80 mL) cornstarch

1¼ cups (310 mL) sugar + 1 Tbsp (15 mL) to
    sprinkle on top of the pie

2 Tbsp (30 mL) unsalted butter, chilled and
    chopped into small pieces

1 Tbsp (15 mL) whipping cream or 1 egg
    lightly beaten, for brushing the pastry

SPECIAL EQUIPMENT

9-inch (23 cm) pie plate

FRESH GINGER imparts a lovely warm and spicy note to this classic pie.

If you enjoy baking, weaving together a lattice topping is entirely satisfying and easier than you might imagine. Don't fret if your lattice is a little wonky at first, it's all fixable and by the time you're on your second pie, you'll be a pro.

....

■ You'll need to first prepare the pastry dough according to the instructions on page 262.

Preheat the oven to 350°F (175°C).

Roll half of the pastry dough about ⅛ inch (3 mm) thick on a sheet of lightly floured parchment. Line the pie plate with the pastry, trim the edges, cover with plastic wrap and refrigerate.

Re-dust the same piece of parchment with flour and roll the balance of dough to about ⅛ inch (3 mm) thick. Shape into a circle with a 10-inch (25 cm) diameter, then cut into sixteen ½-inch (1 cm) wide strips (a ruler comes in handy for perfectly straight strips). Cover with plastic wrap and refrigerate.

Combine the rhubarb, apples, ginger, cornstarch and 1¼ cups (310 mL) sugar in a large bowl, stirring to coat the fruit.

Tip the fruit into the chilled pastry shell and mound the fruit up in the centre. Place a tea towel on your work surface and gently tap the bottom of the pie plate onto the towel to distribute and settle the fruit. Dot the fruit with the pieces of chopped butter.

To create the lattice top, place 8 strips of pastry loosely across the pie in one direction, leaving a ½-inch (1 cm) gap between each strip. Do not press the dough in place.

To weave in the first pastry strip, gently fold back every other pastry strip to the pastry's edge and lay a perpendicular strip of pastry over the remaining strips. Fold the strips back in place and you'll see that you've created your first weave.

Repeat the process with each new strip, pulling back alternating strips of pastry to weave in the strips of dough, allowing a ½-inch (1 cm) gap between each.

When the weaving is complete, pinch together the edges of the pie to form a seal. Brush the pastry with the cream or beaten egg and dust with 1 Tbsp (15 mL) sugar.

Transfer the pie to a foil or parchment-lined baking sheet and bake for 1¼–1½ hours, until the fruit is tender when pierced with the tip of a knife and the pie is bubbling over. Give the pie a half-turn once during baking and tent with foil when sufficiently browned.

Allow pie to rest for 1 hour before cutting in.

CARAMEL CRÈME BRÛLÉE

makes 8 crème brûlées

....

3 cups (750 mL) whipping cream
½ cup (125 mL) sugar + extra for torching
8 egg yolks

SPECIAL EQUIPMENT
Eight ½-cup (125 mL) ramekins or
    ovenproof containers
Baking dish deep enough to hold the
    ramekins, with at least a 1-inch (2.5 cm)
    space between each
Blow torch
Pastry brush

Wondering what to do with all those leftover egg whites? Try Sweet Wafers (page 52) or Cranberry Meringue (page 233).

I'VE ALWAYS loved the flavour of crème caramel but preferred the creamy texture of crème brûlée. This retro custard combines the best of both. And what better way to end a fine meal than to pass along a blowtorch?

Crème brûlée can be refrigerated for up to three days before serving—as if you needed another excuse to make it.

....

■ Preheat oven to 350°F (175°C).

Line the baking dish with a dishtowel to insulate and secure the ramekins.

Heat the cream in a small saucepan until it just starts to boil; remove from the heat.

Pour the sugar into a deep saucepan and moisten with ¼ cup (60 mL) of water. Cook the sugar over medium heat, undisturbed, until the sugar melts and turns deep golden, about 7–10 minutes. As the sugar boils you'll notice tiny bits of sugar sticking to the sides of the pan; to prevent the sugar from crystallizing, dip your pastry brush in water and brush the sides of the pan to remove them. When the sugar has turned deep gold in colour, remove the pan from the heat and swiftly and carefully pour the warm cream into the sugar. The mixture will bubble madly; when it subsides, stir the mixture. (If bits of caramel stick to the bottom, reheat the mixture and stir until the sugar has completely dissolved.)

In a large bowl, whisk the egg yolks until completely smooth then add 1 cup (250 mL) of the warm caramel cream and stir until combined. Add the remaining cream in a narrow stream, whisking until well combined. Strain the custard into a spouted container.

Bring a kettle of water to a boil.

Place the ramekins on the prepared baking dish positioned near the oven (for easy transport). Pour the strained custard into the ramekins, filling them almost to the rim. Pour the hot water into the baking dish around the custards, until the water reaches halfway up the sides of the ramekins, being careful not to splash water into the custards.

Cover the baking dish with foil then poke about a dozen scattered holes into the foil with a skewer or the tip of a knife. Carefully transfer the baking dish to the oven and bake for about 25 minutes for small or shallow ramekins, or about 40 minutes for larger containers. Rotate the pan halfway during baking.

Remove the custards from the oven when they're barely set and the centre is ever-so-slightly wobbly. Transfer the ramekins to a rack to cool before chilling in the refrigerator for at least 3 hours.

Just before serving, generously dust each custard with sugar. Tilt the ramekin from side to side to disperse the sugar. Using the blowtorch, burn (brûlée) the sugar until the top of each custard is nicely browned.

HAZELNUT HONEYCOMB

makes about 2 cups (500 mL)

....

1 cup (250 mL) sugar

½ cup (125 mL) honey

1 Tbsp (15 mL) white (light) corn syrup

1 Tbsp (15 mL) water

2 tsp (10 mL) baking soda

¾ cup (185 mL) roughly chopped
   skinned hazelnuts

THIS RECIPE pays tribute to Caroline's favourite treat, an Australian candy bar called Violet Crumble. Our Canadian equivalent is a Crunchie bar, minus the chocolate coating.

Hazelnut Honeycomb provides a sugar hit your dentist might not appreciate but it's a special treat and one that's strangely addictive. It's a quick, easy recipe and makes for a unique party snack, hostess gift or crunchy addition to ice cream.

This recipe uses light corn syrup but you can substitute dark corn syrup for a more pronounced flavour. Serve Hazelnut Honeycomb the same day you make it.

....

■ The recipe comes together quickly, so you'll need your equipment and ingredients measured and in place near the stove before you start. You're working with cooked sugar, which is serious business indeed, so read and visualize the entire process before you start.

Combine the sugar, honey, corn syrup and water in a deep, heavy-bottomed saucepan, and stir to combine. Heat the mixture over medium heat, brushing down any sugar that splatters on the sides of the pot with a pastry brush dipped in water.

The sugar will melt and turn pale, then amber—then black, within minutes, so man the stove without distraction. Pick up and swirl the pan occasionally to colour the sugar evenly.

When the sugar turns deep gold, remove the pan from the heat and swiftly and carefully add the baking soda and hazelnuts, stirring with a long spoon. The mixture will bubble madly to the surface of the pot.

Immediately pour the molten mixture onto the parchment-lined sheet or pan. The thickness of the crumble depends on how thick or thin you spread the hot molten candy as you pour it; aim for anywhere from ½ to 1½ inches (1–4 cm) thick. Leave to cool then chop or break into pieces.

Store in an airtight container and consume the same day.

Local hazelnuts were plentiful when I was developing recipes for this book. Sadly, as of this writing, hazelnut orchards have been ravaged by the Eastern Filbert Blight, an airborne fungus that's destroyed much of the province's orchards. Until a new blight-resistant seedling is developed, Ontario's hazelnuts will see us through.

SUMMER

....

Farmers' markets come alive, fruit and vegetable stands pop up, pick-your-own farms open their gates and seafood is plentiful. These are the days for picnics, cherries by the handful and homemade ice cream.

....

I love the summer ritual of hauling out the patio furniture and inviting friends for casual backyard picnics with Cranberry Fig Pulled Pork (page 88), Crispy Oysters (page 68), and Spicy Fish in Homemade Tortillas (page 84). Or bringing the party indoors with poached salmon in a delicate tomato broth (page 87) or a light seafood stew with a medley of salmon, halibut and spot prawns (page 76).

When shellfish is on the menu, it has likely been harvested from the pristine waters surrounding Comox Valley, Vancouver Island. Every June seafood lovers gather in Comox to celebrate the ocean's bounty at BC's Shellfish & Seafood Festival. Visitors can tour oyster farms, forage for wild edibles, meet growers and processors and learn about BC's sustainable aquaculture practices.

Much of our summer fruit comes from the Thompson-Okanagan, one of the largest fruit-growing regions in the country. The area is blessed with plenty of sunshine, fertile soil and a sloping terrain—near perfect conditions for orchards and vineyards. It boasts the largest production of sweet cherries, pears and apricots in Canada and is famous for its apples, peaches, plums, nectarines and grapes.

The Okanagan may have orchard fruit but the Fraser Valley has berries. BC's true blue valley is one of the top blueberry producing regions in the world, yielding more than 150 million pounds each year—enough for about 65 million pies. Fresh blueberries are harvested the old fashioned way: hand-picked, one by one. Processed berries (for preserves, juices and such) are harvested by machine.

There are plenty of places to pick berries in BC but Westham Island, just 30 minutes south of Vancouver, is a magical place worth the visit. The island is a rich nugget of rural land situated in the Fraser Estuary. To get there, you cross a century-old wooden truss bridge where a hamlet of colourful float homes cluster at the water's edge. Hand-painted signs point the way to fields of fruit—and vegetables, too. Emma-Lea Farms, a fourth generation family farm, provides fruit buckets and handy wagons to transport your berries back to the cashier for weighing. It's easy to feel like a kid again as you pull your little wagon along neat rows of strawberries, raspberries and blueberries as big as grapes. If you manage to get your berries home without eating them first, you'll enjoy arranging them on tarts, tossing them into custards and ice cream or piling them high on cheesecake.

SUMMER | *savoury*

VEGETABLES POACHED *in a* WINE BROTH
makes 6 cups (1.5 L)

....

BROTH

½ cup (125 mL) extra virgin olive oil + extra
   for drizzling

2 tsp (10 mL) whole coriander seeds

2 tsp (10 mL) whole cumin seeds

3 onions, roughly chopped

Four 1-inch (2.5 cm) pieces fresh
   ginger, peeled

2 Thai chilies, left whole, seeds intact or
   1 tsp (5 mL) hot red pepper flakes

4 cloves garlic, peeled and halved

1 large or 2 small fennel bulbs, roughly
   chopped, including core and stalks

4 cups (1 L) dry white wine

3 cups (750 mL) water

1 Tbsp (15 mL) + 1 tsp (5 mL) white
   wine vinegar

Bundle of fresh parsley stems (about 1 inch
   [2.5 cm] thick)

VEGETABLES

8 cups (2 L) raw vegetables (suggestions:
   zucchini, squash, fennel bulb, carrots,
   shallots, pearl onions, cauliflower or
   mushrooms), washed, peeled (and cored,
   if necessary) and cut into uniform slices

GARNISH (OPTIONAL)

1 large ripe tomato, peeled, seeded
   and diced

Olive oil

¼ cup (60 mL) freshly chopped parsley

POACHING VEGETABLES in an aromatic wine broth, called a court-bouillon, is a classic cooking technique I first learned in culinary school. It's a terrific way to prepare vegetables in advance and the broth is superb for poaching seafood too.

The vegetables make a lovely side dish, a fine addition to an antipasto platter or a light starter served over pasta or gnocchi. They can be served warm or at room temperature and they're especially flavourful when drizzled with a reduction of the wine broth and finished with olive oil.

Poached vegetables last up to a week, refrigerated and stored in their broth.

....

■ BROTH Heat the oil in a large soup pot over medium heat; add the coriander and cumin seeds, stirring to prevent burning. When the spices are aromatic, add the onions, ginger, chilies, garlic and fennel. Cook until the onion is translucent, about 6–8 minutes, stirring occasionally.

Add the remaining broth ingredients and simmer, uncovered, for 30–40 minutes. Pour the broth through a fine-mesh strainer into a clean saucepan and discard the solids.

VEGETABLES In a medium skillet, poach the vegetables, one variety at a time, in enough broth to completely submerge the vegetables. Simmer until the vegetables are cooked through but still slightly firm, adding additional broth as the liquid evaporates.

Firm vegetables, like carrots and fennel, can take up to 20 minutes to cook; tender vegetables like squash and pearl onions take far less time.

Remove the cooked vegetables with a slotted spoon and add the next variety to the pan, adding more broth as necessary to just cover the vegetables.

If not serving immediately, store the vegetables covered in the remaining broth for up to 1 week in the refrigerator.

SERVING When ready to serve, strain the broth into a medium skillet and transfer the vegetables to a serving dish. Heat the broth over medium-high heat and reduce the liquid until it has thickened slightly—just enough to lightly coat the back of a spoon. Taste and season with a bit of salt if necessary.

Add the diced tomato to the vegetables, if desired, and serve at room temperature, drizzling with a bit of broth and olive oil. Garnish with freshly chopped parsley.

CURED SALMON
makes 8–10 appetizer-sized servings

1½ lb (700 g) fresh salmon fillet, preferably
 Sockeye, skin on

Fennel fronds from 1 fennel bulb

2½ cups (625 mL) kosher salt

2½ cups (625 mL) sugar

1 Tbsp (15 mL) fennel seeds, crushed

1 fresh lemon, sliced

2 Tbsp (30 mL) capers, rinsed

1 shallot, thinly sliced

Freshly ground black pepper

CURED SALMON is a nice change from smoked salmon. If you've never cured fish before you'll be surprised how easy it is.

There are many ways to cure salmon, but the principles are pretty much the same: bury the fish in seasoned salt and sugar, add a few pounds of weight (compressing salmon in the cure helps to draw out its moisture) and refrigerate 24–48 hours.

In this recipe, salt is mixed with fennel fronds and fennel seeds, which impart a warm and subtle hint of liquorice. You could also use dill or parsley or a combination of your favourite herbs and spices. Just stay away from strong herbs like rosemary because they'll overpower the fish.

I serve cured salmon with crackers or dark rye and let guests help themselves to shallots, fresh dill, capers and lemon. Cured salmon will keep for about a week in the refrigerator, but never seems to last that long.

■ Coarsely chop the fennel fronds and set aside the bulb for another use. (Thinly sliced raw fennel is delicious in salads.)

Remove any pin bones from the salmon.

Toss the chopped fennel fronds into a bowl with the salt, sugar and crushed fennel seeds. (The salmon releases plenty of liquid as it cures, so select a container at least 2 inches [5 cm] deep.) Scatter half the curing mixture in an even layer in the container, nestle the salmon on top and cover with the balance of the mixture.

Cover the salmon and curing mixture with plastic wrap then place a flat object, like a small plastic cutting board, on top. Weight the board with 2–3 cans or other suitable objects, weighing about 5 lb (2.2 kg) in total. Refrigerate for 24 hours.

Remove the salmon from the curing mixture and rinse thoroughly in cool water. The salmon's texture will be firm. Pat completely dry with paper towels.

Using a sharp knife, slice the salmon thinly at a 45-degree angle, holding a corner of the skin to keep it in place. Discard the skin.

Serve with fresh lemon, capers, shallots and freshly ground black pepper.

CRISPY OYSTERS
makes 6–8 appetizer-sized servings

24 shucked oysters (about 2 lb [900 g])

¾ cup (185 mL) all-purpose flour

½ tsp (2.5 mL) kosher salt

¼ tsp (1 mL) freshly ground black pepper

Dash of cayenne pepper

3 eggs

1 Tbsp (15 mL) freshly squeezed lemon juice

2 Tbsp (30 mL) water

2½ cups (625 mL) panko bread crumbs

1 cup (250 mL) vegetable oil + extra
  as needed

Kosher salt

SPICY MAYO

½ cup (125 mL) homemade Mayonnaise
  (page 296)

1 tsp (5 mL) lemon juice

1 Tbsp (15 mL) hot sauce (such as Sriracha
  or Sambal Olek)

Freshly ground black pepper

SPECIAL EQUIPMENT

Instant-read thermometer (optional)

WHEN I think of oysters, I think of my pal Karri in her pink plastic Crocs, lugging a pail of oysters up a rocky embankment to her cottage on Mudge Island. These superb crispy fried oysters are Karri's recipe, a Mudge speciality.

Shallow-frying oysters transforms their slippery and chewy character (loved by many) into a texture reminiscent of a fine pâté. Raw oyster purists might balk but then again, they don't need a recipe.

Best served with spicy mayo and an ocean view.

Rinse the oysters and place on paper towels to blot dry.

Place 3 shallow bowls on your work surface. In the first bowl, mix together the flour, salt, black pepper and cayenne pepper. In the second bowl, whisk together the eggs, lemon juice and water. Place the panko breadcrumbs into the third bowl.

Working with 1 oyster at a time, dredge each oyster in the flour (shake off the excess), coat in the egg mixture and finish with the panko bread crumbs. Chill for 1 hour.

Bring the oil slowly to temperature in a medium heavy-bottomed skillet, until an instant-read thermometer reaches 350°F (175°C) or when a cube of bread dropped into the oil turns golden in a minute.

Working in batches so as not to crowd the pan, fry the chilled oysters until golden brown, about 4–5 minutes per side, adjusting the heat as necessary. (You may need to add more oil to the skillet.) Transfer the oysters to a paper towel to drain and sprinkle immediately with a pinch of kosher salt.

For the spicy mayo, mix together the mayonnaise, lemon juice, hot sauce and 1 pinch each salt and pepper in a small bowl. Serve oysters with spicy mayo on the side.

I love the challenge of shucking an oyster but after struggling to pry open a few, I don't mind turning my shellfish over to more experienced hands. I have friends who can shuck oysters with astonishing speed without breaking a sweat or damaging the meat.

If you're not accustomed to shucking your own but want to give it a go, first move away from any oyster-shucking show-offs. This will help you focus on the oyster rather than your soon-to-be-damaged ego.

Second, wear a protective glove or hold the oyster in a kitchen towel. When your oyster knife slips, and it will, you'll be grateful for the protection.

Holding an oyster knife in your dominant hand and an oyster in the other, work the knife into the shell's hinge. Slide the knife back and forth, without plunging it into the oyster, and twist it until you've pried the shells open. Remove the meat by sliding the knife along the shell to cut the muscle attached to it.

GARLICKY MISO BEANS

makes 6–8 servings

2 lb (900 mL) fresh green and yellow beans,
   tops trimmed

GARLICKY MISO DRESSING
2 cloves garlic, sliced
2 anchovy fillets, lightly rinsed
Kosher salt
2 Tbsp (30 mL) shiro miso (also referred to
   as white or light miso)
2 Tbsp (30 mL) white wine vinegar
1 tsp (5 mL) Dijon-style mustard
½ cup (125 mL) vegetable oil
1-2 Tbsp (15-30 mL) water

SPECIAL EQUIPMENT
Mortar and pestle (optional)

*Leftover anchovies can be used in Olive and
Caper Butter (page 290) or covered with oil and
refrigerated in an airtight container for up to
2 months.*

THESE LIGHTLY dressed beans show up on our dinner table more often
than any other vegetable during the summer. My daughter, Elise, can't seem
to get enough. Fortunately, she can whip up a batch of dressing faster than I
can cook the beans.

Miso, fermented soybean paste, enhances this dressing with a subtle,
earthy tang.

▪ Plunge the beans into a large pot of rapidly boiling, generously salted
water (about 2 tsp [10 mL] kosher salt per quart of water) for about
4–6 minutes, until just tender. Remove the beans with a slotted spoon and
transfer to a bowl of ice cold water; drain.

For the miso dressing, use a mortar and pestle to pound the garlic,
anchovies and a pinch of salt into a paste. (Alternatively, you can finely chop
the garlic and anchovies.) Scrape the paste into a small bowl and whisk in
the miso, vinegar and mustard. Add the oil in a narrow stream, whisking
constantly. Thin the dressing with a bit of water, if necessary. Alternatively,
combine the ingredients in a small, lidded jar and shake well.

Drizzle enough on the beans to just lightly coat them. Serve remaining
dressing on the side.

Serve the beans at room temperature. Leftover dressing can be stored in
the refrigerator up to 5 days.

DEEP DISH HAM & VEGETABLE QUICHE
makes 1 quiche (about 8 servings)

....

Flaky Pastry Dough (page 262)

2 tomatoes, cut into ⅓-inch (8 mm)
    thick slices

1 zucchini or 2 pattypan squash
    (cut into ⅓-inch [8 mm] thick slices)

2 Tbsp (30 mL) vegetable oil

Kosher salt

1 cup (250 mL) finely diced onion
    (about 1 onion)

1 cup (250 mL) finely diced carrots
    (about 2 carrots)

½ cup (125 mL) finely diced celery
    (about 2 stalks)

2 cloves garlic, finely chopped

1 tsp (5 mL) hot red pepper flakes

¾ cup (185 mL) finely diced black
    forest ham

1 cup (250 mL) crumbled goat cheese

½ cup (125 mL) freshly grated
    Parmesan cheese

10 large eggs

1½ cups (375 mL) whole or 2% milk

1½ cups (375 mL) whipping cream

Pinch of nutmeg

SPECIAL EQUIPMENT
9-inch (23 cm) springform pan

To make sure the vegetables fan out nicely on the
quiche, as pictured, select tomatoes and zucchini
about the same width.

LIKE MANY recipes, this summer quiche came about by accident. My family and I were staying in a beautiful 300-year-old home in Bordeaux during a home exchange a few years ago and I decided to make a quiche. I couldn't find a pie shell in my host's kitchen, so I used her springform pan instead. Not a novel container by any stretch, but it was my first attempt at a deep dish quiche and the results were memorable.

Caroline was working in London and was able to join us in Bordeaux. We enjoyed this impromptu dish and decided if a cookbook was in our future, this quiche would be proudly featured.

....

■ You'll need to first prepare the pastry dough according to the instructions on page 262.

Preheat oven to 375°F (190°C).

Roll out the dough to about a ⅛-inch (3 mm) thickness on a sheet of lightly floured parchment paper and form a circle. Transfer the dough to a springform pan, pressing against the sides to form a smooth fit; trim the dough to the top of the pan so that there is no overhang. Cover with plastic wrap and refrigerate for 1 hour. (Leftover dough can be frozen.)

Place the sliced tomatoes in a single layer on one of the prepared baking sheets, and the zucchini (or squash) slices on the another. Brush each sheet of vegetables with 1 Tbsp (15 mL) oil and season with a pinch of kosher salt. Roast the vegetables until they shrink and lose their moisture, about 15–25 minutes. Turn the zucchini over once during roasting, and remove when the edges have browned.

Increase the oven temperature to 425°F (220°C).

Heat 1 Tbsp (15 mL) oil in a large skillet and add the onion, carrots and celery, stirring to combine. Add ¼ tsp (1 mL) salt and cook over medium heat, stirring occasionally, until the carrots are just tender, about 5 minutes. Add the garlic and red pepper flakes, cook for half a minute until aromatic, then transfer to a medium bowl. Add the diced ham, crumbled goat cheese and ¼ cup (60 mL) Parmesan cheese, stirring gently to combine all of the ingredients.

In a large bowl, whisk together the eggs, milk, cream, 1½ tsp (7.5 mL) salt and nutmeg. Set aside.

Preheat an empty baking sheet in the oven. (The heat from the baking sheet helps to firm the pastry's base.)

. . . recipe continued

. . . Deep Dish Ham & Vegetable Quiche (cont.)

Sprinkle the base of the pastry-lined springform pan with 2 Tbsp (30 mL) Parmesan. Add the vegetables, ham and cheese filling, spreading it evenly around the pan. Sprinkle with 2 Tbsp (30 mL) Parmesan and pour the custard on top.

Top the custard with the roasted vegetables, overlapping and alternating the tomato and zucchini slices (they'll sink a bit). Sprinkle with the remaining Parmesan.

Reduce the oven temperature to 325°F (160°C) and place the quiche on the preheated tray. Bake for about 1½–2 hours or until the centre of the quiche is only slightly jiggly. If the pastry is browning too quickly during baking, cover loosely with foil.

Allow to cool for at least 2 hours before removing from the spring-form pan.

Serve at room temperature.

JALAPEÑO & CILANTRO COLESLAW
makes 5–6 cups (1.5 L)

5–6 cups (1.25–1.5 L) cabbage, thinly sliced (about ½ small cabbage)

3 green onions, thinly sliced

½–¾ cup (125–185 mL) homemade Mayonnaise (page 296)

2 tsp (10 mL) freshly squeezed lime juice

1 jalapeño pepper, seeded and finely chopped or 1 tsp (5 mL) hot sauce (such as Sriracha)

¼ tsp (1 mL) kosher salt

⅓ cup (80 mL) freshly chopped cilantro

COOL, REFRESHING coleslaw complements so many recipes in this book that we had to include it. Tuck it into fish tacos, pulled pork sandwiches or serve it alongside crab and leek timbales, potato croquettes or mushroom tarts. Cabbage never had it so good!

■ Toss the cabbage and green onions into a large bowl.

Whisk together ½ cup (125 mL) mayonnaise, lime juice, jalapeño pepper (or hot sauce) and salt in a small bowl. Scrape the mayonnaise mixture into the bowl of cabbage and green onions and toss to combine. Add additional mayonnaise, if the mixture is too dry. Taste the coleslaw and season with additional salt or lime juice, if desired.

Toss in the cilantro just before serving.

Cover and refrigerate for up to 2 days.

CHUNKY SEAFOOD STEW

makes 4 servings

....

2 Tbsp (30 mL) vegetable oil

½ lb (250 g) raw shrimp, shells removed and set aside for the broth

6 cups (1.5 L) Halibut Stock (page 261)

1 Thai pepper or 2 Serrano peppers, halved, seeds removed

1 bundle parsley stems (about as thick as a finger), tied together with kitchen string

1¾ cups (435 mL) diced red potatoes (in ½-inch [1 cm] pieces), skin on

½ lb (250 g) halibut, skin removed

½ lb (250 g) salmon, skin and pin-bones removed

4-5 slices uncooked bacon (about ¼ lb [125 mL]), diced

¼ cup (60 mL) dry white wine or water

2 medium onions, diced

Kosher salt

2 cloves garlic, minced

3 Tbsp (45 mL) Cilantro and Jalapeño Butter (page 290) or plain butter mixed with 1 tsp (5 mL) freshly squeezed lemon juice and a pinch of salt

THIS RUSTIC chunky stew combines the best of the season—halibut, salmon and spot prawns—in a flavourful fish broth made from halibut stock. The chowder is dairy-free but richly flavoured thanks to a bit of bacon and hint of pepper.

Call your guests to the table before you poach the fish—it only takes minutes to cook and you'll want to serve it straight away.

....

■ Heat 1 Tbsp (15 mL) oil in a wide saucepan over medium heat. Add the reserved shrimp shells and sauté for 1–2 minutes, being mindful not to burn the shells. Add the halibut stock, Thai pepper and parsley. Simmer until the liquid is reduced to about 4 cups (1 L). Use a slotted spoon to remove and discard the shrimp shells, pepper and parsley. Set aside the broth.

Place the diced potatoes in a saucepan of water with a generous pinch of salt and bring to a simmer. Cook until the potatoes are just tender when pierced with a knife. Strain and set aside.

Cut the halibut and salmon into 1½- to 2-inch (4 to 5 cm) chunks and bring to room temperature, along with the shelled shrimp.

Fry the bacon in a medium soup pot until completely cooked through. Remove and set bacon aside. Reserve fat for the next step.

Add ¼ cup (60 mL) wine (or water, if using) to the soup pot, scraping the bottom of the pan to dislodge any bits of bacon stuck to the pan. When the wine has all but evaporated, add 1 Tbsp (15 mL) bacon fat, the onions and a pinch of salt. Cook over medium heat, stirring occasionally, until the onions are completely soft.

Add the garlic and stir until aromatic, about half a minute.

Add the reduced stock, cooked bacon and another pinch of salt; stir to combine.

Before you poach the fish, be prepared to serve it immediately. Poaching takes only minutes, and you risk overcooking your fish if you leave it in the hot broth for too long.

Bring the stock to a simmer then poach the halibut for 2 minutes making sure the fish is completely sumberged; add the salmon, shrimp and cooked potatoes for an additional 2–3 minutes.

Test the fish for doneness with the tip of a knife; if not completely cooked, leave the fish in the hot broth for 1–2 minutes longer until cooked through.

Swirl a slice of flavoured butter into the broth, being careful not to break up the fish. Taste and season with additional salt if desired.

Ladle broth and fish into warmed bowls. Serve immediately.

SUMMER SQUASH

makes 4 servings

....

2 Tbsp (30 mL) vegetable oil

1½ lb (700 g) patty pan or zucchini squash,
   sliced ⅛ inch (3 mm) thick

Kosher salt

½ lemon, sliced into wedges

SPECIAL EQUIPMENT

Mandoline or hand-held vegetable slicer
   (optional)

THESE PAN-FRIED wafers of squash are so thin and delicate they crisp at the edges. It's a quick and easy way to enjoy the abundance of squash this time of year. A pinch of salt and a squeeze of lemon juice are all the seasoning required.

A mandoline or hand-held vegetable slicer comes in handy if you want perfectly even slices. Some box graters have a panel for slicing small vegetables, but a sharp knife and a patient hand does the job too.

You'll need to cook the squash in batches so as not to crowd the pan, which would steam, rather than brown them. Each batch takes only minutes, so arm yourself with a pair of tongs and mind the skillet without distraction.

....

▪ Preheat your oven to the lowest temperature to keep the squash warm.

Heat 1 tsp (5 mL) oil over medium-high heat in a nonstick skillet, tilting the pan to distribute the oil. Add just enough squash slices to cover the pan in a single layer. Cook until the edges just start to soften, about 1–2 minutes. Turn the squash with a pair of nonstick tongs, add a pinch of salt and cook just until the edges have darkened and the squash are paper thin, another 1–2 minutes.

Transfer to a plate lined with paper towels, add a pinch of salt and keep warm in the oven while preparing the next batch. Repeat until all the squash slices are cooked.

Serve immediately with lemon wedges on the side.

CRAB & LEEK TIMBALES

makes 8 timbales

....

6 Tbsp (90 mL) unsalted butter, divided
+ extra for molds

½ cup (125 mL) freshly grated Parmesan
cheese + extra for molds

2 leeks, white parts only, sliced thinly
(about 2 cups [500 mL])

Kosher salt

¼ cup (60 mL) all-purpose flour

1 cup (250 mL) whole or 2% milk

4 egg yolks, room temperature

2 Tbsp (30 mL) freshly squeezed
lemon juice

Pinch of nutmeg

¼ tsp (1 mL) hot red pepper flakes, or more
if desire

¾ cup (185 mL) cooked crab, picked
over (approx.)

6 egg whites, room temperature

Pinch cream of tartar

SPECIAL EQUIPMENT

Eight 6-oz (175 g) ramekins or
ovenproof containers

Electric mixer

THIS SAVOURY timbale combines sweet crab and slow-cooked leeks in a creamy sauce, lightened with whipped egg whites. If that sounds like the makings of a soufflé, you're right—it is a soufflé, but one that's upended to expose a cheesy crust. There's no need to sprint from the oven to the table to show off your timbale before it deflates—they're inverted onto a plate after they've settled.

Makes a lovely starter, light lunch or a welcome addition to a brunch buffet.

....

■ Brush ramekins with butter and generously dust with freshly grated Parmesan cheese; tap out excess cheese. Refrigerate until ready to use.

Preheat oven to 400°F (200°C).

Melt 2 Tbsp (30 mL) butter in a skillet over medium heat. Stir in the leeks, ½ tsp (2.5 mL) salt and a spoonful of water; cover and cook over low heat, stirring occasionally until very tender, about 30 minutes.

Melt ¼ cup (60 mL) butter in a medium saucepan. Add the flour and cook over medium heat, stirring constantly, about 3–5 minutes, until the mixture turns golden.

Add the milk and stir constantly until smooth and thickened. Remove the pan from the heat and mix in the egg yolks one at a time. Mix in the Parmesan, lemon juice, ½ tsp (2.5 mL) salt, nutmeg and hot red pepper flakes, as well as the cooked crab and leeks; stir until well combined. (If you're not serving the timbales immediately, the sauce can be covered and refrigerated. Bring the sauce to room temperature before proceeding with the recipe.)

In a meticulously clean bowl, whisk the egg whites with pinch of cream of tartar on medium speed until a small network of tiny bubbles have formed, about 1 full minute. Gradually increase the speed to high and whip until the whites have expanded and formed billowy, firm glossy peaks. Be mindful not to over-whip the whites otherwise they'll turn grainy and lose their shape.

Gently fold the egg whites into the sauce in 3 or 4 batches, mixing until well combined. Place the prepared ovenproof containers on a baking sheet and fill about three-quarters full with the sauce; smooth the tops with the back of a spoon.

Reduce the oven heat to 375°F (190°C) and bake the timbales for 25–30 minutes or until they have risen and the tops are golden.

Allow the timbales to rest and deflate for a few minutes, then invert onto a plate and serve warm.

VEGETABLE POT PIES

makes 6 pot pies

....

¾ lb (375 g) Handcrafted Puff Pastry
    (page 266)
½ cauliflower (about ½ lb [250 g]), florets
    broken into bite-sized pieces
2 medium carrots, peeled and diced into
    bite-sized pieces
3 Tbsp (45 mL) vegetable oil, divided
Kosher salt
½ small broccoli (about ½ lb [250 g]),
    florets broken into small bite-sized pieces
¼ cup (60 mL) unsalted butter
3 Tbsp (45 mL) all-purpose flour
2¼ cups (560 mL) whole or 2% milk
⅓ cup (80 mL) freshly grated
    Parmesan cheese
½ tsp (2.5 mL) hot sauce (such as Sriracha)
2 Tbsp (30 mL) freshly squeezed lemon
    juice (or to taste)
4 cups (1 L) very thinly sliced leeks
    (about 3–4 stalks, white and light green
    parts only)
1½ cups (375 mL) finely diced fennel
2 celery stalks, thinly sliced
2 cloves garlic, minced
½ cup (125 mL) dry white wine
½ cup (125 mL) frozen peas, thawed
1 egg, lightly beaten or 1 Tbsp (15 mL) cream

SPECIAL EQUIPMENT
Six 8-oz (230 g) ovenproof containers

....

*Leftover puff pastry dough can be used to make
Pastry Straws (page 48).*

....

THESE VEGETABLE pies rival chicken pot pies in our house. They're brimming with roasted cauliflower and carrots and bound in a creamy lemon sauce flavoured with fennel and leeks.

The pies are topped with puff pastry but flaky pastry would work nicely as well. Both the filling and pastry can be prepared in advance, making these pies ideal for guests.

....

■ You'll need to first prepare the Handcrafted Puff Pastry dough according to the instructions on page 266. Preheat the oven to 365°F (185°C).

Roll the pastry about ⅛ inch (3 mm) thick and cut into 6 shapes, making sure each shape is ½ inch (1 cm) larger than your containers' rim. If desired, cut six 1-inch (2.5 cm) circles for a pastry garnish. Cover with plastic wrap and refrigerate.

Toss the cauliflower and carrots in a bowl with 1 Tbsp (15 mL) oil and ¼ tsp (1 mL) salt. Spread the vegetables onto a parchment-lined baking sheet in a single layer and roast in the oven 30–40 minutes or until cooked through, stirring occasionally to prevent burning.

Remove the vegetables and increase the oven temperature to 425°F (220°C). Plunge the broccoli into a pot of heavily boiling salted water for about 3–4 minutes, until cooked but slightly firm. Drain and set aside.

Melt the butter in a medium saucepan over medium heat; add the flour, stirring constantly, until the mixture turns golden and smells nutty, about 3–5 minutes. Add the milk and stir continuously until thickened, about 5 minutes. Remove from heat and stir in the cheese, hot sauce, lemon juice and 1 tsp (5 mL) salt.

In a saucepan large enough to hold the vegetables and sauce, heat 2 Tbsp (30 mL) oil. Add the leeks and ¼ tsp (1 mL) salt, stirring to coat the leeks with oil. Cook over medium-low heat, partially covered, about 8–10 minutes, stirring occasionally.

Add the fennel, celery and ½ tsp (2.5 mL) salt and continue cooking, partially covered, for another 10 minutes, stirring occasionally to prevent burning.

Add the garlic and stir until aromatic, about half a minute, then add the wine and continue to cook until the wine has evaporated and no liquid remains. Add the sauce, cooked vegetables and thawed peas, and stir to combine. Taste and season with additional salt or lemon, if desired.

Ladle into ovenproof containers and top with a disc of chilled pastry, pressing the pastry firmly to the container's edge. Add a pastry circle garnish, if using. Score the pastry with a knife, brush with egg or cream and place on a baking sheet.

Bake for 15–20 minutes or until the pastry is puffed and golden, rotating the pan halfway during baking.

SPICY FISH *in* HOMEMADE TORTILLAS
makes 6 filled tortillas

6 Flour Tortillas (page 278)

3 cups (750 mL) Jalapeño and Cilantro
   Coleslaw (page 75)

SPICE MIX

1 Tbsp (15 mL) chili powder

1 Tbsp (15 mL) coriander

1 Tbsp (15 mL) ground cumin

1 Tbsp (15 mL) sweet smoked paprika
   (not hot)

1½ tsp (7.5 mL) garlic powder

1½ tsp (7.5 mL) sugar

2 tsp (10 mL) salt

1½ tsp (7.5 mL) curry powder

¼–½ tsp (1–4 mL) cayenne (adjust heat
   to taste)

6 fillets fresh red snapper (also called
   rockfish), halibut or lingcod (about 4 oz
   [120 g] per fillet)

2 Tbsp (30 mL) vegetable oil, divided

6 Tbsp (90 mL) unsalted butter or
   Compound Butter (page 290)

Freshly squeezed orange or lemon
   juice (optional)

2 small fresh nectarines or peaches, sliced
   just before serving

½ cup (125 mL) freshly chopped cilantro

*Leftover seasoning mix can be used to liven-up
chicken, chili, ribs, steak, eggs or just about
anything else that could use a flavour boost. Store
in an airtight container, away from direct heat.*

THIS IS my idea of a perfect informal summer meal: spicy pan-fried snapper, sweet nectarine and creamy coleslaw wrapped in a homemade flour tortilla. You'll needs loads of napkins, but it's worth the mess.

Homemade tortillas make all the difference to this dish and beat the store bought variety hands down.

All but the fish can be prepared in advance.

■ Prepare tortillas according to the instructions on page 278 and make the coleslaw using the recipe on page 75. Set both aside.

Combine the spices in a small bowl and set aside.

Run your fingers along the fish to check for bones; remove any with a pair of tweezers. Remove the skin from the fish with a sharp knife.

Place a fillet on a cutting board and lightly sprinkle each side with about ½ tsp (2.5 mL) spice mix. Too much spice will spoil your fish, so don't be tempted to saturate the fish. Repeat with the remaining fillets.

Heat 1 Tbsp (15 mL) oil in a non-stick skillet, over medium-high heat until the oil is hot and simmering, but not smoking. Working in batches, place the seasoned fish in the hot pan, without crowding, and cook about 2–3 minutes on each side, adding the remaining oil for the next batch. Remove the fish before it's completely cooked, add 1 Tbsp (15 mL) butter to each fillet and loosely tent with foil. The residual heat will finish cooking the fish.

Place a tortilla on your work surface; add a generous heap of coleslaw and top with the warm fish. Squeeze a bit of orange or lemon juice on the fish, if desired. Garnish with nectarines or peach slices and fresh cilantro. Wrap the tortilla around the filling and repeat with the balance of ingredients. Serve immediately.

POACHED SALMON
in a TOMATO WINE BROTH
makes 4 servings

....

1½ lb (675 g) fresh salmon (preferably
   from the belly, rather than the tail),
   pin bones removed
2 large fennel bulbs, including stalks
   and fronds
3 Tbsp (45 mL) vegetable oil
4 onions, roughly chopped
6 stalks celery, roughly chopped
2 Tbsp (30 mL) whole coriander seeds
Kosher salt
4 large very ripe tomatoes,
   roughly chopped
4 cups (1 L) dry white wine
4 cups (1 L) water
5 Tbsp (75 mL) Sun-Dried Tomato Butter
   (page 290) or unsalted butter

SIMPLE, FRESH and vibrant is how I'd sum up this dish. Salmon is gently poached in a light vegetable and wine broth and topped with a zesty sun-dried tomato butter. This recipe was inspired by an elegant dish my friend Chef Castro Boateng demonstrated at my former cooking school, French Mint.

Only the freshest fish will do in this recipe, so ask your supplier for the catch of the day. Salmon is lovely in this recipe but halibut, sablefish and lingcod are excellent choices too. Fresh is always best.

Both the broth and the tomato butter can be made well in advance.

....

■ Cut the salmon into 4 portions and remove the skin. Cover with plastic wrap and bring to room temperature.

Before chopping the fennel bulbs (for the broth), set aside 12 thin slices for the pan-fried fennel topping, as pictured. The fronds can also be used for garnish.

Roughly chop the remaining fennel, including the core, stalks and fronds. Heat 2 Tbsp (30 mL) oil in a large saucepan or stockpot (if you don't have one large enough, use 2 pans). Add the chopped fennel, onions, celery, coriander seeds and a generous pinch of salt. Cook the vegetables over medium heat for about 5 minutes, stirring occasionally to prevent browning. Add the tomatoes, stir and cook for another 1–2 minutes.

Add the wine and water, bring to a boil then reduce the heat and simmer, uncovered, for about 40 minutes. Strain the broth and discard the vegetables.

Pour the broth into a shallow saucepan, wide enough to hold the salmon in a single layer. Taste the broth and season with a pinch of salt. Reheat the broth and adjust the temperature to a bare simmer (about 160–180°F [71–82°C]). Do not boil the broth otherwise the fish will break.

Season the salmon with a generous pinch of salt and place it in the broth, making sure it's completely submerged. Gently poach until the fish is almost, but not completely cooked, about 5 minutes. (The fish will continue to cook as it rests.)

Transfer the fish to a plate or shallow bowl and top each portion with 1 Tbsp (15 mL) sun-dried tomato butter and loosely tent with foil. Swirl 1 Tbsp (15 mL) sun-dried tomato butter into the broth then taste the broth, adding additional salt if desired.

Heat 1 Tbsp (15 mL) oil in a small skillet over medium-high heat. Add the reserved fennel slices and cook briefly on both sides, until the edges are golden; add a pinch of salt.

Portion the salmon into 4 heated bowls. Ladle the broth around the salmon, add the seared fennel and garnish with fronds, if desired.

....

There are five species of wild salmon in British Columbia: sockeye, chinook (also called spring or king), coho, pink and chum. Chinook and sockeye are the most popular species, not only for their rich flavour but because they're forgiving to cook and hold up to just about every cooking technique. Pink and chum are often overlooked by home cooks but they're lovely delicate fish and definitely worth trying.

....

CRANBERRY-FIG PULLED PORK

makes about 12 servings

....

SPICE MIX

1 Tbsp (15 mL) cumin

1 Tbsp (15 mL) hot smoked paprika

1 tsp (5 mL) garlic powder

1 Tbsp (15 mL) chili powder

1 tsp (5 mL) kosher salt

1 tsp (5 mL) sugar

1 boneless pork shoulder
   (about 4 lb [1.8 kg])

SAUCE

1½ cups (375 mL) dried figs, preferably
   Black Mission

1 cup (250 mL) dried cranberries

1 Tbsp (15 mL) vegetable oil

8–10 slices uncooked bacon (about ½ lb
   [250 g]), diced

2 large onions, finely chopped

4 cloves garlic, finely chopped

¼ tsp (1 mL) kosher salt

One 27-oz (765 g) can puréed tomatoes

¼ cup (60 mL) tomato paste

3 Tbsp (45 mL) puréed or finely mashed
   chipotle peppers (from a small can of
   chipotle peppers in adobo sauce)

1 Tbsp (15 mL) red wine vinegar
   (not balsamic)

¼ cup (60 mL) soy sauce

1 Tbsp (15 mL) Worcestershire sauce

SPECIAL EQUIPMENT

Casserole pot, dutch oven or slow cooker
   large enough to fit the pork with about
   1 inch (2.5 cm) room to spare (about
   7 quarts [6.5 L])

Food processor or blender

....

Leftover chipotle peppers can be frozen in ice cube trays for later use.

....

THIS IS one of the greatest pulled pork recipes you will ever try, with beautifully balanced sweet-tart flavours from the classic marriage of fruit with pork. Though it can be tricky to achieve big flavours with streamlined techniques (a recipe tester quipped of my original, lengthy write-up, "I've had relationships that were shorter"), I've managed to keep things simple enough here so you can recreate this dish with ease.

I knew I succeeded when my friend Noreen announced: "Robbie and I are thinking of stealing this recipe to start a food truck. Best pulled pork ever!"

As with all braised meats, plan to make it a day or two in advance. The flavours only get better after sitting in the fridge for a couple days.

Best served with Jalapeño and Cilantro Coleslaw (page 75).

....

▪ Preheat oven to 300°F (150°C).

Combine the spices in a small bowl and massage into the pork. Place the pork in a casserole pot or slow cooker and fill ½ inch (1 cm) deep with water.

If using a casserole pot, cover the pork and place in the oven for about 4–5 hours or until tender enough to shred easily, turning the meat over once during cooking. Check the pork in the oven after about 40 minutes; the juices should be bubbling at a low steady simmer, if not, regulate the heat. (If using a slow cooker, set the temperature on high until the liquid starts to simmer, then reduce to low.)

While the pork is cooking, start on the sauce. Place the figs and cranberries in a bowl and cover with 2 cups (500 mL) boiling water; let stand for 30 minutes. Heat oil in a large heavy saucepan over medium heat; add the bacon and cook until the fat has rendered and the bacon is partially cooked. Add the onions and stir occasionally until they are soft and golden. Add the garlic, stirring for half a minute until aromatic. Set aside.

Purée the dried fruit and the soaking water in a blender or food processor until smooth. Pour the purée into the saucepan with the onions and add the remaining ingredients, stirring to combine. Re-warm the sauce and taste; season with additional salt if desired. The sauce will be thinned later with the braising liquid from the pork.

When the pork is fork-tender, transfer to a cutting board, reserving the braising liquid. When the pork is cool enough to handle, shred it into bite-sized pieces, discarding any chunks of fat or gristle. Add the shredded pork to the sauce and mix well. Refrigerate overnight.

Strain the reserved braising liquid and refrigerate overnight. The next day, remove the layer of chilled fat from the liquid's surface.

Reheat the pulled pork sauce and thin as necessary with the braising liquid (now fat-free and somewhat gelatinous).

RATATOUILLE PIE

makes 1 pie (6–8 servings)

Flaky Pastry Dough (page 262)

RATATOUILLE FILLING

1 large eggplant (about 1½ lb [700 g]),
    peeled and sliced ½ inch (1 cm) thick
6 Tbsp (90 mL) olive oil, more as necessary
1 large onion, diced
1 large zucchini (about 12 oz [360 g]),
    cut in half lengthwise, then into ¼-inch
    (6 mm) slices
1 large red pepper, diced
¼ tsp (1 mL) kosher salt
2 cloves garlic, minced
One 14-oz (420 g) can good quality
    plum tomatoes
One 6-oz (175 g) jar marinated artichoke
    hearts, drained and finely chopped
18 large Kalamata olives, pits removed and
    coarsely chopped
1 tsp (5 mL) hot sauce (such as Sriracha)
3 Tbsp (45 mL) freshly chopped parsley
1 Tbsp (15 mL) freshly chopped basil

CHEESE FILLING

1¾ cups (435 mL) ricotta cheese, strained
    in a sieve to remove excess water
1 cup (250 mL) crumbled feta cheese
½ cup (125 mL) freshly grated
    Parmesan cheese
1 egg, slightly beaten + an extra beaten egg
    for brushing the pastry

SPECIAL EQUIPMENT

9-inch (23 cm) springform pan

LONG BEFORE marriage, children and culinary school, there was The Great Canadian Pie Contest.

Years ago, I entered a pie contest on a whim. Months later, long after I'd forgotten about it, I received happy notice that my recipe had been short-listed. I was invited to join the other finalists to demonstrate my pie at the Canadian National Exhibition in Toronto.

After a nerve-wracking public demonstration alongside the other contestants, my pie took first place in the savoury category and I was suddenly surrounded by photographers and shoved in front of a television camera. For one brief thrilling moment, I was a pie celebrity.

This recipe is a much-improved version of the original, made with a standard pie shell. A springform pan creates a larger pie and a more impressive presentation. The pastry and fillings can be made in advance and assembled the next day.

If you're not in the mood for making pastry, the ratatouille filling is marvellous over pasta, gnocchi, rice or baked potatoes.

◾ Preheat the oven to 350°F (175°C).

PASTRY Prepare the pastry dough according to the instructions on page 262. Roll out the dough for the base, lid and decorative braid as per the instructions on the following page.

EGGPLANT PREP Before chopping all the vegetables, first spread the eggplant slices onto a paper towel and sprinkle with ½ tsp (2.5 mL) kosher salt. Leave undisturbed for at least 30 minutes for the salt to draw-out any bitterness. Blot the eggplant slices dry.

RATATOUILLE FILLING Heat 2 Tbsp (30 mL) oil in a large nonstick skillet and, working in batches, cook the eggplant over medium heat until browned, about 3 minutes per side. Add additional oil as necessary to prevent sticking. Set aside to cool.

In the same pan, heat 1 Tbsp (15 mL) oil, add the onion and cook over medium heat for about 5 minutes until translucent. Add the zucchini, red pepper and salt and cook until just tender, about 5 minutes. Add the garlic and stir for about half a minute until aromatic, then add the tomatoes, breaking them up with a wooden spoon. Add the artichokes, pitted olives, hot sauce and herbs. Simmer uncovered over medium heat, until the liquid has completely evaporated and the mixture has thickened, about 15–20 minutes. (A watery mixture will seep through the pastry). Taste and season with additional salt if desired. Set aside to cool completely.

. . . recipe continued

. . . Ratatouille Pie (cont.)

CHEESE FILLING   Combine the strained ricotta, feta, Parmesan and egg in a medium bowl and mix well.

PASTRY BASE   Roll about two-thirds of the dough onto a sheet of lightly floured parchment and form a circle about ⅛ inch (3 mm) thick. Transfer the dough to a springform pan, pressing against the sides for a smooth fit; trim the dough at the top of the pan so that there is no overhang. Cover with plastic wrap and refrigerate for 1 hour.

PASTRY LID   Roll out the balance of the dough into a ⅛-inch (3 mm) thick circle to shape the lid; trim the dough to the size of the springform pan with a scant ¼-inch (6 mm) trim. Cover with plastic wrap and refrigerate for 1 hour. When the dough is chilled, cut vents into the pastry lid, as pictured.

PASTRY BRAID   Gather and roll the remaining pastry into a long narrow strip about 3 inches (8 cm) wide. Cut the dough into 2 long strips, each about ¾ inch (2 cm) wide. Place the strips side by side on a sheet of lightly floured parchment and gently braid them together: right strip over the left, left over right, and so on. (You may need to join a couple braids to fit the circumference of the pan.) Cover with plastic wrap and refrigerate for 1 hour.

PUTTING IT ALL TOGETHER   Spread the cheese mixture evenly along the base of the pastry-lined springform pan. Cover with a layer of cooled eggplant, then the cooled ratatouille filling.

Brush the edges of the exposed pastry with the beaten egg, then place the pastry lid over the filling, pressing the edges of the dough together to form a seal. Brush the edges of the pastry lid with the beaten egg, then run the braid along the edge, pressing gently so that it adheres to the pastry lid. Brush the remaining pastry with the egg.

Place the pie on a baking sheet and bake for 50–60 minutes until the pastry is golden; rotate the pie once during baking. You may have to cover the pie with foil, to prevent excessive browning.

Allow to rest for 1 hour before serving.

Olives are tastier with the pits intact. Purchase them from a deli if possible and stay away from olives sold in a jar or can.

To pit olives, place them on a sheet of parchment and tap them gently with the bottom of a small saucepan just until they crack slightly open. Remove the pits, noting number of pits to olives; it's easy to miss one.

SUMMER | *sweet*

BLUEBERRY CHEESECAKE *with* HAZELNUT CRUST 96

APRICOT PAVLOVA 99

RUMPOT 100

RASPBERRY MOUSSE 103

PATCHWORK TARTS 104

STRAWBERRY ICE CREAM *with* SOUR CHERRY SORBET 106

RASPBERRY TRUFFLE CAKES 108

PEACH TARTS *with* HONEY RUM MASCARPONE 111

SUMMER BERRIES *with* FRUIT COULIS *&* CUSTARD 115

BLUEBERRY CHEESECAKE
with HAZELNUT CRUST
makes 1 cheesecake (10–12 servings)

HAZELNUT CRUST

½ cup (125 mL) skinned hazelnuts

½ cup (125 mL) unsalted butter at room
temperature + extra for greasing the pan

¼ cup (60 mL) light brown sugar

3 Tbsp (45 mL) liquid honey + 2 Tbsp
(30 mL) for glaze (optional)

½ cup (125 mL) all-purpose white flour

½ cup (125 mL) whole wheat flour

½ tsp (2.5 mL) baking powder

¼ tsp (1 mL) baking soda

½ tsp (2.5 mL) ground cinnamon

CHEESE FILLING

2 cups (500 mL) cream cheese
(room temperature)

2 cups (500 mL) ricotta cheese, strained in
a sieve to remove excess water

1 tsp (5 mL) freshly squeezed lemon juice +
finely grated zest from 1 lemon

¾ cup (185 mL) sugar

2 Tbsp (30 mL) all-purpose flour

¼ tsp (1 mL) kosher salt

4 large eggs

1½ cups (375 mL) fresh blueberries, washed

2 Tbsp (30 mL) liquid honey (optional)

Blueberry Sauce (recipe follows)

SPECIAL EQUIPMENT

9-inch (23 cm) springform pan

Food processor or blender (for the
berry sauce)

*Blueberries have a natural dusty sheen that
helps protect the berry—it's an indication the
berries are fresh. Don't rinse them until you're
ready to enjoy them.*

RICOTTA AND cream cheese make an exceptional cheesecake that is creamy but not overly rich or sweet.

Cheesecake provides a delicious platform to showcase the plump blueberries of the season. Strawberries, raspberries and blackberries work nicely too.

As one friend sighed, *"If you were to tell me this cake is low in calories, I'd say this is the perfect food!"*

The cake freezes very well, without the berries.

◼ Preheat the oven to 350°F (175°C).

Remove the base from the springform pan and lightly brush the base and the sides with butter. Line both with parchment paper, cut to size. The butter helps the parchment stay in place. (The pan will be assembled later.)

HAZELNUT CRUST Pulse the hazelnuts in a food processor, about 15–20 seconds, or until the nuts are mostly fine-textured with some irregular coarse pieces.

Blend the butter with the brown sugar and honey in a medium bowl or the bowl of a standup mixer. Add the ground hazelnuts and remaining ingredients and mix until combined.

Place the hazelnut dough onto the base of the prepared pan. Cover with plastic wrap, and using a rolling pin, or the bottom of a small pan, smooth the dough evenly into place. Discard the plastic, then reassemble the springform pan.

CHEESE FILLING Blend together the cream cheese, ricotta, lemon juice and zest in a medium bowl or in the bowl of a standup mixer. Add the sugar, flour and salt and mix until combined. Add the eggs, one at a time, mixing after each addition until well combined.

Pour the cheese mixture on top of the hazelnut dough and bake on a baking sheet for about 60 minutes or until the mixture has firmed and the edges are golden, rotating the pan once during baking. Cool and refrigerate for at least 4 hours before serving. The cheesecake sometimes cracks as it cools but the berries will conceal any imperfections.

PUTTING IT ALL TOGETHER Decorate the chilled cheesecake with the fresh blueberries. Glaze with honey thinned with 1 Tbsp (15 mL) water, if desired.

Serve with the berry sauce on the side.

BERRY SAUCE *makes about 2 cups (500 mL)*

⅓ cup (80 mL) sugar
⅓ cup (80 mL) water
2 tsp (10 mL) lemon juice
1½ cups (375 mL) fresh blueberries,
    washed

■ Combine the sugar and water in a saucepan and bring to a simmer, stirring until the sugar has dissolved. Add the lemon juice and blueberries and cook about 3–5 minutes or just until the berries have softened. Tip the berries and liquid into a blender or food processor and blend until smooth. Pour the mixture through a strainer into a clean spouted container. Cover and refrigerate until ready to use.

APRICOT PAVLOVA

makes 10–12 pavlova

4 egg whites, with no traces of yolk,
   at room temperature
1 cup (250 mL) superfine or berry sugar
1½ tsp (7.5 mL) cornstarch
½ tsp (2.5 mL) white vinegar
10–12 ripe apricots
1 cup (250 mL) whipping cream, chilled
½ cup (125 mL) apricot jam

SPECIAL EQUIPMENT
Electric mixer

ALTHOUGH MERINGUE has been around for centuries it continues to be a stylish dessert.

These are mini versions of a traditional cake-size pavlova, a simple meringue dessert topped with whipping cream and fresh fruit. I scaled down the meringue's size to show off the season's finest apricots.

Meringues are easy to make but can be as temperamental as the weather—don't attempt them on a humid day. They are meant to be dried rather than baked, but not all ovens are created equal; you may have to adjust the temperature.

Uncooked meringues are brilliant white but turn ivory with heat. With practice, you'll learn to recognize the colour of a perfectly cooked meringue.

■ Preheat the oven to 250°F (120°C).

For uniform meringues, draw circles onto a sheet of parchment paper, using a teacup as a template and leaving about a 1-inch (2.5 cm) space between each circle. Turn the parchment over (ink or pencil can mar the meringue) onto a baking sheet and use as a guide when spooning or piping the meringue onto your tray.

Whisk the egg whites in a meticulously clean bowl at medium speed for 1 minute or until a small network of tiny bubbles have formed. Gradually add the sugar and increase the speed to high; whip until the whites have expanded and formed billowy, firm glossy peaks. Be mindful not to over-whip, otherwise the whites will turn grainy and lose their shape. Reduce the speed to low and add the cornstarch and vinegar until just blended.

Pipe or spoon the meringue onto your prepared tray (if using a pastry bag, fit with a ¾-inch [2 cm] tip), using the template as a guide.

Using the back of a large spoon, create an indentation in 1 meringue, just deep enough to hold an apricot in place. Test the meringue with an apricot first to gauge the size before shaping the rest. Remove the apricot after testing.

Bake for about 1 hour on a rack in the lower third of your oven or until the meringues are dry. Turn the heat off and leave the meringues in the oven until cooled. The meringues will crack slightly. If not using immediately, store in an airtight container in a cool dry place.

To easily remove the skin from the apricots, bring a pot of water to a boil. Score the circumference of each apricot with a sharp paring knife and carefully lower them into the water for about 10–15 seconds; remove with a slotted spoon and transfer to a bowl of ice cold water. If the skin doesn't peel off easily, repeat the process. (If the skin refuses to come loose, the apricots are not ripe enough.) Slice the bottom quarter from each apricot and carefully remove the pit, keeping the apricot whole.

Just before serving, whip the cream to a firm peak.

Add a dollop of whipping cream, a spoonful of apricot jam and a peeled, pitted apricot to each meringue. Serve immediately.

Wondering what to do with leftover yolks? Try your hand at homemade ice cream (page 106), Caramel Crème Brûlée (page 56) or Crème Anglais (page 293).

RUMPOT
makes 1 gallon (4 L)

15 cups (3.75 L) ripe, unblemished summer
    fruits, washed (and pitted, if necessary)
5 cups (1.25 L) superfine or berry sugar
3 cups (750 mL) white rum
1 vanilla pod, split into 2 halves

SPECIAL EQUIPMENT
Glass gallon jar with a lid, or a traditional
    rumpot container
Cherry pitter (handy if you're including
    cherries, but not essential)

*You can find traditional stoneware rumpots,
or rumtopfs, on eBay. If you're lucky, you might
come across one in your local vintage or
second-hand boutique.*

I FIRST tasted rumpot, or rumtopf, when my friend, Noreen, gave me a jar from her stash. It was like nothing I'd tried before: the fruit was sweet, fragrant, complex and boozy. I spooned it over everything in sight, from ice cream to roast duck.

Traditionally, rumpots are made with an assortment of fruits, one variety stacked atop another, as the seasons unfold. I have a preference for cherries and berries, so I stick to these. Some cooks insist that keeping the cherry pits adds flavour and a hint of almond. If you opt to remove the pits, as I do, a cherry pitter makes the job easy enough to delegate to the smallest of hands. Just make sure your little assistant is wearing the biggest of aprons.

Some fruits, like blueberries and saskatoon berries, do not work well; their skins become tough and unpleasant. Tender fruits, like strawberries, turn too spongy for my taste but I don't mind raspberries that disintegrate over time. Rumpots are as personal as your palate.

For every 1 lb (450 g) of fruit, you'll need ½ lb (250 g) of sugar and enough rum to cover the fruit. I use white rum, but that's a personal choice rather than a rule.

Your summer rumpot will be ready by Christmas. It pairs beautifully with the Spiced Hazelnut Loaf on page 229.

■ Fill your container with fruit and pour the sugar on top, resisting the temptation to stir or otherwise disturb the fruit. It will seem like an alarming amount of sugar but it will settle, eventually, at the bottom of your container. Pour the rum over the sugar, making sure the fruit is completely covered. (It's important to keep the fruit completely submerged with rum, otherwise mold can form on any fruit that bobs to the surface.) Add the split vanilla pod.

If using a traditional rumpot container, the opening is wide enough to place a small plate over the fruit to keep it submerged. If you're using a jar, as pictured, fill a heavy-duty freezer bag with pie weights and arrange the bag on top of the fruit to prevent any fruit from bobbing to the surface. Alternatively, fashion a flexible disc from a plastic container and place it over the fruit.

If you don't have a cool cellar, you'll need to set aside room in your refrigerator to store your rumpot for 3 to 4 months.

RASPBERRY MOUSSE

makes eight 3-oz (90 mL) servings

....

3¾ cups (930 mL) fresh or frozen
    raspberries (thawed if frozen) + extra
    for garnish
½ cup (125 mL) granulated or superfine
    sugar + extra as needed
1 Tbsp (15 mL) unflavoured gelatin
    (usually 1 packet)
1 cup (250 mL) whipping cream

SPECIAL EQUIPMENT
Food processor, blender or food mill

A FEW ingredients is all it takes to create this light, delicate raspberry mousse. Topped simply with plump raspberries, this dessert is the perfect ending to a summer's meal. If you don't have raspberries on hand, this recipe can be made with strawberries or blackberries instead.

Mousse can be prepared up to two days in advance, covered and refrigerated.

....

■ Process the raspberries in a food processor or blender until smooth, then press the purée through a fine-mesh strainer into a bowl, using the back of a ladle or large spoon to extract as much juice as possible. Discard the seeds. Measure out 1¼ cups (310 mL) strained purée.

Add the sugar to the purée, mix well and set aside for the sugar to dissolve, about 5 minutes. Taste the purée; if your berries are tart, you may need to add additional sugar.

Bring 1 cup (250 mL) of water to a boil (you'll only use a small amount).

Pour the packet of gelatin into a small bowl or teacup. Cover with 3 Tbsp (45 mL) boiling water and mix continuously with a small spoon until the gelatin is completely dissolved with no lumps, about 1 minute.

Scrape the gelatin into the berry purée and mix until well combined.

Whip the cream in a large bowl until soft peaks form, being mindful not to over-whip the cream.

Pour the fruit purée into the whipping cream, in 3 batches, gently folding the purée into the cream after each addition. Mix until the mousse is uniform in colour.

Transfer the mixture into a spouted jug (for easy pouring) and distribute into containers immediately, before the mousse sets. Refrigerate until firm, about 2 hours. Garnish with fresh raspberries.

PATCHWORK TARTS

makes twelve 3-inch (8 cm) tarts

....

3 lb (1.35 kg) chilled Handcrafted Puff
    Pastry (page 266)
Flour for dusting the dough
1 egg, lightly beaten
1½ cups (375 mL) Pastry Cream
    Lightened with Whipping Cream
    (page 293)
1½ cups (375 mL) ripe seasonal fruit

I FIRST made these puff pastry tarts as my contribution to a memorable farm-to-table dinner, in beautiful Metchosin on Vancouver Island. I wanted a dessert that would highlight the fruit of the summer and this colourful, edible quilt proved to be the perfect offering.

The hosts, Noreen and Robbie, had joined several long tables together overlooking their vegetable garden and rolling farmland below, beyond which stretched an expansive blue ocean. The tables were covered with white linen and decorated with bright sunflowers and every dish had been sourced locally, most from Noreen's garden. We clinked our glasses in thanks and the heavens responded with a sudden downpour.

We enjoyed these very special tarts indoors.

....

■ You'll need to first prepare the Handcrafted Puff Pastry dough according to the instructions on page 266.

Preheat the oven to 385°F (195°C).

Roll half the dough onto a sheet of parchment paper dusted with flour.

Shape the dough into a rectangle measuring 16 × 12 inches (40 × 30 cm), about ⅛ inch (3 mm) thick.

Cut the pastry into twelve 3- × 3-inch (8 × 8 cm) squares. If the pastry is too soft to cut easily, place it in the fridge for 20 minutes to firm it up.

Place the squares of dough onto the parchment-lined baking sheet, cover with plastic and refrigerate while you roll out the remaining dough for the tarts' edges.

Roll out the balance of the dough and shape into another 16- × 12-inch (40 × 30 cm) rectangle, about ⅛ inch (3 mm) thick. Cut the pastry into 12 strips, with each strip measuring 12 inches (30 cm) in length and between ¼ and ½ inch (0.6–1 cm) in width. Cut the strips into 3-inch (8 cm) lengths, to cover the tart's square edges. You'll need 48 in total, or 4 strips per tart.

Working in batches, remove a few squares of dough from the refrigerator and brush the edges with the beaten egg. Place the 3-inch (8 cm) strips of dough along the egg-moistened edges, overlapping the dough at each corner. Trim any excess dough.

Score the corners with an "X" using the dull side of your knife. Holding a tart in front of you, score the outer edges of each tart by etching vertical lines every ¼ inch (6 mm) with the dull side of a knife. This helps the dough to rise evenly. Finally, poke holes into the base of each tart with a fork.

Cover and refrigerate while you assemble the remaining tart shells. If desired, refrigerate or freeze the entire batch until ready to bake.

Place the tarts onto a parchment-lined baking sheet with an inch (2.5 cm) between each. Brush the edges of the tarts with the beaten egg. Bake the chilled dough in the preheated oven on the middle rack for 10–15 minutes, or until golden, rotating the pan halfway during baking.

Cool the tart shells on a wire rack. Just before serving, fill each tart with about 2 Tbsp (30 mL) Pastry Cream Lightened with Whipping Cream and top with your favourite summer fruit.

STRAWBERRY ICE CREAM
with SOUR CHERRY SORBET
makes 4 cups (1 L)

¾ cup (185 mL) whole milk

¾ cup (185 mL) whipping cream

4 egg yolks

6 Tbsp (90 mL) sugar

3½ cups (875 mL) fresh strawberries,
  washed and hulled

3 cups (750 mL) Sour Cherry Sorbet
  (recipe follows)

SPECIAL EQUIPMENT

Ice cream machine

Food processor or blender

Food mill or potato ricer

If you have the freezer space, store your ice cream canister in the freezer so it's ready to use when you are.

FROSTY SORBET and velvety ice cream come together in this flavourful blending of sweet juicy strawberries and sassy tart cherries.

The ice cream machine's canister insert must be frozen for at least 24 hours before using. If you're making the sorbet too, keep in mind you'll need to re-freeze the canister again before using.

Add an easy-to-make tuile wafer (page 52) for a little crunch.

■ Before you get started, place a fine-mesh strainer over a bowl or pitcher to strain the hot custard. You'll also need a larger bowl filled with ice water to quickly cool the container of custard.

Heat the milk and cream in a medium saucepan over medium heat, until the mixture just begins to boil. Remove from heat.

Whisk the yolks and sugar in a medium bowl. Add about half of the warm milk and cream mixture and whisk until well combined. Pour the yolk mixture into the saucepan of milk and cream. Bring to a bare simmer, whisking continuously, being mindful not to boil.

The custard is ready when the mixture is thick enough to lightly coat the back of a spoon.

Pour the mixture through a strainer into a bowl or pitcher, then place the container into the bowl of ice water to cool the custard quickly. Cover the custard with plastic wrap, touching the custard so as not to form a skin, and refrigerate until well chilled.

Purée the strawberries in a food processor or blender, scrape into a bowl and refrigerate until well chilled.

Mix together the chilled strawberry purée and custard; pour into a frozen ice cream canister and churn according to manufacturer's instructions. Transfer to a freezer-safe container and freeze until ready to serve. Serve with Sour Cherry Sorbet.

SOUR CHERRY SORBET *makes 3 cups (750 mL)*

3 cups (750 mL) sour cherries
  (about 1½ lb [250 g]), washed, pitted and
  stems removed

3 cups (750 mL) sweet cherries
  (about 1½ lb [250 g]), washed, pitted and
  stems removed

1 cup (250 mL) sugar

1 cup (250 mL) water

1–3 tsp (5–15 mL) balsamic vinegar

THIS RECIPE calls for half tart sour cherries but you can use sweeter cherries and decrease the overall amount of syrup accordingly.

■ Working in batches, press the pitted cherries through a food mill or potato ricer. You'll need to extract about 2 cups (500 mL) juice. Discard the cherry pulp (or freeze and use to flavour muffins or cakes).

Pour the juice through a fine-mesh strainer into a jug or jar and refrigerate until well chilled.

Place the sugar and water in a small saucepan over medium-low heat until the sugar is completely dissolved. Cool the syrup to room temperature, then refrigerate until well chilled.

The juice and syrup are combined but the amount of syrup will depend on the tartness of your cherries. Start with half the syrup and add more by the tablespoon until it's sweet, but not cloying. (I often use ¾ cup [185 mL] syrup for 2 cups [500 mL] juice.)

Add balsamic vinegar sparingly to taste, 1 scant tsp (about 5 mL) at a time, tasting the mixture after each addition.

Pour the sweetened cherry juice into a frozen ice cream canister and churn according to manufacturer's instructions. Transfer to a freezer-safe container and freeze until ready to serve.

RASPBERRY TRUFFLE CAKES

makes about forty-eight 2-inch (5 cm) cakes

....

12 oz (360 g) best-quality bittersweet
    chocolate, chopped, divided
¼ cup (60 mL) unsalted butter,
    softened, divided
½ cup (125 mL) whipping cream
4 yolks at room temperature
8 egg whites at room temperature
Pinch cream of tartar
¼ cup (60 mL) sugar
1½ cups (375 mL) fresh raspberries

SPECIAL EQUIPMENT
2-inch (5 cm) flexible silicone muffin mold
    or 2-inch (5 cm) muffin tins lined with
    cupcake liners
Electric mixer

I FIRST created these delicate, flourless cakes while on a home exchange. I was unsure what I'd find in my host's kitchen so I stashed a few easy-to-carry kitchen tools in my suitcase, including my flexible silicone muffin mold.

It wasn't long before I was using the mold for these little chocolate cakes with truffle centres. My daughter, Lucie, was in charge of topping each cake with a fresh raspberry, while the truffle centre was still warm. Before I had a chance to enjoy a single one, Lucie's twin sister, Elise, polished them off.

All to say, these cakes should be hidden from children until serving time.

....

■ Place 4 oz (120 g) chocolate and 2 Tbsp (30 mL) butter in a medium-sized bowl. Heat the cream in a small saucepan until just boiling then pour the hot cream over the chocolate and stir until the chocolate and butter are melted and thoroughly blended. Refrigerate until the chocolate is just firm enough to hold its shape.

Spoon the chocolate into a pastry bag (fitted with a plain tip) or a freezer bag with a small hole cut from a corner. Pipe the chocolate truffles onto the prepared baking sheet, small enough to fit the centre of your muffin wells but with enough room for the batter to completely surround the chocolate. If the truffles are too large, the cakes will collapse.

Cover the truffles with plastic wrap and freeze until firm enough to peel from the parchment.

Preheat the oven to 375°F (190°C).

Place a heat-resistant bowl over a saucepan filled with 1 inch (2.5 cm) simmering water. Place 8 oz (230 g) chocolate and 2 Tbsp (30 mL) butter in the bowl and stir until just melted. Remove from heat and add the egg yolks, stirring until well blended. Set aside.

Whisk the egg whites with the cream of tartar in a meticulously clean bowl at medium speed until a small network of tiny bubbles have formed, about 1 full minute. Gradually add the sugar and increase the speed to high; whip until the whites have expanded and formed billowy, firm glossy peaks. Be mindful not to over-whip, otherwise the whites will turn grainy and lose their shape.

Using a large spatula, gently fold the egg whites into the melted chocolate mixture in 3 batches, folding until no white streaks remain.

Spoon the batter into the muffin wells until three-quarters full. Place 1 truffle in the centre of each well, pressing gently to ensure the batter surrounds each truffle but not to the bottom of the muffin well.

Bake for about 10 minutes or until a toothpick inserted into the cake's outer edge comes out clean. Add a raspberry to the centre of each cake while the chocolate is still warm. Cool on a wire rack.

PEACH TARTS *with* HONEY RUM MASCARPONE

makes 4 tarts

....

2 ripe, firm peaches

½ lb (250 g) Handcrafted Puff Pastry
 (page 266)

¼ cup (60 mL) sugar

Honey Rum Mascarpone (recipe follows)

1 Tbsp (15 mL) whipping cream

PEACHES ARE cradled in sugared puff pastry and baked until golden in this simple summer dessert. These tarts are especially scrumptious served with a great dollop of mascarpone cheese sweetened with honey and fortified with rum.

The tarts come together quickly and can be assembled ahead of time and baked just before serving. They're ideal for casual summer get-togethers.

....

■ You'll need to first prepare Hancrafted Puff Pastry according to the instructions on page 266.

To easily remove the peach skin, bring a pot of water to a boil. Score the circumference of each peach with a sharp paring knife then carefully lower the peaches into the water for about half a minute; remove with a slotted spoon and transfer to a bowl of ice cold water. If the skin doesn't peel off easily, repeat the process. (If the skin refuses to come loose, the peaches are not ripe enough.) Cut the peach in two and remove the pit.

Roll the dough out to about a ⅛-inch (3 mm) thickness on a sheet of flour-dusted parchment. Using a 4-inch (10 cm) diameter cup or bowl as a guide, cut the dough into 4 circles. Refrigerate until ready to use. Roll and cut any leftover dough and freeze for later use.

Place a circle of pastry in the palm of your hand and centre half of a peach on top, cut side up. Mold the pastry around the peach half, leaving the cut side exposed. The pastry's edges will pucker as you shape the dough around the peach.

. . . recipe continued

. . . Peach Tarts with Honey Rum Mascarpone (cont.)

Working over your prepared baking tray, dust the peach with ½ tsp (2.5 mL) sugar then invert the pastry onto the tray, peach side down.

Continue with the remaining peaches and dough, cover with plastic wrap and refrigerate for at least 45 minutes, or up to 24 hours, before baking. Prepare the Honey Rum Mascarpone (recipe follows).

When ready to bake the tarts, preheat the oven to 425°F (220°C).

Remove the pastry from the fridge and brush each pastry "dome" with whipping cream and sprinkle with ½ tsp (2.5 mL) of sugar.

Using a sharp knife, score the pastry domes with an "X" from edge to edge through the centre, being careful not to cut into the peach.

Bake, peach side down, on a baking sheet for about 15–20 minutes or until the pastry is well browned; rotate the pan once during baking.

Remove the baking sheet from the oven and turn the pastry over with a spatula so that the peach faces up.

Continue to bake for another 5–10 minutes until the edges of the pastry are golden. Transfer to a wire rack to keep the pastry firm.

Best served fresh from the oven with Honey Rum Mascarpone on the side.

HONEY RUM MASCARPONE *makes about ¾ cup (185 mL)*

¾ cup (185 mL) mascarpone cheese
2–4 tsp (10–20 mL) honey
2 tsp (10 mL) dark rum (or more as desired)

In a small bowl, combine the mascarpone cheese with 2 tsp (10 mL) of honey and the rum. Taste and add additional honey, if desired. Cover and refrigerate until ready to serve.

SUMMER BERRIES
with FRUIT COULIS *&* CUSTARD
makes 6–8 servings

Pastry Cream Lightened with Whipping
   Cream (page 293)
5 cups (1.25 L) fresh berries, divided
½–¾ cup (125–185 mL) granulated or
   superfine sugar

SPECIAL EQUIPMENT
Blender, food processor or food mill

*Refrigerate fresh berries and wash just before
using. Bring fruit to room temperature before
serving to enhance its natural flavours.*

THIS SIMPLE, yet scrumptious make-ahead dessert is ideal for showing off the season's berries. The custard is laced with a quick blender coulis made of sweet raspberries and tart currants, but feel free to use whatever fruit you have on hand.

This dessert pairs exceptionally well with Pastry Straws (page 48) or Sweet Wafers (page 52).

The custard and fruit coulis can be made up to three days in advance.

■ Prepare the Pastry Cream Lightened with Whipping Cream according to instructions on page 293.

To make the fruit coulis: process 3 cups (750 mL) berries in a blender or food processor until smooth, then press the purée through a fine-mesh strainer into a bowl, using the back of a ladle or large spoon to extract as much liquid as possible; discard the solids. Add ½ cup (125 mL) sugar to the purée, mix well and taste. Add additional sugar as desired—the coulis should be sweet with a slightly tart edge. Transfer the coulis to a spouted container. Cover and refrigerate until ready to use.

To serve, portion the custard into individual bowls. Swirl a generous spoonful of coulis into each serving and top with the remaining fresh berries. Serve extra coulis and berries on the side.

FALL

....

Fall is cozy-sweater food: chowders, stews and heart-warming soups. Bring on the sweet roasted root vegetables, baked apples and potato dumplings. Rainy weekends are made for kneading dough and enjoying fresh-from-the-oven pastries.

....

The first time I drove through the Lower Mainland and the Fraser Valley in the fall, I was stunned by a landscape blanketed in crimson. When the leaves on the blueberry bushes turn colour, you realize just how much land is devoted to the fruit.

Fall kicks off harvest celebrations throughout the province—we pay tribute to everything from mushrooms to garlic to cranberries. The University of British Columbia in Vancouver hosts one of many annual apple festivals at their Botanical Garden, where you can sample some 60 varieties from all over the province.

Much of BC's orchard land is devoted to apples, one of our province's most valuable tree-fruit crops. The Okanagan-Similkameen region produces the vast majority, an astounding 89,000 tons of apples each year.

BC apples are featured in a number of recipes: pan-roasted until golden and served alongside sausages and sauerkraut (page 149), stuffed with nuts and goat cheese and baked whole (page 171), fanned out on an tart (page 158) and bundled in puff pastry (page 168).

Fall pears add a hint of sweetness to savoury foods like Roasted Squash Soup (page 132) and smoked duck salad (page 136). You'll also find them tucked into crêpes (page 175) and sweet soufflés flavoured with cardamom and ginger (page 161) or sliced paper-thin and baked into crisp delicate chips (page 179).

Autumn brings a wild abundance of mushrooms, and there's no better place to forage for fresh ones than the damp coastal forests of Vancouver Island. Find a knowledgeable guide to explore BC's most hidden treasures and you'll be rewarded with the earthy, intoxicating flavours of chanterelles, pine, lobster, ruffled cauliflower, porcini and more. (I've shared our mushroom foraging adventures on page 120.) You'll find recipes for Mushroom and Wine Ragù (page 150) and a Mushroom Lover's Tart (page 145), perfect for fall get-togethers.

This is also the season when BC's cranberry farmers flood their bogs. You can see just how unique the harvest is on page 118. Local dried cranberries are featured in a variety of baked goods from Sticky Buns (page 164) to Whole Wheat Cranberry Scones (page 172).

Lastly, potatoes are one of my favourite go-to staples when the weather turns cool. The majority of BC's potatoes come from the Fraser Valley. Brian Faulkner of BC Fresh says, "Most people don't realize when they drive from Vancouver to Tsawwassen, they're passing thousands of tons of potatoes." The potatoes are piled up to 20 feet high and housed in simple steel farm buildings. You'll find recipes for potatoes in many guises including decadent fritters (page 124), spicy croquettes (page 131) and kale gnocchi (page 215). There's nothing like kneading warm gnocchi dough to soften autumn's chill.

BERRIES IN MOTION

CAROLINE AND I are perched atop a cranberry pump at Hopcott Farms in scenic Pitt Meadows, where the autumn air is fragrant with damp soil. We have a bird's eye view of the flooded bog below and the workers wading through a sea of millions of floating cranberries in every shade of red. The workmen drag 100-foot-long foam-padded bands, called booms, through the berries to corral them. With one man at each end of the boom and one in the centre, they work in perfectly choreographed movements to encircle the berries, creating a mesmerizing pattern of colour and movement.

The robust workers, many with long grey beards, have been harvesting cranberries for Hopcott Farms for years. Many don't need the work anymore, says owner Bob Hopcott, but they come every year out of a sense of loyalty, and to show appreciation for having had work when they did need it.

Hopcott Farms is one of seventy cranberry farms in the Lower Fraser Valley. The valley is ranked among the top four cranberry-producing regions in the world. It's prized for its soil—cranberries thrive in peat, gravel, sand and clay—and its flat level terrain; ideal conditions for reservoirs and irrigation systems that serve to flood the bogs at harvesting time. Cranberries are not grown in water; the bogs are flooded only at harvest time as an efficient means of gathering berries. Farmers drive huge tractors, called beaters, through the flooded field to agitate the water and loosen the cranberries from the vines. Miraculously, this doesn't damage the fruit.

Cranberries float to the surface due to tiny air pockets in each berry (this is also the reason fresh cranberries "pop" when they're cooked). The floating berries are siphoned to an overhead pump, or moved along a conveyor belt, onto a truck destined for a receiving station where they are weighed, cleaned and sent for processing. Most cranberries are destined for the processed market as dried cranberries and juice. Fresh cranberries—those sold during the holidays—represent a small percentage of the market. They are harvested on dry land with a machine resembling a lawn mower that combs the berries from the vines.

For all this action, you might not even notice a cranberry field off-season. The vines are low, scraggly and altogether unremarkable. Even when the berries start to appear, they're barely discernible under the cover of vines. It's only when the fields are wet-harvested and the berries float to the surface that it becomes a spectacular sight. Most farmers, if you ask permission, will allow you to watch the harvest unfold. You'll never look at cranberries in the same way again.

Hopcott Farms is a third generation family farm. The business started off in 1932 as a dairy farm but later switched to cattle. Over the years the farm diversified to include cranberries, corn and numerous other fruits and vegetables. Hopcott Meats is their full service butcher shop, produce market and deli. What they don't grow themselves, they source locally. It's a great food destination anytime.

HUNT AND GATHER

CAROLINE MEETS me at the café bundled in a puffer vest with her camera bag slung over one shoulder. She's grinning—the damp autumn morning has cleared into perfect mushroom foraging weather.

We're meeting our friend Castro Boateng and his colleague Janusz Urban, two chefs as comfortable cooking over a campfire as they are in a commercial kitchen. We pile into a waiting van with other curious foragers and head toward the ancient rainforest along the southwest coast of Vancouver Island.

It's late in the season and many of the mushrooms, the easily accessible ones anyway, have already been harvested. We trudge deeper into the forest, where the moss hangs from the branches in shaggy green tresses and the air is fragrant with damp cedar and musty soil. The only sounds are the creaks of the towering trees.

Janusz has been foraging mushrooms for as long as he can remember, a pursuit passed down by his father and enriched through wild food studies. He bounds over rocks and fallen trees and up the steep terrain, while we follow behind cautiously negotiating slippery stones and clutching narrow trees to pull ourselves onto higher ground. Occasionally one of us stumbles backward with a rotted uprooted tree in one hand, basket in the air.

Before we collect any mushrooms, Janusz first identifies them. With so many species, some with sinister names like Satan's Bolete and Death Cap, we dare only pick those he recognizes.

When Janusz announces he's found a hedgehog, Caroline and I race to join him, only to discover a mushroom, not an animal, and one that looks suspiciously like every other chanterelle we've encountered along the way. Janusz is animated as he shows us the underside of the mushroom cap, which contains the smallest of spines, rather than gills. Ah well, it's this kind of passion that separates the foragers from those of us who toss shrink-wrapped mushrooms into our grocery carts.

After a couple hours of foraging we're shuttled to French Beach Provincial Park where Castro and Janus have set up camp under a wooden shelter. While we sip hot tea from mason jars and brush the dirt from our precious stash, the two chefs toss assorted mushrooms in butter, whip up chanterelle soup and sear wild salmon in pans heated over propane burners. We sit around a fire pit with plates balanced on our laps, our appetites sharpened by the autumn chill.

Mushroom foraging is a great adventure, but one to take seriously. Wild mushrooms can be deadly. Forage with an experienced guide and only consume mushrooms identfied as safe to eat.

FALL | *savoury*

POTATO FRITTERS

makes about 28 fritters

....

1½ medium Russet potatoes (about 1 lb
    [450 g]), peeled and diced

⅓ cup (80 mL) whole or 2% milk

⅓ cup (80 mL) water

6 Tbsp (90 mL) unsalted butter

1½ tsp (7.5 mL) kosher salt

1 tsp (5 mL) sugar

1 cup (250 mL) all-purpose flour

3 large eggs + 1 extra, if necessary

Freshly ground black pepper (optional)

8 cups (2 L) vegetable oil (approx.)

SPECIAL EQUIPMENT

Potato ricer or food mill (optional)

Instant-read thermometer (optional)

Spring-loaded ice cream scoop for round,
    rather than oval, fritters (optional)

*If the thought of deep-frying puts you off, you
can bake the dough instead, a discovery made by
Gail, one of our clever recipe testers. Portion the
dough onto a baking tray using a small ice cream
scoop, brush with melted butter and bake in a
375°F (190°C) oven for 30 minutes.*

CRISP ON the outside and somewhere between Yorkshire pudding and mashed potatoes on the inside, these heavenly fritters are a French classic, traditionally called *pommes Dauphine*. They are surprisingly light and make a superb appetizer or side dish paired with chicken or meat.

If you plan to serve potato fritters to guests, you'll be pleased to know the dough can be prepared entirely in advance, refrigerated and brought to room temperature before deep-frying. I've offered instructions on how to shape the fritters into lovely ovals, as pictured, but they can also be shaped into perfect rounds using a spring-loaded ice cream scoop.

....

■ Place the potatoes in a saucepan with enough lukewarm water to cover the potatoes by 1 inch (2.5 cm). Bring to a simmer, uncovered, until the potatoes are tender and you can pierce them with a knife. Drain the potatoes and process them through a ricer or food mill into a large bowl. Alternatively, mash them as smooth as possible with a potato masher.

Combine the milk, water, butter, salt and sugar in a medium saucepan. Bring the mixture to a boil then remove from heat and add the flour all at once. Stir vigorously with a wooden spoon until the mixture forms a ball and pulls away from the sides of the pan.

Tip the dough into a large bowl or a standup mixer fitted with a paddle attachment. Add the eggs, one at a time, mixing after each addition. The dough is ready when it hangs from your mixing utensil in a thick, sticky paste. If the mixture is too firm, add an additional egg. Add the mashed potatoes and stir to combine. Season with freshly ground black pepper, if desired.

Pour at least 4 inches (10 cm) vegetable oil into a deep saucepan. Bring the oil slowly to temperature until an instant-read thermometer reads 350°F (175°C) or when a cube of bread dropped in the oil turns golden in 1 minute.

To form the dough into oval shapes (called *quenelles*), you'll need 2 identical spoons and a cup of water to rinse them in, between each quenelle. They are shaped one at a time and lowered into the oil before the next one is shaped.

Take a generous spoonful of dough with a spoon and, with your free hand, hold another spoon. Holding the spoons near to the scoop end, alternate the dough from spoon to spoon, using the contour of the spoons to shape the dough into neat ovals. Rinse the spoons in water between each quenelle.

If that sounds too fussy for you, simply drop the batter from a 1 Tbsp (15 mL) spoon or a spring-loaded ice cream scoop.

. . . recipe continued

. . . Potato Fritters (cont.)

Carefully lower the shaped batter into the hot oil, using a spoon to release the dough from your utensil; be mindful not to crowd the pan. Fry until golden brown, about 3–4 minutes, turning occasionally to colour evenly. Remove with a slotted spoon and transfer to a paper towel. Sprinkle with salt while still warm. Serve immediately.

POTTED MEAT

POTTED PORK, salmon and duck, also called rillettes (rē'yets), are wonderful to have on hand for last-minute appetizers and quick snacks. They're like pâtés, as smooth or coarse as you wish, made from inexpensive cuts of meat. Spiced pork and duck are slowly poached in fat until the meat is fork-tender. It's an easy process that brings out a great deal of flavour.

Salmon is steamed, seasoned and bound with cream, an old technique from culinary school that left me smitten. I was inspired to add cured or smoked salmon after reading Thomas Keller's salmon rillette recipe in *Bouchon*, one of my favourite French inspired cookbooks. It elevates the texture of the salmon to another level entirely.

Properly sealed potted meats and fish last for a week, refrigerated.

PORK RILLETTES *makes about 1½ cups (375 mL)*

1 Tbsp (15 mL) whole cumin seeds, crushed

1 Tbsp (15 mL) whole coriander seeds, crushed

½ tsp (2.5 mL) ground allspice

Kosher salt

1½–2 lb (700–900 g) fresh side pork, cut into 1½-inch (4 cm) chunks

4 cloves garlic, peeled and left whole

1½ cups (375 mL) pork or duck fat, melted

1 pitted prune, chopped finely (optional)

SPECIAL EQUIPMENT
Food processor (optional)

▪ Preheat the oven to 320°F (157°C).

Mix the spices and 1 tsp (5 mL) salt together in a medium bowl. Add the pork and toss to coat.

Place the pork in a snug ovenproof container in a single layer. Add the garlic cloves and cover with the melted fat. Cook for about 2½–3 hours or until fork-tender. Check the oven after 20 minutes to ensure the fat is simmering gently; you may need to regulate the heat.

When the pork is done, strain the melted fat through a fine-mesh strainer lined with cheesecloth. Cool and reserve the fat.

When the pork is cool enough to handle, separate the meat from the fatty layers; discard the fat.

Chop the pork finely, by hand or with a food processor, and scrape into a bowl. Add 1 Tbsp (15 mL) of the strained cooled fat, ½ tsp (2.5 mL) salt and the prune, if using. The rillettes should be spreadable so add additional fat if necessary. Taste and season with additional salt, if desired.

Portion the cooled pork into small containers. Seal with the partially cooled fat, when it is thick enough to settle on top of the pork, rather than sink to the bottom. Refrigerate until ready to use.

. . . recipe continued

. . . Potted Meat (cont.)

SALMON RILLETTES *makes about 2 cups (500 mL)*

1 lb (450 g) fresh salmon fillet, skin on,
    pin-bones removed

Kosher salt

4 oz (120 g) cured or smoked salmon,
    roughly chopped

¼ cup (60 mL) whipping cream

4 tsp (20 mL) freshly squeezed lemon juice

1 Tbsp (15 mL) capers, rinsed and chopped

½ cup (125 mL) Clarified Butter
    (page 289), melted

■ Cut the salmon to fit a steamer in a single layer.

Season the salmon with a generous pinch of salt and place in a lightly oiled steamer basket over a saucepan filled with 1–2 inches (2.5–5 cm) boiling water. Cover and steam the salmon for 7 minutes then transfer to a bowl. If there are any parts of the salmon that are uncooked, return these to the steamer and cover, but turn off the heat; leave for a few minutes until cooked through.

When the fish is cool enough to handle, remove the skin and break the salmon into small pieces in a medium bowl. Add the smoked or cured salmon, whipping cream, lemon juice and capers; mix well. Taste and season with additional salt or lemon if necessary.

Portion the cooled salmon into small containers. Seal with melted and partially cooled clarified butter when it is thick enough to settle on top of the salmon, rather than sink to the bottom. Refrigerate until ready to use.

DUCK RILLETTES *makes about 1½ cups (375 mL)*

8 oz (230 g) Duck Confit (about 3 legs;
    see page 200 to prepare your own.
    Alternatively, purchase fresh or frozen at
    finer grocery stores.)

¼ cup (60 mL) duck fat, room temperature

Freshly cracked black pepper

SPECIAL EQUIPMENT

Food processor (optional)

■ Pull the meat from the bone, discarding the skin and bone. Chop the duck finely, by hand or with a food processor. Scrape the duck into a bowl, add 2 Tbsp (30 mL) fat and a generous grinding of pepper.

The rillettes should be spreadable, so add additional fat if necessary. The duck should be salty enough from the curing, but taste to make certain and, if necessary, add a pinch more salt.

Portion the duck into small containers. Warm the balance of fat in a small saucepan until it is semi-liquid or just thick enough to pour onto the rillettes and stay put, rather than sink to the bottom. Refrigerate until ready to use.

SPICY POTATO CROQUETTES
makes about 18 croquettes

3 large russet potatoes (about 2 lb [900 g]), peeled and diced

1 tsp (5 mL) whole coriander seeds

1 tsp (5 mL) whole cumin seeds

¼ cup (60 mL) unsalted butter

2 tsp (10 mL) kosher salt

2 tsp (10 mL) freshly squeezed lemon juice, more if desired

¾ tsp (4 mL) ginger, finely grated

½ tsp (2.5 mL) garlic, finely grated

1 serrano pepper, seeds removed and finely chopped

½ tsp (2.5 mL) ground turmeric

BREADING

⅔ cup (160 mL) all-purpose flour

¼ tsp (1 mL) kosher salt

2 eggs, lightly beaten

1½ cups (375 mL) panko bread crumbs

Vegetable oil

SPECIAL EQUIPMENT

Spice blender or mortar and pestle

Microplane zester (optional but ideal for finely grating ginger and garlic)

Instant-read thermometer (optional)

POTATO CROQUETTES are crispy fried morsels usually made with leftover mashed potatoes, but this Indian-spiced version is so flavourful, I don't mind making them from scratch.

Croquettes make a terrific side dish and a popular appetizer, especially when served with Cilantro Mint Sauce (page 17).

They can be prepared up to a day in advance, refrigerated and fried just before serving.

■ Place the potatoes in a medium saucepan with enough water to cover by 1 inch (2.5 cm). Bring to a gentle boil then reduce and simmer, uncovered, until the potatoes are easily pierced with a knife.

While the potatoes are cooking, toast the coriander and cumin seeds in a small dry skillet over medium-high heat until just fragrant. When they have cooled, grind them in a spice blender or with a mortar and pestle.

Drain the water from the potatoes and mash them in a large bowl or mill them through a potato ricer. Add the ground spices, butter, salt, lemon juice, ginger, garlic, pepper and turmeric; blend until well combined. Taste and season with additional salt or lemon juice, if desired.

Scoop about 3 Tbsp (45 mL) of the potato mixture onto your work surface and, using the palm of your hand, gently roll into a log measuring 4 × ¾ inches (10 × 2 cm). Trim the edges and place on a parchment-lined baking sheet. Repeat with the remaining mixture, shaping the croquettes as uniformly as possible. Cover with plastic wrap and refrigerate for at least 30 minutes.

Place 3 shallow bowls on your work surface. Place the flour and salt in the first bowl and mix to combine; the beaten eggs go into the second and panko bread crumbs into the third.

Working with 1 chilled croquette at a time, dredge first in the flour, then gently coat with eggs, then the panko crumbs. If a croquette starts to fall apart, reshape it, chill completely in the refrigerator and coat it again. Cover with plastic wrap and refrigerate for at least 1 hour or up to 24 hours.

Pour enough oil in a heavy skillet to cover the croquettes halfway. Bring the oil slowly to temperature, until an instant-read thermometer reaches 350°F (175°C) or when a cube of bread dropped in the oil turns golden in a minute. Carefully lower the croquettes into the oil, being mindful not to overcrowd the pan, which will render your croquettes soggy rather than crisp. Rotate the croquettes with tongs or a fork to brown evenly.

Transfer to a paper-towel to drain, and sprinkle lightly with salt while warm. Place in a warm oven while cooking the remaining croquettes.

ROASTED SQUASH SOUP

makes 6 – 8 servings

2 medium acorn squash (about 2 lb [900 g] each), halved and seeds removed (and set aside, if roasting)

2 Tbsp (30 mL) vegetable oil

3 large carrots, peeled and chopped into 1-inch (2.5 cm) chunks

Kosher salt

2 Tbsp (30 mL) unsalted butter

1 Granny Smith apple, peeled, cored and diced

1 onion, peeled and diced

1 large ripe pear, peeled, cored and diced

3-4 cups (0.75–1 L) chicken stock (page 257)

1 cup (250 mL) whipping cream

¾ cup (185 mL) crumbled blue cheese (about 3 oz [85 g])

Roasted squash or pumpkin seeds (for garnish; see sidebar)

SPECIAL EQUIPMENT

Food processor or blender

To make your own squash seeds, rinse the squash seeds to remove the fibres and place on a lightly oiled, parchment-lined baking sheet. Roast in a 350°F (175°C) oven until crisp and lightly golden, turning the seeds over occasionally to prevent burning. Sprinkle with salt while still warm.

IT'S HARD to go wrong with a creamy soup that brings together the best of the season: roasted squash, sweet pear and tart apple. This comforting soup is finished with a drizzle of cream, flavoured with blue cheese, a tip I picked up from my friend Castro Boateng, a chef with a gift for balancing flavours. Select a blue cheese as mild or as sharp as you wish. If you don't care to make the cream, simply crumble the cheese over the soup instead.

I've garnished the soup with roasted squash seeds, but toasted pumpkin seeds work nicely too.

This soup, like most, tastes even better the day after preparation.

■ Preheat the oven to 350°F (175°C).

Brush the cut sides of the squash with 1 Tbsp (15 mL) oil. Place cut side down on a prepared baking sheet. Bake for about 1–1½ hours, until completely tender.

Toss the carrots with 1 Tbsp (15 mL) oil and sprinkle with a pinch of salt. After the squash has baked for about 30 minutes, add the carrots to the baking tray. Turn the carrots occasionally to encourage even cooking.

If the vegetables have browned but are still firm, cover them with foil and continue to bake until completely soft. The soup will not be silky if the vegetables are undercooked.

When the squash is cool enough to handle, scoop out the pulp and discard the skin.

Melt the butter in a medium saucepan over medium heat and add the diced apple. Cook the apple until it softens and starts to turn golden. Add the onion, a pinch of salt and the diced pear and cook for about 5 minutes or until the onion is translucent.

Process the roasted vegetables and the apple mixture in a food processor, in batches if necessary, adding enough stock to form a smooth purée. Thin the soup with additional stock until it reaches a smooth creamy consistency. Taste and season with additional salt, if desired.

If you prefer a soup with an ultra-smooth, velvety texture, pour it through a fine-mesh strainer into a clean pot and use the back of a ladle to press the solids against the strainer, extracting as much liquid as possible. Reheat the soup and thin, if necessary, with additional stock. Taste and season with additional salt if desired; set aside.

Heat the cream in a small saucepan, over low heat. Crumble the cheese into the cream and stir until combined and warmed through. Do not boil the cream.

To serve, ladle the warm soup into heated bowls and add a generous swirl of blue cheese cream. Sprinkle with roasted squash or pumpkin seeds.

CROUTONS *makes about 2 cups (500 mL)*

1–2 slices day-old bread, crusts removed

2 tsp (10 mL) vegetable oil

Pinch of ground cumin

Pinch of kosher salt

■ Preheat the oven to 375°F (190°C). Cube the bread and transfer to a bowl; drizzle with oil and toss with cumin and salt. Spread onto a baking sheet and bake until crisp, about 3–5 minutes, turning the croutons once or twice to brown evenly.

CLAM CHOWDER *with* SMOKY CHORIZO

makes 4 servings

....

½ cup (125 mL) dry white wine

3 lb (1.4 kg) fresh clams, cleaned

½ lb (250 g) best quality chorizo
sausage links

1 Tbsp (15 mL) vegetable oil

1 onion, chopped

2 stalks celery, chopped

3 cloves garlic, finely minced

2 Thai chilies, halved with seeds removed

1½ Tbsp (22.5 mL) all-purpose flour

1½ cups (375 mL) whole or 2% milk

½ cup (125 mL) whipping cream

1 cup (250 mL) diced potatoes with a
½-inch [1 cm] thickness (about 1 Yukon
Gold or red-skinned potato), washed but
not peeled

1 tsp (5 mL) freshly squeezed lemon juice

Kosher salt

Croutons (recipe on previous page)

1 Tbsp (15 mL) minced parsley

....

*If not using clams straight away store them in
the fridge nestled atop a colander filled with ice,
with a plate or large shallow bowl underneath to
catch the melting ice. Cover with a damp towel.*

*Although cultivated clams have been purged of
sand, I still soak them in a saltwater solution to
remove any chance traces of grit before cooking.
I may be overly cautious but it's not much work:
Soak clams in sea water or a solution of 1 part
kosher salt and 16 parts water for a couple of
hours. If you notice any sand at the bottom of
the bowl, remove the clams, drain the water and
repeat with a new solution of salt water.*

*Rinse (don't soak) the purged clams in cool
tap water before using.*

*If you find an open clam, give it a tap on
your work surface. If it closes, it's still alive. If
it doesn't, it's dead and must be discarded.*

....

CHORIZO SAUSAGE and Thai chilies impart a spicy, smokey finish to this
deeply flavoured soup. I love the texture of this silky chowder; it's rich
without being thick and heavy.

You'll want to use the freshest of clams and the best chorizo sausage you
can find, preferably from a deli. We have plenty of artisan charcuteries in B.C.
Beast & Brine in South Surrey and Choux Choux Charcuterie in Victoria are
personal favourites, where sausage making is a craft still revered.

....

■ Pour the wine into a pot large enough to steam the clams. Bring the wine
to a boil, add the clams and steam, covered, just until the shells open, about
3–5 minutes. Discard any shells that have have not opened.

Using a slotted spoon, transfer the clams to a clean bowl. Pour the
residual wine/clam broth into the cheesecloth-lined measuring cup.
Separate the meat from the shells, working over a bowl to catch any residual
clam broth. Pour any broth from the bowl into a fine-mesh strainer lined
with cheesecloth, set over a 2-cup (500 mL) container and set aside.

Pierce the sausages in several places with the tip of a knife to prevent
them from bursting. Heat the oil in a medium skillet and cook the sausages
over medium-low heat until cooked through, turning occasionally to
encourage even browning. Remove the sausages and drain all but 1 Tbsp
(15 mL) oil from the pan. Cut the sausages lengthwise and dice into ½-inch
(1 cm) pieces and set aside.

Add the onion and celery to the skillet and cook over medium heat,
scraping up any dark bits on the bottom of the pan. After about 5 minutes,
or when the onion has softened, add the garlic and chilies and stir constantly
for about half a minute. Add the flour and stir for another minute until the
vegetables are coated and the flour lightly cooked.

Add the strained clam broth, milk, cream and diced potatoes. Simmer,
uncovered, for 8–10 minutes, until the potatoes are just cooked through.
Remove the chilies and add the sausage, clams and lemon juice, stirring
to combine. Taste and adjust the seasoning with a pinch of salt only if
necessary—keep in mind the clams and sausage are already salty.

Serve the chowder in warm bowls and garnish with croutons and parsley.

SMOKED DUCK *with* AUTUMN SALAD

makes 4 main-course servings

....

DUCK-CURING MIXTURE

2 boneless duck breasts

½ cup (125 mL) firmly packed light
    brown sugar

¼ cup (60 mL) kosher salt

1 star anise

1 tsp (5 mL) peppercorns

1 tsp (5 mL) coriander seeds

½ Tbsp (7.5 mL) cinnamon powder

1 sprig thyme

2 bay leaves

SALAD

½ cup (125 mL) mild blue cheese (such as
    Stilton or Cambozola), thinly sliced and
    warmed to room temperature

1 ripe pear, cored and sliced just
    before serving

Pear Dressing (recipe follows)

5 cups (1.25 L) baby arugula, washed

½ cup (125 mL) whole walnuts or pecans,
    toasted on a dry skillet until aromatic

SPECIAL EQUIPMENT

2 cups (500 mL) wood chips

1 cup (250 mL) heat-resistant container
    filled with water–for the smoker

Deep metal roasting pan (about 4 inches
    [10 cm] deep)

Food processor or blender (for the
    pear dressing)

I FIRST enjoyed this salad in Victoria when my talented friend Chef Castro Boateng demonstrated it at my former cooking school French Mint. The flavour combination of smoked duck, sweet pear and tangy blue cheese is extraordinary. Castro generously shared his recipe for this book and I didn't even have to beg.

If you've never smoked duck, or any food for that matter, you'll be surprised how easy it is to rig up a smoker in your kitchen. You only need a roasting pan with a lid, wood chips from the hardware store and a metal rack or grill to prop over the wood chips.

I straddle my makeshift smoker over two burners, throw open the windows, and in less than half an hour I have the most succulent duck imaginable. If you're concerned about the smoke, you can place the smoker directly on an outdoor gas or charcoal grill.

The duck is first cured (that is, seasoned with salt, sugar, spices and herbs) for 24 hours before it is smoked. You'll need to plan ahead.

If you can't find fresh duck breasts, frozen and thawed work just as well. Smoked duck breasts last for up to 3 days in the refrigerator.

....

■ CURING THE DUCK Using a sharp knife, trim any silver skin (the sinewy iridescent membrane) from the meat side of each breast. Score the skin in a cross-hatch fashion, as deep as possible without cutting through to the meat.

Place the sugar, salt, spices and herbs in a small bowl, tossing to combine. Pour half the mixture into a container into which the duck breasts can fit side by side. The duck releases moisture as it cures, so use a container that's at least 2 inches (5 cm) deep.

Spread the remaining mixture over the breasts, cover with plastic wrap, and refrigerate for 24 hours.

. . . recipe continued

Pear Dressing

. . . Smoked Duck with Autumn Salad (cont.)

SMOKING THE DUCK Rinse the curing mixture from the breasts with cold water, pat dry with paper towels and set aside to bring to room temperature.

Soak half the wood chips in water for 20 minutes, then drain.

Line a deep metal pan with foil (for easy clean-up). Combine the soaked wood chips with the dry ones and scatter on top of the foil. Place a rack on top of the pan, making sure the rack is about 3–4 inches (8–10 cm) above the wood chips. Place a cup of water on the rack, along with the cured duck breasts, skin side up. Cover with a lid. To minimize the smoke, fashion a temporary seal with tinfoil, crimping the foil where the lid joins the base.

Place your makeshift smoker on the stovetop, straddling 2 burners if necessary, on medium-low heat or in a preheated barbecue if you prefer. In about 10–12 minutes the smoke will fill the container; at this stage, turn the heat to the lowest possible setting and allow the smoke to infuse the duck for 15 minutes. Turn off the heat, remove the duck from the smoker and tent it loosely with foil. Let it rest 5–10 minutes before slicing into the meat. The duck should be rosy-coloured and medium-rare. If not, return it to the smoker and repeat the process.

SERVING THE SALAD When ready to serve, slice the cheese and raw pear. Remove the fat from the duck and slice the breast as thin as possible. Whisk the dressing and, just before serving, toss the greens with just enough dressing to lightly coat them; too much will wilt the salad. Combine the dressed greens with, or serve alongside, the smoked duck, cheese, nuts and pear slices. Serve immediately with additional dressing on the side.

PEAR DRESSING *makes about 1 cup (250 mL)*

1 Tbsp (15 mL) unsalted butter

1 Tbsp (15 mL) light brown sugar

1 ripe pear, cored, peeled and diced

5 Tbsp (75 mL) champagne vinegar or white wine vinegar

¼ tsp (1 mL) kosher salt

¾ cup (185 mL) vegetable oil

◼ Heat the butter in a medium skillet; when it starts to foam add the brown sugar and diced pears, turning often to prevent them from burning. When the pears have turned golden, tip them and the buttery juices into a blender or food processor. Add the vinegar and salt and purée until smooth. With the motor running, slowly add the vegetable oil in a narrow stream. The dressing should be the consistency of light cream—if it's too thick, thin it with a bit of water by the spoonful, with the motor still running. Taste the dressing and season with additional salt and vinegar, if desired.

POTATO GRATINS

makes 4 servings

....

4 medium Yukon Gold or new potatoes
   (about 1 lb [450 g]), peeled and washed
¼ cup (60 mL) unsalted butter, melted +
   extra for buttering the ramekins
¼ cup (60 mL) whipping cream
1 tsp (5 mL) kosher salt
½ cup (125 mL) freshly grated
   Parmesan cheese

SPECIAL EQUIPMENT
Four 4-oz (120 g) ceramic ramekins or
   ovenproof containers
Mandoline or hand-held vegetable slicer
   (optional but very handy)

THIS IS one of the most comforting dishes imaginable, and easy to put together—especially if you own a mandoline or hand-held vegetable slicer.

Gratins are great for company because they can be made ahead of time, refrigerated and reheated when needed. They can be served directly from the oven in their containers or inverted onto a plate, as pictured. Either way, potatoes, cheese and cream never disappoint.

....

■ Lightly butter ramekins and set aside.

Preheat oven to 350°F (175°C).

Slice the potatoes ⅛ inch (3 mm) thick, as uniform as possible, preferably with a mandoline or vegetable slicer. (Some food processors come equipped with a handy slicing attachment.)

Place the sliced potatoes in a large bowl with the melted butter, cream and salt, tossing with tongs or a spatula to coat the potatoes evenly.

Stack the potato slices into the prepared ramekins and trim the edges as necessary for a snug fit. Sprinkle every third layer with about ½ tsp (2.5 mL) grated Parmesan, ending with the cheese on top. The potatoes can be stacked to the container's rim; they'll puff up a bit during cooking then deflate slightly when removed from the oven.

Place the ramekins on a baking sheet and bake for about 30–40 minutes, or until the potatoes are tender when tested with a skewer or the tip of a knife. If the gratins brown before they're tender, cover with foil and continue baking.

Serve directly from the containers or run a knife around the ramekin's edge and carefully invert onto a plate, protecting your hands with an oven-mitt or tea towel.

Leftover gratins can be cooled in their ramekins, covered with plastic wrap and stored in the refrigerator for up to 3 days. To reheat, remove the plastic wrap, place the ramekins on a tray, cover with foil and reheat in a 325°F (160°C) oven until warmed through.

BUTTERMILK ROASTED CHICKEN
makes 4–6 servings

1 cup (250 mL) buttermilk

1 tsp (5 mL) finely minced garlic

1 tsp (5 mL) finely minced ginger

Kosher salt

2½ lb (1.2 kg) chicken legs or thighs (about 10 legs or 6–8 thighs)

1 Tbsp (15 mL) ground coriander

1 Tbsp (15 mL) ground cumin

⅓ cup (80 mL) all-purpose flour

2–3 Tbsp (45 mL) vegetable oil

For a low-calorie alternative to this recipe, marinate boneless, skinless chicken breasts in the buttermilk mixture for an hour and steam or grill.

WHEN CHICKEN is marinated in buttermilk infused with ginger and garlic, the meat becomes incredibly moist and flavourful. This simple dish is a weeknight favourite at our house and is especially good served with Chickpea and Vegetable Stew (page 154).

The chicken must be marinated overnight, so be sure to plan ahead.

■ Mix together the buttermilk, garlic, ginger and 1 tsp (5 mL) salt in a small bowl.

Rinse the chicken pieces with cold water and pat dry. Place the chicken in a freezer bag and pour the buttermilk marinade over the chicken; seal the bag. Place the bag in a bowl (to safeguard against leaks) and refrigerate overnight, or up to 48 hours, turning the bag occasionally to distribute the marinade.

When you're ready to cook the chicken, preheat the oven to 375°F (190°C).

Combine the ground spices, flour and 1 tsp (5 mL) salt in a medium-sized bowl.

Drain the chicken and thoroughly pat dry. Discard the marinade. Toss the chicken, a few pieces at a time, in the seasoned flour.

Heat the oil in a large nonstick skillet. Brown the chicken in batches, over medium heat, until golden, being mindful not to crowd the pan.

Transfer the seared chicken to the prepared baking sheet and roast in the preheated oven for about 20–30 minutes, or until the chicken is cooked through. Turn the chicken pieces over once during baking.

MUSHROOM LOVER'S TART
makes 3–4 serving

1 lb (450 g) Handcrafted Puff Pastry
    (page 266)

1 egg, lightly beaten

3 Tbsp (45 mL) freshly grated
    Parmesan cheese

½ cup (125 mL) grated Gruyère cheese

¼ cup (60 mL) goat cheese

2–3 Tbsp (45 mL) whole or 2% milk

1–1½ lb (450–700 g) assorted wild or
    cultivated mushrooms (chanterelle,
    button, shiitake, oyster, portobello, etc.)

¼ cup (60 mL) unsalted butter, divided

1 cup (250 mL) chopped shallots

1 tsp (5 mL) fresh thyme leaves

Kosher salt

¼ cup (60 mL) vegetable oil + extra
    as needed

¼ cup (60 mL) white wine vinegar

2 tsp (10 mL) soy sauce

Beautiful large portobello mushrooms are just grown up button mushrooms.

THREE DIFFERENT cheeses combined with mushrooms and shallots make for a heady combination in this richly flavoured tart.

The secret to flavourful mushrooms is allowing them to brown in the skillet until they fully develop their flavours. Don't crowd the pan, you'll end up with bland tasting, pale, steamed mushrooms.

Plan to make this tart shell in advance or prepare it when you're in the mood for an afternoon of leisurely cooking. This tart can be made in advance and reheated just before serving.

■ You'll need to first prepare the Handcrafted Puff Pasty according to the instructions on page 266.

Roll the dough about ⅛ inch (3 mm) thick on a sheet of lightly floured parchment paper. Cut the pastry into 5 pieces: one 12- × 5-inch (30 × 12 cm) rectangle for the tart base, 2 strips measuring 12 × ¾ inches (30 × 2 cm) and 2 strips measuring 5 × ¾ inches (12 × 2 cm). Brush the border of the pastry's base with the egg and place the pastry strips along the border to form the tart's edges. Cover the pastry with plastic and refrigerate for 30 minutes.

Preheat the oven to 425°F (220°C).

Remove the tart from the fridge and prick the base several times with a fork (to prevent the pastry from buckling in the oven) then sprinkle with Parmesan cheese. Brush the tart's edges with the egg.

Reduce the oven temperature to 350°F (175°C). Transfer the tart to a parchment lined baking sheet and bake for 15–20 minutes, or until the edges are golden, rotating the pan once.

Combine the Gruyère and goat cheese in a small bowl and thin with 2–3 Tbsp (30–45 mL) milk, until spreadable. Set aside.

Wipe the mushrooms clean with a damp cloth or rinse briefly in cold water and pat dry. Shiitake mushroom caps can be left whole, but remove the tough stems. Tear chanterelles and oyster mushrooms in half or, if small, keep whole. Slice or quarter the button mushrooms.

Melt 1 Tbsp (15 mL) butter in a medium skillet over medium heat; add the shallots, thyme and a pinch of salt and cook, stirring frequently, until the shallots are translucent. Transfer to a medium bowl.

Cook the mushrooms in batches, starting with the heartier ones and ending with the delicate, quick-cooking mushrooms. Heat 1 Tbsp (15 mL) each butter and oil in the same skillet, over medium-high heat. Add a handful of mushrooms to the skillet along with a pinch of salt, being mindful not to crowd the pan. Shake the pan to coat then cook, undisturbed, until the mushrooms have coloured on one side; adjust the heat as necessary to prevent burning. Toss the mushrooms and continue to cook until brown all over. Add 1 Tbsp (15 mL) vinegar, ½ tsp (2.5 mL) soy sauce, stir and allow the liquid to evaporate. Transfer to the bowl of cooked shallots.

Cook the balance of mushrooms in the same manner, starting with butter and oil and ending with vinegar and soy sauce after the mushrooms have browned. If the pan becomes too dry, add a splash of water.

. . . recipe continued

. . . Mushroom Lover's Tart (cont.)

Combine the cooked mushrooms and shallots; taste and season with additional soy sauce or vinegar if desired.

Spread the cheese mixture over the base of the partially cooked tart. Top with the shallot and mushroom mixture.

Bake on a parchment-lined baking sheet for about 15 minutes or until warmed through. Serve warm or at room temperature.

GNOCCHI *in a* PARMESAN SAUCE *with* ROASTED TOMATOES *&* FENNEL

makes 6–8 servings as a main course, 8–10 as an appetizer

Potato Gnocchi (page 277)

SAUCE

⅓ cup (80 mL) unsalted butter

⅓ cup (80 mL) all-purpose flour

1 cup (250 mL) whole or 2% milk

2¼ cups (560 mL) chicken stock (page 257)

¼ cup (60 mL) freshly squeezed lemon juice (more if desired)

½ cup (125 mL) grated Parmesan cheese

½ tsp (2.5 mL) kosher salt

1 tsp (5 mL) Dijon-style mustard

½ tsp (2.5 mL) hot red pepper flakes

VEGETABLES

2 cups (500 mL) cherry tomatoes, sliced in half

1 tsp (5 mL) freshly chopped rosemary

1 tsp (5 mL) freshly chopped thyme

3 Tbsp (45 mL) vegetable oil, divided

Kosher salt

2 small fennel bulbs, cored and thinly sliced

1 Tbsp (15 mL) coriander seeds, crushed

Freshly cracked black pepper

I OWE my love of handcrafted gnocchi to my daughter, Elise. Years ago, while grocery shopping, she picked up a vacuum-sealed package of gnocchi and asked me what it was. I told her they were heavy, dense dumplings and that I didn't think she'd like them. She pestered until I agreed we'd have gnocchi for dinner, but only if we made them from scratch. Our first attempt produced a gnocchi so light and tender they've been part of our dinner repertoire ever since.

In this recipe, the gnocchi is tossed in a savoury cheese sauce and topped with roasted tomatoes and caramelized fennel. It makes for a perfect fall appetizer or hearty main dish.

The gnocchi can be prepared and cooked days in advance and reheated when serving. The sauce, too, can be prepared ahead of time.

■ You'll need to first prepare and cook the gnocchi according the instructions on page 277. You'll have more than you need for this recipe, so plan to freeze the rest.

Preheat oven to 350°F (175°C).

SAUCE Melt the butter in a medium saucepan over medium-low heat. Whisk in the flour and cook for a few minutes, stirring constantly until the mixture is golden and smells slightly nutty. Add the milk, stirring constantly until the mixture is smooth and very thick. Add the stock and continue to stir until completely smooth. Add the remaining sauce ingredients and gently simmer until the mixture has reduced and is thick enough to coat the back of a spoon. Taste the sauce and season with additional salt and lemon if necessary. Keep warm until ready to serve.

VEGETABLES Combine the tomatoes, rosemary, thyme, 1 Tbsp (15 mL) oil and ½ tsp (2.5 mL) kosher salt, in a medium bowl and toss to coat. Spread the tomatoes onto a baking sheet (lined with foil or parchment), cut-side up. Roast for about 15–30 minutes, or until the tomatoes are tender and have started to collapse. Reserve any tomato liquid to pour over the gnocchi just before serving.

. . . recipe continued

. . . Gnocchi in a Parmesan Sauce with Roasted Tomatoes and Fennel (cont.)

Heat 2 Tbsp (30 mL) oil in a medium saucepan until very hot, but not smoking. Add the sliced fennel in batches, being mindful not to crowd the pan. Season each batch with a pinch of salt and a generous pinch of coriander. Cook a few minutes on each side until the edges are crisp and golden brown. Drain on a paper towel and keep warm in a low-temperature oven.

SERVING To reheat the gnocchi, bring a pot of water to a boil and briefly plunge the cooked gnocchi into it, being mindful not to overcook the dumplings. Remove with a slotted spoon and portion into heated bowls.

Serve gnocchi with a generous spoonful of sauce and top with fennel, roasted tomatoes and any residual tomato liquid.

Garnish with freshly cracked black pepper, if desired.

SAUSAGES & SAUERKRAUT *with* APPLE
makes 4–6 servings

1 Tbsp (15 mL) vegetable oil

8 bratwurst sausages (about 1½ lb [700 g])

6-7 slices bacon (about ½ lb [250 g]), diced

2 medium onions, diced

¼ tsp (1 mL) kosher salt, divided

3 cups (750 mL) good quality sauerkraut, rinsed and drained

1 cup (250 mL) chicken stock (page 257)

2 sprigs thyme

2 bay leaves

2 Granny Smith apples

1 Tbsp (15 mL) unsalted butter

Dijon-style mustard

I REDISCOVERED sauerkraut a few years ago at Relish, one of my favourite restaurants in Victoria. I was so taken with their sauerkraut, which was paired with cod of all things, I asked the chef-owner, Jamie Cummins, to teach at my cooking school. He did and this sauerkraut is an adaptation of Jamie's recipe.

The success of this simple dish relies on the quality of the ingredients. If you're lucky enough to live near a deli or charcuterie, that's where you'll find the best quality bacon and bratwurst. And where there's bratwurst, sauerkraut is never far behind. Some delis even make their own. If you can't find deli-made, opt for sauerkraut sold in glass jars rather than tins.

■ Preheat the oven to a low temperature to keep the sausages warm while you're preparing the rest of the dish.

Heat the oil in a large skillet over medium heat; add the sausages and prick them in several places with the tip of a knife to prevent them from bursting. Brown the sausages until the meat is firm and cooked through. Transfer to an ovenproof plate, cover with foil and hold in the warm oven until ready to serve.

Drain the skillet of all but 1 Tbsp (15 mL) of fat. Add the bacon and cook over medium-high heat until the fat has rendered and the bacon is cooked through. Transfer to a plate lined with paper towels.

Drain the skillet of all but 1 Tbsp (15 mL) of fat, reserving the excess fat. Add the onions and a pinch of salt and cook over medium heat until the onions are soft and starting to brown. Add the rinsed sauerkraut, chicken stock, thyme, bay leaves, cooked bacon and another pinch of salt. Stir the mixture until well-combined and simmer, uncovered, until the stock has completely evaporated and the sauerkraut is just moist.

. . . recipe continued

. . . Sausages and Sauerkraut with Apple (cont.)

While the stock is reducing, peel, core and slice the apples. Melt 1 Tbsp (15 mL) of the reserved bacon fat in a medium skillet over medium heat. Place the apple slices in the skillet in a single layer and cook in batches until browned on one side before turning them over. The apples are done when they are tender and browned on both sides.

Just before serving, remove the sprigs of thyme and bay leaves from the sauerkraut. Add the butter and combine thoroughly. Taste and season with additional salt, if desired. Serve the sauerkraut and sausages with the cooked apple and Dijon-style mustard on the side.

MUSHROOM & WINE RAGÙ *with* HANDCRAFTED PASTA

makes 2–4 servings

1 lb (450 g) cooked Fresh Pasta (page 270)

1 lb (450 g) assorted wild and/or cultivated mushrooms (chanterelle, button, shiitake, oyster, portobello, etc.)

¼ cup + 1 Tbsp (75 mL) unsalted butter, divided + extra if needed

½ cup (125 mL) shallots or onions, chopped

2 cloves garlic, finely chopped

¼ cup (60 mL) vegetable oil + extra if needed

Kosher salt

¾ cup (185 mL) dry red wine, divided

1 cup (250 mL) Roasted Chicken or Beef Stock (page 257) + extra as needed

¼ cup (60 mL) whipping cream

¼ cup (60 mL) freshly grated Parmesan cheese + extra if desired

½ tsp (2.5 mL) fresh thyme leaves

Freshly cracked black pepper

When sautéeing mushrooms, or anything cooked in a fair bit of fat (oil, butter or duck fat), keep an empty bowl nearby with a fine-mesh strainer placed over it. If you find your skillet has too much oil, tip the mushrooms and fat into the strainer then return the drained mushrooms to the skillet. The excess fat can be reused when needed.

THIS RICH, hearty mushroom ragù is deeply satisfying when served over homemade pasta. It also makes a superb topping for pizza and pairs beautifully with steak or eggs.

While technically not a ragù, the word has become my default tag for any rustic, richly flavoured sauce. When I asked my friend Terra what she calls it, she responded: "Most Excellent *%$#%@ Mushroom Sauce Ever!"

Call it what you will, just be sure to use mushrooms that are fresh and firm, within a few days of foraging or purchasing.

■ You'll need to first prepare the pasta according to the instructions on page 270. Cook pasta just before serving, it's ready in minutes.

Wipe the mushrooms clean with a damp cloth or rinse briefly in cold water and pat dry. Shiitake mushroom caps can be left whole but remove the tough stems. Tear chanterelles and oyster mushrooms in half or, if small, keep whole. Slice or quarter button mushrooms.

Melt 1 Tbsp (15 mL) butter in a medium skillet over medium heat; add the shallots and cook over medium heat until soft and translucent. Add the garlic and cook until aromatic, about half a minute. Transfer to a clean bowl.

Cook the mushrooms in batches, starting with the heartier ones and ending with the delicate, fragile mushrooms, which cook quickest. For each batch, heat 1 Tbsp (15 mL) each butter and oil in the same skillet over medium-high heat. Add a handful of mushrooms to the skillet along with a pinch of salt, being mindful not to crowd the pan (crowding the pan will steam the mushrooms rather than colour them). Shake the pan to coat the mushrooms in butter and oil, then cook, undisturbed, until the mushrooms have coloured on one side. Toss the mushrooms and continue to cook until brown all over. Transfer to the bowl containing the shallots.

You'll notice the bottom of your pan developing a golden patina—this contains the mushroom's flavourful essence. Add a generous splash of wine to your empty skillet and scrape the bottom of the skillet clean with a heat-resistant spatula. Pour the liquid into the bowl of shallots and mushrooms.

. . . recipe continued

. . . Mushroom and Wine Ragù with Handcrafted Pasta (cont.)

Continue cooking the mushrooms in batches adding a pinch of salt with each batch. Add a splash of wine to the skillet whenever the pan darkens.

Return all the cooked mushrooms, shallots and any liquid to the skillet. Add the remaining wine, increase the heat and continue to cook until the liquid has all but evaporated.

Add the stock and bring to a boil, allowing the liquid to evaporate by about half. Reduce the heat, add the whipping cream, cheese and thyme, and simmer until the sauce reduces enough to lightly coat the back of a spoon. Taste and season with additional salt if desired.

Serve over fresh pasta and garnish with additional Parmesan cheese and freshly cracked pepper.

ROASTED CAULIFLOWER
& BROCCOLI PESTO PIZZA
makes two 9-inch (23 cm) pizzas

Whole Wheat Pizza Dough (page 273)

1 small head cauliflower
   (about 1½ lb [250 g])

2 Tbsp (30 mL) vegetable oil, divided

¼ tsp (1 mL) kosher salt

Broccoli Pesto (recipe follows)

1 cup (250 g) crumbled feta (about 4 oz
   [120 g]), divided

2 Tbsp (30 mL) freshly grated
   Parmesan cheese

½ lemon, sliced

SPECIAL EQUIPMENT

Pizza stone (optional)

Food processor (for the broccoli pesto)

THIS MAKES a nice change from a typical tomato-based pizza. The dough is easy to make and comes together quickly. The dough tastes even better after a day in the fridge.

The crust is slathered with a vibrant garlic-lemon broccoli pesto and topped with feta and sweet roasted cauliflower. The pesto, which also doubles as a great pasta topping, can be made in advance.

If you have a pizza stone, use it; it distributes the heat evenly and makes for a crisp crust.

■ You'll need to first prepare the pizza dough according to the instructions on page 273.

Preheat a pizza stone or baking sheet in a 375°F (190°C) oven.

Divide the pizza dough in half and place each portion on a sheet of parchment dusted with flour. Stretch and shape the dough with your hands or a rolling pin to fashion 2 pizzas about 9 inches (23 cm) each in diameter. Cover and set aside while you prepare the toppings.

Trim and core the cauliflower; slice the florets to a ¼-inch (6 mm) thickness and break into bite-sized pieces. Transfer to a large bowl, drizzle with 1 Tbsp (15 mL) oil and sprinkle with salt. Toss to combine, then spread onto a parchment-lined baking sheet in a single layer. Bake for about 20–30 minutes, tossing occasionally, or just until the cauliflower starts to turn golden around the edges. (The cauliflower will be baked again with the pizza.) Meanwhile, prepare the pesto (page 154). Remove the cauliflower and increase the oven temperature to 450°F (230°C).

Spread each pizza with about ¼ cup (60 mL) pesto, leaving a ½-inch (1 cm) border. Distribute the feta over the pesto, then top with the roasted cauliflower. Brush the pizza border with oil.

Transfer each pizza, along with the parchment, to the preheated pizza stone or baking sheet in the oven; bake for about 10–12 minutes or until the edges are crisp.

. . . recipe continued

. . . Roasted Cauliflower & Broccoli Pesto Pizza (cont.)

Sprinkle with freshly grated Parmesan and serve with lemon slices on the side.

BROCCOLI PESTO *makes 1 cup (250 mL)*

2 cups (500 mL) broccoli florets (about 1 small crown), broken into 2-inch (5 cm) pieces

½ cup (125 mL) flat-leaf parsley

½ cup (125 mL) fresh basil leaves

1 clove garlic, sliced

2 anchovies, lightly rinsed

½ tsp (2.5 mL) kosher salt

4 tsp (20 mL) freshly squeezed lemon juice

6 Tbsp (90 mL) vegetable oil

■ Blanch the broccoli florets in heavily salted boiling water (about 2 tsp [10 mL] salt per 4 cups [1 L] water) for about 2 minutes; remove with a slotted spoon and transfer to a bowl of very cold water and drain.

Place the broccoli and remaining pesto ingredients into the bowl of a food processor and pulse to a spreadable consistency, leaving some irregular pieces. Alternatively, chop the ingredients finely with a knife. Taste and season with additional salt and lemon juice if desired.

Pesto keeps in the fridge for up to 1 week.

Broccoli pesto is lovely slathered on sandwiches or spooned over poached eggs, pasta and gnocchi.

CHICKPEA & VEGETABLE STEW
makes 4 servings

1½ tsp (7.5 mL) freshly ground coriander

1½ tsp (7.5 mL) freshly ground cumin

1½ Tbsp (22.5 mL) all-purpose flour

Kosher salt

1 Tbsp (15 mL) vegetable oil

1 onion, diced

2 medium carrots, peeled and chopped

2 celery ribs, chopped

5 cloves garlic, peeled and left whole

Three 1-inch (2.5 cm) pieces fresh ginger, peeled

1 large very ripe tomato, chopped

1 Tbsp (15 mL) tomato paste

1 cup (250 mL) dry white wine

1–1½ cups (250–375 mL) chicken stock (page 257)

1 cup (250 mL) cooked chickpeas (preferably from dried; cooking instructions on page 246)

1 tsp (5 mL) white wine vinegar

1 tsp (5 mL) fish sauce

1 tsp (5 mL) hot sauce (such as Sriracha)

2 Tbsp (30 mL) plain Greek yogurt

2 Tbsp (30 mL) freshly chopped cilantro

THIS EASY stew combines the warm and earthy flavours of cumin and coriander, with tart tomato and fresh ginger. I love the texture of chickpeas in this dish, but feel free to substitute your favourite bean. Like all stews, the flavours intensify after a day in the fridge.

Delicious served over quinoa or rice and paired with Buttermilk Roasted Chicken (page 142).

■ Combine the spices, flour and ½ tsp (2.5 mL) salt in a small bowl.

Heat the oil in a large skillet and add the onion, carrots, celery, garlic, ginger and ¼ tsp (1 mL) salt; cook over medium heat for about 3 minutes, stirring occasionally. Add the seasoned flour and stir for about a minute to coat the vegetables and cook the flour. Add the tomato and tomato paste and stir to coat; add the wine and simmer to reduce for about 2 minutes, scraping the bottom of the pan to dislodge any bits stuck to the bottom. Add 1 cup (250 mL) stock and simmer, uncovered, for about 30 minutes or until the vegetables are tender and the sauce has thickened. Add additional stock, or water, as necessary to prevent the stew from drying out.

Discard the chunks of ginger and add the chickpeas. Remove skillet from the heat and add the vinegar, fish sauce and hot sauce, stirring to combine. Mix in the yogurt and taste, adding additional salt or hot sauce if desired. Garnish with cilantro.

FALL | *sweet*

FALL APPLE TART

makes one 10-inch (25 cm) tart

Sweet Tart Dough (page 265; you'll only
    need half for this recipe, freeze the rest)

7 Granny Smith apples, divided

4 tsp (20 mL) freshly squeezed lemon
    juice, divided

6 Tbsp (90 mL) sugar, divided

3 Tbsp (45 mL) unsalted butter, divided

3 egg yolks

¾ cup (185 mL) whipping cream

1 Tbsp (15 mL) apple jelly or 1 Tbsp (15 mL)
    honey thinned with ½ tsp (2.5 mL) hot
    water (optional)

SPECIAL EQUIPMENT

10-inch (25 cm) fluted tart pan with a
    removable bottom.

*If you've ever wrestled with keeping foil secure
around a tart's edge, while leaving the centre
exposed, you'll appreciate this tip: Cover the
entire empty tart shell with foil, secure the edges
in place, then cut-out the centre with scissors,
leaving only an inch (2.5 cm) border of foil. Set
aside until needed.*

COOKS LOVE talking about food and sometimes these conversations spark
an idea for a recipe. My sister-in-law Nicky, an avid cook, asked if I'd ever
made an apple custard tart. At the time I had not, but I loved the idea of
combining tart apples with sweet custard. This open-faced tart is a result of
that sweet exchange.

The pastry for this recipe is made with Sweet Tart Dough, a firm, cookie-
like dough that can be made well in advance.

The elegant apple spiral is simple to create with a little patience. The key
is to slice the apples thinly, otherwise they don't cook through or fan out
properly on the tart.

Once baked, this tart freezes exceptionally well.

◼ PASTRY Prepare the Sweet Tart Dough according to the instructions
on page 265. Place the dough onto a sheet of parchment dusted with flour;
cover with a sheet of plastic wrap and roll into a circle ⅛ inch (3 mm) thick.
Fit the dough into the tart pan, trimming excess dough from the edges;
cover with plastic and refrigerate until ready to fill.

FILLING Preheat oven to 375°F (190°C). Peel, quarter and core 4 apples. Slice
½ inch (1 cm) thick, place in a large bowl and toss with 2 tsp (10 mL) lemon
juice and 3 Tbsp (45 mL) sugar.

Melt 2 Tbsp (30 mL) butter in a large skillet over medium heat and add
the sugar-coated apple slices. Toss the apples in the butter and cook for
about 10 minutes, or until the apples turn golden on one side, shaking the
pan occasionally to prevent sticking.

Turn the apple slices over and cook, partially covered, until soft and
golden, about another 10 minutes, adding a spoonful of water as necessary
to prevent sticking. Transfer the apples into a bowl.

CUSTARD In a 2-cup (500 mL) jug, whisk the yolks, then stir in the cream
and 2 Tbsp (30 mL) sugar. Pour the custard over the cooked apples, stir to
combine and set aside to cool.

TOPPING Peel, quarter and core the remaining apples. Slice the apples as
uniformly as possible, a mere ⅛ inch (3 mm) thin. Place the slices in a large
bowl and toss with the remaining (2 tsp) lemon juice.

. . . recipe continued

Despite the speed with which the soufflés were dispatched from the oven to the camera, they started their inevitable collapse before Caroline could photograph them at their loftiest height. We cursed their descent, then Caroline sighed and said, "Well, they're real, Denise." Real is what we went with.

. . . Fall Apple Tart (cont.)

PUTTING IT ALL TOGETHER Remove the tart shell from the fridge and fill with the cooled apple-custard mixture, patting the apples smooth with a spatula. Starting in the centre of the tart, fan a small spiral of raw apple slices, with each slice slightly overlapping the next. Fan a second spiral to the tart's edge. Sprinkle the apples with remaining (1 Tbsp [15 mL]) sugar and dot with remaining (1 Tbsp [15 mL]) butter.

Cover the tart's edge completely with foil to prevent the pastry from burning.

Place the tart on a baking sheet and bake for 45–50 minutes or until the apple slices are tender with golden-tinged edges, rotating the pan once during baking.

Brush with glaze, if desired, and cool completely before serving.

PEAR SOUFFLÉS
with CARDAMOM *&* GINGER
makes 6 – 8 soufflés

1 cup (250 mL) whole or 2% milk

½ cup (125 mL) sugar, divided + extra for molds

Two 3-inch (8 cm) cinnamon quills (also referred to as "sticks")

1 cardamom pod, lightly bruised with the side of a knife or the bottom of a small pot

1 clove

3 medium or 4 small firm but ripe pears, peeled, cored and diced

2 Tbsp (30 mL) light brown sugar

1 tsp (5 mL) finely grated fresh ginger

2 tsp (10 mL) freshly squeezed lemon juice

2 Tbsp (30 mL) unsalted butter

4 egg yolks, room temperature

¼ cup (60 mL) all-purpose flour

6 egg whites, room temperature

Pinch of cream of tartar

SPECIAL EQUIPMENT

Six to eight 6-oz (175 g) soufflé molds or ramekins

Electric mixer

CARAMELIZED PEAR and ginger form the base for these delicate soufflés, flavoured with cinnamon, cardamon and cloves. If the thought of preparing soufflés makes you nervous, you'll be pleased to know all but the whipped egg whites can be prepared the day before serving.

If you really want to indulge your guests, serve the soufflés with Crème Anglaise (page 293).

▪ Brush the molds or ramekins with butter and generously dust with sugar; tap out excess sugar. Refrigerate until ready to use.

Preheat the oven to 375°F (190°C).

Heat the milk with ¼ cup (60 mL) sugar, cinnamon quills, cardamom and clove in a small saucepan over medium heat. Bring to a simmer then turn off the heat, set aside to allow the spices to infuse the milk.

Place the diced pears, brown sugar, ginger and lemon juice in a medium-sized bowl and toss until the fruit is evenly coated.

Melt the butter in a large nonstick skillet over medium heat then add the pears.

Cook the pears until golden, about 8–10 minutes, turning the fruit occasionally until the liquid has evaporated. When the fruit has cooled, divide it among the prepared molds. (If not using immediately, cover with plastic wrap and refrigerate up to 24 hours. Bring to room temperature before using.)

. . . recipe continued

. . . Pear Soufflés with Cardamom and Ginger (cont.)

Whisk the egg yolks with the balance of white sugar in a medium bowl, until the yolks turn a paler shade of yellow. Add the flour and mix well. The mixture will be very stiff at this stage.

Strain the milk mixture and discard the solids. Return half the milk to the saucepan and warm it over medium heat. Pour the balance of the milk into the yolk mixture, mix until smooth, then return it to the saucepan of warm milk.

Whisk continuously over medium heat until the mixture firms to a thick custard and just starts to boil. Transfer the hot custard to a medium bowl to cool slightly. (If not using immediately, cover with plastic and refrigerate up to 24 hours. Bring to room temperature and re-mix to loosen, before using.)

In an exceptionally clean bowl, whisk the egg whites with a pinch of cream of tartar at medium speed until a network of tiny bubbles have formed, about 1 full minute. Gradually increase the speed to high and whip until the whites have expanded and formed billowy, firm glossy peaks. Be mindful not to over-whip, otherwise the whites will turn grainy and lose their shape.

Gently fold the egg whites into the bowl of custard in 3 to 4 batches, mixing until well incorporated. Scoop the mixture into the pear-lined containers, up to about three-quarters full. Smooth the custard with the back of a spoon.

Place on a baking sheet and bake for about 15–20 minutes or until the soufflés have risen and the tops are golden.

STICKY BUNS
makes 12 large buns

DOUGH

1 Tbsp (15 mL) quick-rise (instant) yeast

1½ cups (375 mL) lukewarm water

¼ cup (60 mL) sugar

3 Tbsp (45 mL) vegetable oil

1 tsp (5 mL) table salt

1 eggs (room temperature)

3½ cups (875 mL) all-purpose flour + extra
   as needed

1 Tbsp (15 mL) unsalted melted butter

SYRUP BASE

¾ cup (185 mL) unsalted butter

¾ cup (185 mL) light brown sugar

¾ cup (185 mL) whipping cream

3 Tbsp (45 mL) honey

3 Tbsp (45 mL) maple syrup

¼ tsp (1 mL) kosher salt

NUTTY FILLING

½ cup (125 mL) firmly packed light
   brown sugar

¼ cup (60 mL) white sugar

2 tsp (10 mL) ground cinnamon

Pinch ground nutmeg

¼ tsp (1 mL) kosher salt

2 Tbsp (30 mL) unsalted butter

¾ cup (185 mL) chopped hazelnuts

¾ cup (185 mL) chopped walnuts

¼ cup (60 mL) chopped dried cranberries

SPECIAL EQUIPMENT

9- × 12-inch (23 × 30 cm) baking dish

ANYONE WITH a sweet tooth will appreciate these sticky buns stuffed with dried cranberries, hazelnuts and walnuts, smothered in a rich honey-maple topping.

This recipe is made in three easy steps: the dough, syrup base and nutty filling. It's important to pre-measure all the ingredients before you start. While the dough is rising, you'll prepare the syrup and filling. If your ingredients are organized and ready to go, you won't risk over-rising the dough which can compromise the texture of the buns.

Rest assured this recipe was tested by novice bakers with "definitely-going-to-make-this-again" results.

This versatile dough is also used for the Dinner Buns recipe (page 274).

■ Preheat oven to 360°F (180°C).

Before you get started, butter the sides of the baking dish (it isn't necessary to butter the base).

DOUGH In the bowl of a standup mixer, or a deep mixing bowl if mixing by hand, combine the yeast with the water, sugar, oil, salt and eggs; whisk together until there are no traces of yeast. Using the dough hook attachment (or a sturdy wooden spoon if mixing by hand) start with about 3 cups (750 mL) flour and gradually add more as necessary for the dough to come together and pull away from the edge of the bowl, about 3–4 minutes. The dough will be very sticky.

Whether you're using a machine or not, finish kneading the dough by hand. Turn the dough out onto a lightly floured surface, incorporating more flour as needed until the dough is smooth, about 5–7 minutes. The dough will be slightly sticky.

Shape the dough into a ball and place into a lightly oiled bowl; rotate the dough to cover it with a light film of oil. Loosely cover with a damp towel and allow the dough to rise in a warm draft-free area.

When the dough has doubled in size, after about 20 minutes, gently punch the dough down a few times to deflate it. Reshape the dough into a ball, cover, and allow it to rise until it has doubled again, about 20 minutes.

While the dough is rising, prepare the syrup base and filling.

SYRUP BASE Combine the syrup ingredients in a small saucepan. Stir over medium heat until the butter has melted and the sugar has dissolved. Pour all but ½ cup (125 mL) syrup into the prepared baking dish and set aside.

NUTTY FILLING Mix together the sugars, spices and salt in a medium bowl. Blend in the butter using a fork or your fingertips until the mixture is fairly uniform. Add the nuts and fruit and mix until well combined; set aside.

PUTTING IT ALL TOGETHER On a generously floured work surface, roll out the dough (or stretch it with your hands) into a rectangle about 11 × 16 inches

. . . recipe continued

. . . Sticky Buns (cont.)

(28 × 40 cm). The dough tends to spring back but will stay in place with additional rolling.

Brush the dough with melted butter, then distribute the nutty filling evenly over the dough, leaving a 1-inch (2.5 cm) border along one of the long (16 inch [40 cm]) ends. Work quickly to prevent the dough from over-rising.

Working from the end with no border, carefully roll the dough around the filling as snugly as possible, ending with the dough seam-side down. Cut the dough with a serrated bread knife into 12 equal portions and transfer to the pan with the syrup base, spiral facing up.

Bake in a preheated oven for 30–35 minutes until well browned, rotating the pan once. Cover with foil and bake for an additional 10–15 minutes, until golden.

Brush the warm buns with the remaining syrup.

APPLE CRANBERRY BREAD PUDDING
makes 6 bread puddings

1 cup (250 mL) Crème Anglaise (page 293)

1 day-old baguette (I like ciabatta but you can use any type of bread)

1½ Tbsp (22.5 mL) unsalted butter + extra for coating the muffin wells

2 Tbsp (30 mL) sugar + extra for the muffin wells

2 tsp (10 mL) ground cinnamon

1 Granny Smith apple, peeled, cored and diced

¼ tsp (1 mL) kosher salt

⅓ cup (80 mL) chopped dried cranberries

3 eggs

¾ cup (185 mL) whole or 2% milk

¾ cup (185 mL) whipping cream

SPECIAL EQUIPMENT
Six 2½-inch (6 cm) muffin wells

FRESH-FROM-THE-OVEN bread pudding flavoured with caramelized apples, cinnamon and cranberries makes an excellent dessert or breakfast treat.

Bread pudding is a fine way to use up old bread. Traditionally considered a poor man's comfort food, it makes a luxurious treat, especially when served fresh from the oven with Crème Anglaise.

Bread pudding can be prepared in advance and kept in the refrigerator until ready to bake. Crème Anglaise can be made up to three days in advance.

■ Preheat oven to 350°F (175°C).

Prepare the Crème Anglaise following the instructions on page 293.

Coat the muffin wells generously with butter then dust with sugar; knock out excess sugar.

Trim the crust from the bread and cut into 1-inch (2.5 cm) cubes; you should have about 5–6 cups (1.25–1.5 L) bread. Place into a large bowl.

Melt the butter in a medium nonstick skillet over medium heat and add the sugar, cinnamon, diced apple and salt. Cook until the apples are soft and golden brown, about 6–8 minutes, shaking the pan or turning the apples with a spatula occasionally to colour them evenly.

Transfer the cooked apples to the bowl of bread, add the cranberries and mix to combine.

Crack the eggs into a medium bowl and mix lightly with a fork; add the milk and cream and stir to combine. Pour the custard over the bread and fruit and mix well.

Divide the mixture among the prepared muffin wells, piling the bread high above the rim. Sprinkle generously with sugar.

Bake for about 30–40 minutes or until the tops are nicely toasted. Serve warm, drizzled with Crème Anglaise.

APPLE TURNOVERS

makes 12 turnovers

....

1 lb (450 g) Handcrafted Puff Pastry
(page 266) or Flaky Pastry Dough
(page 262)

4 cups (1 L) diced Granny Smith apples
(about 3 large apples), peeled, cored and
cut into ½-inch (1 cm) cubes

1 Tbsp (15 mL) freshly squeezed lemon juice

2 Tbsp (30 mL) unsalted butter

6 Tbsp (90 mL) brown sugar

1 egg, lightly beaten or 1 Tbsp (15 mL)
whipping cream

1 Tbsp (15 mL) sugar

SPECIAL EQUIPMENT

Round cookie cutter 3½–4 inches (9–10 cm)
in diameter (optional)

FRESH-FROM-THE-OVEN turnovers will have your kitchen smelling like a bakery.

The apple filling is precooked to avoid soggy pastry and to keep the turnover light and crisp. I've prepared these with puff pastry, but they could be made with flaky pastry dough too.

Turnovers can be prepared in advance and refrigerated until you're ready to bake them.

If you plan to serve them warm, make a double batch. They won't last.

....

■ You'll need to first prepare the Handcrafted Puff Pastry or Flaky Pastry Dough according to the instructions on pages 266 or 262.

Preheat oven to 375°F (190°C).

Toss the apples and lemon juice together in a medium bowl.

Melt the butter in a large skillet over medium heat; add the apples and brown sugar, stirring to coat the apples.

The apples will turn soft in about 5 minutes; it will take another 15–20 minutes to turn golden. Turn them every so often to colour them evenly—be gentle, you want nice cubes of apples, not applesauce. The apples will reduce to about half their original size and the liquid must be evaporated completely, otherwise the pastry will get soggy. Cool the apples before using.

Roll the pastry onto a floured work surface to a thickness of about ⅛ inch (3 mm). Cut the pastry into 12 rounds using a cookie cutter measuring 3½–4 inches (9–10 cm) in diameter (a small bowl works too).

Add a generous spoonful of cooled apples to the centre of each pastry round. Brush the edge of the pastry with a bit of beaten egg or whipping cream and fold the dough over to create a half circle. Seal the edges, gently with your fingers first, then with the tines of a fork. Repeat with the remaining pastry.

Place the turnovers on a parchment-lined baking sheet. Cover with plastic wrap and chill until firm, at least 30 minutes or up to 24 hours.

When ready to bake, brush the pastry lightly with the beaten egg or whipping cream and sprinkle with a bit of white sugar. Using a sharp knife, score the top of the pastry to create 3 air vents. Bake for 15–20 minutes or until the pastry is golden, turning the pan once.

BAKED APPLES

makes 4 baked apples

....

4 medium baking apples, washed

2 Tbsp (30 mL) unsalted butter, softened

4 tsp (20 mL) light brown sugar

¼ cup (60 mL) chopped walnuts

¼ cup (60 mL) raisins or cranberries or a
  combination of both

¼ cup (60 mL) goat cheese

¼ cup (60 mL) pure maple syrup

Vanilla ice cream (optional, but highly
  recommended)

SPECIAL EQUIPMENT

Apple corer (optional)

FRAGRANT BAKED apples stuffed with fruit, nuts and cheese are so simple they hardly merit a recipe. Crystallized ginger, pecans, dried cherries, apricots, hazelnuts—I've baked them all in apples at one time or another. Consider this a nudge to find inspiration in your pantry rather than a firm recipe.

Most apples can be baked, so select your favourite variety—just avoid Red Delicious as they don't hold up well to heat.

Baked apples are especially flavourful served warm with a scoop of vanilla ice cream. It's like apple pie without all the fuss.

....

■ Preheat oven to 350°F (175°C).

Remove the core from each apple with an apple corer or paring knife and create an opening about 1 inch (2.5 cm) in diameter, being careful to leave the bottom of each apple intact. Place the cored apples on a parchment-lined baking sheet.

Combine the butter, brown sugar, nuts and raisins in a small bowl. Divide and spoon the mixture into the hollow of each apple. Divide the cheese and press it lightly on top of the nuts and raisins. Drizzle with maple syrup.

Bake the filled apples for 30–40 minutes, or until the apples are soft and easily pierced with the tip of a knife. Baste occasionally with the maple syrup.

Serve warm with vanilla ice cream, if desired.

WHOLE WHEAT CRANBERRY SCONES

makes 12–14 scones

1½ cups (375 mL) whole wheat flour

1½ cups (375 mL) all-purpose white flour

¼ tsp (1 mL) table salt

2 tsp (10 mL) baking powder

½ tsp (2.5 mL) baking soda

½ cup (125 mL) sugar

1 cup (250 mL) cold unsalted butter,
     chopped into ½-inch (1 cm) pieces

½ cup (125 mL) dried cranberries,
     finely chopped

1½ cups (375 mL) whipping cream + extra
     to brush the scones just before baking

2 Tbsp (30 mL) light brown sugar
     (for the topping)

SPECIAL EQUIPMENT
Circle-shaped 2½-inch (6 cm) cookie cutter

WHILE TESTING this recipe I had so many scones in the freezer that my twins were tossing them into their lunch bags. I figured my testing was complete when I learned the scones were a valuable trading commodity during school lunch.

I used to make scones with white flour only but now I use half whole wheat—the texture is more satisfying and without the heaviness often associated with whole wheat baked goods.

I often double the recipe and freeze half. Baked scones freeze well. You can also freeze the shaped dough and thaw before baking.

■ Preheat the oven to 375°F (190°C).

Combine the flours, salt, baking powder, baking soda and white sugar in a large bowl and mix with a whisk or fork.

Cut the butter into the flour using a pastry blender or 2 knives until the mixture is crumbly with some irregular pieces. Add the cranberries and mix to combine.

Add the cream and mix with a fork. When the mixture becomes too unmanageable to mix with a fork, use your hands to gather the dough. If the dough is too dry to gather together, add additional cream by the spoonful until it just comes together.

Turn the dough and any bits of flour onto a floured work surface. Using your hands, shape the dough into a 6-inch (15 cm) diameter disc.

Gently roll the dough to a thickness of 1 inch (2.5 cm) and about 9 inches (23 cm) in diameter.

Dip the cookie cutter into the flour to stamp out each scone. Gather together any remnants of dough and stamp out additional scones.

Place the scones on a parchment-lined baking sheet, leaving at least 1 inch (2.5 cm) between each. Brush each scone with a bit of cream and sprinkle with ½ tsp (2.5 mL) brown sugar.

Cover with plastic wrap and refrigerate for half an hour, or up to 24 hours, before baking.

Bake in a preheated oven until golden, about 15 minutes, rotating the pan once. Best served warm.

HONEY CRÊPES *with* PEARS

makes 10–12 crêpes

CRÊPES

1 cup + 3 Tbsp (295 mL) all-purpose flour

1½ cups (375 mL) whole or 2% milk

4 large eggs, lightly beaten

¼ cup (60 mL) unsalted butter, melted

3 Tbsp (45 mL) honey

¼ tsp (1 mL) kosher salt

CARAMELIZED PEARS

2 medium pears, ripe but firm

1 Tbsp (15 mL) unsalted butter

2 Tbsp (30 mL) sugar

Jam or jelly (optional)

Icing sugar (optional)

SPECIAL EQUIPMENT

Blender or food processor (optional)

Stack leftover crêpes between layers of parchment, store in a freezer bag and freeze up to 1 month.

FALL WEEKENDS are made for crêpes and caramelized pears are the perfect complement. Crêpes are a special treat and they're quick and easy to prepare, especially if you make the batter in a blender the night before.

If you enjoy crêpes, it's worth investing in a nonstick crêpe pan. They're specially designed with a shallow, tapered rim to hold a thin layer of batter. Some pans even come with a wooden (T-shaped) crêpe spreader to evenly distribute the batter but I find swirling the pan works perfectly well.

Delicious served with your favourite jam or jelly and a dusting of powdered sugar.

◼ CRÊPES Place the flour in a medium bowl, add the remaining crêpe ingredients and mix until smooth. Alternatively, place the ingredients in a food processor or blender and process until smooth. Cover the batter with plastic wrap and refrigerate for an hour, or up to 24 hours.

Heat a crêpe pan or nonstick skillet over medium heat. Pour about ⅓ cup (80 mL) of the batter into the pan, tilting the pan to evenly distribute the batter. When the crêpe starts to form tiny bubbles, after about 30 seconds, loosen the edges with a nonstick spatula, peel the crêpe from the pan (I used my fingertips) and flip the crêpe over. Alternatively, loosen the edges and give the pan a quick upward jerk to flip the crêpe, hopefully, back into the pan. Each crêpe takes less than 2 minutes. Hold the crêpes in a warm oven until ready to serve.

CARAMELIZED PEARS Cut the pears in half, leaving the skin intact. Remove the core and slice into wedges. Melt the butter in a medium nonstick skillet over medium heat; add the pears in a single layer and sprinkle evenly with sugar. Cook the pears until golden, about 3–5 minutes per side.

To serve, fold each crêpe in half, fill with warm pears and your favourite jam or jelly if desired, and roll, placing the crêpe seam-side down. Dust with icing sugar, if desired.

CHOCOLATE MOUSSE *with* PEAR CHIPS
makes 4–6 servings

8 oz (230 g) good quality dark chocolate,
  chopped into small chocolate-chip
  size pieces
2 cups (500 mL) whipping cream,
  chilled, divided
4–6 Pear Chips (optional; recipe follows)
4–6 Chocolate Leafs (optional; recipe follows)

SPECIAL EQUIPMENT
Heat-resistant bowl
Electric mixer (optional)

THE KEY to this rich, melt-in-your-mouth mousse is to have your tools close at hand. With only two ingredients, chocolate and cream, the recipe is more about preparation than culinary finesse.

Once the cream and melted chocolate collide, the mousse firms quickly, so have your containers nearby. A piping bag is useful for distributing the mousse into narrow glasses but a small spoon works too.

If you'd like your mousse to peer above the rim of the containers, as pictured, wrap parchment paper around the containers first (as shown on page 179).

The mousse is rich and best served in small sherry or shot glasses.

If you'd like to garnish your mousse with pear chips and chocolate leaves, plan to make these in advance.

■ Place the chocolate and ¼ cup (60 mL) whipping cream in a heat-resistant bowl placed over a saucepan filled with 1 inch (2.5 cm) of simmering water. Stir until the chocolate is just melted then remove from the heat.

Pour the remaining whipping cream into a large bowl or the bowl of a standup mixer fitted with a wire whisk. Whisk the cream until just thick enough to form soft peaks.

Working quickly, pour the melted chocolate into the whipped cream, using a spatula to scrape any remaining melted chocolate left clinging to the bowl. Whisk the chocolate into the cream until the mixture is uniform in colour and has thickened.

Spoon or pipe the mousse into glasses and refrigerate until set.

Take the mousse out of the refrigerator about 20 minutes before serving. Remove the parchment collar, if using, and garnish with a pear chip and chocolate leaf, if desired.

. . . *recipe continued*

. . . Chocolate Mousse with Pear Chips (cont.)

PEAR CHIPS *makes 1 pear's worth*

1 firm, slightly underripe pear, washed

1 cup (250 mL) sugar

1 cup (250 mL) water

Zest of 1 lemon

■ Preheat the oven to 200°F (95°C) and line a baking sheet with parchment paper.

Combine the sugar, water and lemon zest in a small saucepan over low heat until the sugar is completely dissolved.

Slice the pear paper-thin.

Coat both sides of each pear slice with the sugar water mixture and place on a prepared baking sheet without overlapping any slices.

Dry the pear slices in the oven for 2–3 hours, carefully turning them over once. Allow the pears to cool for 10 minutes then gently peel the slices from the parchment. If the pears are not firm and crisp once cooled, continue to dry them in the oven.

The pear chips can be made a few days ahead of time and kept in a covered container.

CHOCOLATE LEAVES *makes 8–12 leaves*

6 oz (175 g) good quality chocolate, chopped into small, chocolate-chip size pieces

8–12 small, firm non-toxic leaves such as holly or rose, washed and completely dried

■ Place the chocolate in a heat-resistant bowl over a saucepan filled with 1 inch (2.5 cm) simmering water. When the chocolate has melted, dip one side of each leaf into the chocolate and place on a parchment-lined baking sheet. Reserve leftover chocolate for another use.

Once the chocolate has firmed, carefully peel the leaves from the chocolate.

WINTER

....

Winter: a time for celebrations and snowmen—or incessant rain, depending on where you live. Kitchen windows steam up from savoury pies or aromatic stew. Come in from the cold, build a crackling fire and enjoy the comforts of hearty winter fare.

....

Winter in British Columbia can be as exciting or relaxing as you choose. Bobsledding the Olympic runs on Whistler Mountain, ice fishing in Kamloops, storm-watching off Tofino's coastline . . . or just curling up with a good book. Whatever your winter joy, nothing caps a blustery day like a steaming mug of cranberry and apple juice laced with rum (page 237).

Cold days are for puttering in the kitchen, and few foods are more comforting than Chicken Pot Pies (page 207) or Minestrone with Tomato Cilantro Pistou (page 188). Both can be made a day or two in advance—just be sure to make plenty, because they won't last.

When the weather turns cold, I tend to cook with meat more often. My winter favourites include Rustic Beef Stew (page 211), Stuffed Pork Loin with Braised Cabbage (page 216) and Slow-Braised Lamb with Polenta (page 203). Much of our local beef comes from the sprawling cattle ranches of the Cariboo in central BC, and the Kootenays to the southeast. Pork and poultry are raised throughout the province, but the majority come from the Fraser Valley. Fortunately, winter farmers' markets are gaining popularity throughout the province, providing greater access to our local bounty all year long.

Holiday entertaining is easy with finger foods like light and airy Cheese Puffs (page 184) and exquisite Nutty Caramel Cream Puffs (page 225). Both are made from the same dough and can be frozen until ready to bake. The antipasto offerings (page 287) provide a variety of quick-pickled vegetables, mushrooms and marinated olives—ideal for grazing and stress-free entertaining. And Frosted Cranberry Jellies (page 234) and Cranberry Meringue (page 223) always make for festive party offerings.

My favourite holiday gifts are the edible sort, and not just the sweet variety. I enjoy giving jars of Duck Confit (page 200), preserved in fat. It makes for a unique gift and I've never met anyone who doesn't like it—even those who have never tried duck. (They'll also have the luxury of using the duck fat to fry potatoes, a gift in itself.) The reduced port sauce used in the Poached Pear recipe (page 226) makes a decadent gift for sweet or savoury tastes. I drizzle it on everything from ice cream to roast pork.

Of course holidays wouldn't feel the same without a few edible traditions like my Christmas morning Swiss Chard & Ham Strada (page 192) and the elegant Root Vegetable Terrine (page 199). Sweet or savoury, these recipes will warm you from the inside out.

View from Whistler cable car, between Whistler and Blackcomb mountains

WINTER | *savoury*

CHEESE PUFFS (GOUGÈRES)

makes about 48 cheese puffs

1 cup (250 mL) whole or 2% milk

1 cup (250 mL) water

¾ cup + 1 Tbsp (200 mL) unsalted butter, cut into pieces

2 tsp (10 mL) (10 mL) kosher salt

2½ tsp (12.5 mL) sugar

2 cups (500 mL) all-purpose flour

4–5 eggs

1 cup (250 mL) Gruyère cheese

1 egg slightly beaten (for egg wash)

SPECIAL EQUIPMENT

Pastry bag fitted with a round tip or a spring-loaded ice cream scoop

Electric mixer (optional)

If you enjoy tinkering, the dough can be flavoured with just about anything: finely chopped herbs, pickled jalapeño peppers, ham, anchovies, spices—to name a few.

To freeze unbaked cheese puffs, place them onto a baking tray, cover with plastic and freeze. Once firmed, transfer them to a freezer bag to save space. When ready to bake, portion the frozen cheese puffs onto a baking tray, leaving at least a 1-inch (2.5 cm) space between each. Thaw about 40 minutes before baking.

WHEN I taught cooking classes in Victoria, I started each lesson by offering warm, freshly baked pastries. It was a happy, fragrant beginning to each class and I never met a student who didn't enjoy them.

Gruyère-flavoured cheese puffs are so light and airy, their centres are all but hollow. They're made of choux (SHoo) pastry, an incredibly versatile dough that's easy to make. And once you've mastered choux pastry, you can create cream puffs (page 225), potato fritters (page 124) and numerous other classic recipes.

For special occasions, you can split the pastries in two and stuff them with your favourite filling. I love them filled with hand-peeled shrimp bound in a lemony mayonnaise, flecked with dill. If the filling is moist, line the baked pastries with a crisp piece of lettuce to prevent them from becoming soggy.

For perfectly shaped cheese puffs, you'll need a pastry bag, fitted with a round tip. A spring-loaded ice cream scoop distributes the dough evenly too.

◼ Preheat oven to 425°F (220°C).

Combine the milk, water, butter, salt and sugar in a medium saucepan. Bring the mixture to a full boil then remove the pan from the heat. Add the flour all at once and stir vigorously with a wooden spoon until the mixture forms a ball and pulls away from the sides of the pan.

Transfer the dough to a large bowl or a mixer fitted with the paddle attachment and allow the dough to cool for 5 minutes. Add the eggs one at a time, at medium speed if using a machine, mixing thoroughly after each addition.

The dough is ready when it hangs from your mixing utensil in a thick sticky paste. It should be supple enough to squeeze through a pastry bag or scoop onto a baking sheet. If the mixture is too firm, add another egg. Finally, add the grated cheese.

If you are using a pastry bag, spoon the dough into a bag fitted with a plain pastry tip. Pipe round mounds about 1¼ inches (3 cm) diameter onto a parchment-lined baking sheet, leaving 1–2 inches (2.5–5 cm) between each mound.

Alternatively, portion the dough using a spoon or an ice cream scoop onto the baking sheet.

If you've used a pastry bag, you'll notice a little peak on each mound where the pastry tip was released; gently smooth it out with the tip of your finger.

Brush the top of each mound with the beaten egg. Set aside for 15 minutes before baking.

Bake for 10 minutes then reduce the temperature to 350°F (175°C) and bake for another 15–25 minutes, rotating the pans halfway through baking. Test 1 gougère; it should be slightly hollow in the centre. If not, turn the oven off and leave the gougères until they are cooked through.

Best served warm.

PAN-FRIED MUSSELS
makes 2–4 servings

2 lb (900 g) mussels, rinsed and beards
    removed (see sidebar)
1 cup (250 mL) dry white wine
3 Tbsp (45 mL) unsalted butter
6 garlic cloves, thinly sliced
1½ tsp (7.5 mL) freshly squeezed
    lemon juice
Kosher salt
1 Tbsp (15 mL) freshly chopped parsley
    or cilantro
Fresh baguette (optional, for serving)

*Select mussels with tightly closed, undamaged
shells. Store in the fridge nestled atop a colander
of ice, with a larger bowl underneath to catch
the melting ice. Cover with a damp towel and
replace the ice as necessary. Because you'll likely
discard a few, it's best to buy a little more than
you need.*

*To clean mussels, rinse (don't soak) them
under cold-running tap water, and remove any
grit with a kitchen brush. If a mussel is open,
give it a tap on your work surface. If it closes,
it's still alive. If it doesn't, it's dead and must
be discarded.*

*Just before cooking, remove the mussel's
beard, the tough stringy threads attached to the
shell, by sharply tugging at it. (This kills the
mussel, so don't do this ahead of time.)*

THIS RECIPE was inspired by a sizzling skillet of mussels I enjoyed at Le Plat à Oreilles, a small but busy café in Bordeaux, France. I met the lone chef, Jean-Philippe, and his hostess wife, Evelyne, who gave me a tour of their neat compact kitchen. My family and I returned to their restaurant so many times we left with a gift of Jean-Philippe's homemade preserves and the inspiration to recreate these exquisite mussels.

I hope this recipe does justice to Jean-Philippe.

■ Place a fine-mesh strainer lined with cheesecloth over a small saucepan and set aside.

In a pot large enough to fit the mussels, bring the wine to a boil. Tip the cleaned mussels into the pot and steam, covered, for about 3–5 minutes or just until the mussels open.

Transfer the cooked mussels to a large bowl and pour the wine broth through the prepared strainer, into the saucepan. Simmer the broth over low heat until the liquid has reduced, about 10 minutes. You'll need only a small amount, about ¼ cup (60 mL). (Leftover broth can be frozen and used in any recipe that calls for seafood broth.)

Separate the meat from the mussel shells and discard the shells. Strain any residual juice from the mussels into the saucepan of simmering broth.

In a skillet just large enough to fit the mussels in a single layer, melt the butter and half the garlic; cook for about a minute over medium heat until aromatic, tilting and swirling the pan to make sure the garlic does not take on any colour.

Add the mussels and balance of the garlic, and swirl the pan to coat the mussels in the butter. Add ¼ cup (60 mL) of the reduced broth and cook on medium to medium-high until the liquid has reduced and the mussels are covered in a syrupy glaze, about 5–6 minutes.

Add freshly squeezed lemon juice and a light pinch of salt and toss to combine. Garnish with freshly chopped parsley or cilantro and serve immediately with a fresh baguette.

MINESTRONE
with TOMATO CILANTRO PISTOU
makes 12–14 servings

....

2 Tbsp (30 mL) olive oil

4 slices bacon, finely chopped

2 medium onions, diced

2 cups (500 mL) green cabbage,
    finely chopped

Kosher salt

2 cloves garlic, chopped

3 medium carrots, peeled and diced

2 stalks celery, diced

10 cups (2.5 L) Roasted Chicken or Beef
    Stock (page 257)

½ lb (250 g) Kielbasa sausage, cut in half

One 14.5 oz (420 g) can diced
    plum tomatoes

1½ cups (375 mL) cooked navy beans
    (preferably from dried; cooking
    instructions on page 246)

Bouquet garni (thumb-size bunch parsley
    [stems included], 2 bay leaves and
    4 sprigs thyme tied together with
    kitchen string)

Parmesan rind (about 3 inches [8 cm];
    optional, but strongly recommended)

GARNISH

1½ cups (375 mL) cooked small pasta shells

1½ cups (375 mL) Tomato Cilantro Pistou
    (recipe follows)

½ cup (125 mL) Parmesan cheese, grated or
    shaved with a vegetable peeler

1 bunch fresh spinach, chopped

Freshly ground black pepper

THIS ROBUST minestrone is made with a roasted chicken stock infused with kielbasa sausage and a generous chunk of Parmesan rind. The rind has loads of flavour and the sausage imparts a smoky, garlicky punch. I add cooked pasta just before serving to prevent it from getting mushy.

I love minestrone served with lots of last-minute garnishes: raw spinach, shaved Parmesan and a great dollop of pistou made with piquant peppers, shallots, lime and freshly chopped cilantro.

This soup gets even better over a day or two. It's worth making a big batch.

....

▪ Heat the oil in a large pot, add the bacon and cook over medium heat until partially cooked; add the onions, stirring occasionally until they start to brown.

Add the cabbage and a pinch of salt and cook until the cabbage starts to turn golden, about 10 minutes. Add the garlic, stir and cook for half a minute until aromatic. Add the remaining soup ingredients and a generous pinch of salt and simmer until the vegetables are tender.

Remove and discard the bundle of herbs, bay leaves and Parmesan rind, if using. Remove the sausage and cut into bite-sized pieces. Taste the soup and season with additional salt, if desired.

To each warmed soup bowl, add a few slices of sausage and a spoonful of cooked pasta. Ladle the hot soup over the pasta and top with a generous dollop of pistou. Garnish with Parmesan, raw spinach and freshly ground pepper.

TOMATO CILANTRO PISTOU *makes about 1½ cups (375 mL)*

1 small shallot, finely chopped

1–2 serrano peppers, sliced in half, seeds removed and finely chopped

1 cup (250 mL) cherry tomatoes, finely chopped

1 large bunch cilantro, washed, stems removed and finely chopped

⅓ cup (80 mL) vegetable oil

¼ tsp (1 mL) kosher salt

Juice from 1 lime + extra if desired

SPECIAL EQUIPMENT
Food processor (optional)

If using a food processor or blender, there's no need to finely chop the ingredients—roughly chopped will do.

■ Combine all ingredients in a small bowl and mix well. Alternatively, toss everything in a food processor and purée until smooth, scraping down the sides of the bowl with a spatula. Taste and season with additional salt or lime, if desired.

WINTER SALAD *with* SESAME DRESSING
makes 6–8 servings

....

3 cups (750 mL) red cabbage
   (about ½ small head), thinly sliced

1 cup (250 mL) red onion (about ½ onion),
   thinly sliced

¼ cup (60 mL) rice vinegar

Kosher salt

½ large head cauliflower (about 14 oz
   [420 g]), chopped into bite-sized pieces

2 Tbsp (30 mL) vegetable oil, divided

1 bunch kale (about 8 oz [230 g]), washed
   and coarsely chopped (reserve the stems
   for soup)

1 cup (250 mL) thinly sliced carrots (about
   2–3 medium carrots)

1 cup (250 mL) thinly sliced celery (about
   2–3 stalks)

⅓ cup (80 mL) goat cheese, crumbled
   (about 3–4 oz [90–120 g])

⅓ cup (80 mL) hazelnuts, skinned and
   toasted in a dry pan

1 Tbsp (15 mL) dried cranberries,
   finely chopped

Sesame Dressing (recipe follows)

THE UNLIKELY combination of my favourite raw and roasted vegetables comes together beautifully in this hearty and vibrant salad.

Roasted kale provides a satisfying chewy texture when moistened with the dressing. It also serves as a last-minute crispy garnish along with the toasted hazelnuts.

This makes a lovely accompaniment to roast chicken or beef and is delicious rolled in handmade Flour Tortillas (page 278).

....

■ Preheat the oven to 375°F (190°C).

Place the cabbage and onion in a medium bowl; add the vinegar and ¼ tsp (1 mL) salt. Toss to combine then set aside while roasting the vegetables.

Toss the cauliflower in a large bowl with 1 Tbsp (15 mL) oil and a pinch of salt. Spread evenly onto a prepared baking sheet and roast for about 30 minutes, or until tender and browned around the edges; turn the cauliflower once during roasting. Transfer to a bowl.

Toss the kale in a large bowl with 1 Tbsp (15 mL) oil and a pinch of salt, spread evenly onto the same parchment-lined baking sheet that the cauliflower was cooked on. Roast until crisp, about 10–15 minutes, turning the kale over once.

Just before serving, tip the cabbage and onion into a sieve to drain the vinegar.

In a large bowl, toss the drained cabbage and onions with the balance of ingredients, reserving a large handful of kale as a crispy garnish. Toss with about 3 Tbsp (45 mL) Sesame Dressing, then transfer to a clean salad bowl. Top with the reserved kale and serve with dressing on the side.

SESAME DRESSING *makes about 1 cup (250 ml)*

½ cup (125 mL) vegetable oil

2 Tbsp (30 mL) sesame oil

¼ cup (60 mL) rice vinegar

1 tsp (5 mL) soy sauce

½ tsp (2.5 mL) each sugar and salt

½ tsp (2.5 mL) freshly grated ginger

½ tsp (2.5 mL) freshly minced garlic (about
   1 clove)

½ tsp (2.5 mL) hot red pepper flakes

SPECIAL EQUIPMENT
Food processor (optional)

■ Combine all of the dressing ingredients in a small bowl and mix well. Alternatively, toss everything in a blender or food processor and purée until smooth. Cover and store in the refrigerator until ready to use. Leftover dressing keeps in the fridge for 2 weeks.

SWISS CHARD & HAM STRADA
makes 8 servings

3 Tbsp (45 mL) unsalted butter, softened,
    divided + extra for the casserole pan
1 onion, diced
Kosher salt
3 cups (750 mL) finely chopped Swiss chard
    leaves (stems reserved for another use)
1 Tbsp (15 mL) freshly squeezed lemon juice
1 loaf day-old white bread, cut lengthwise
    into ½-inch (1 cm) slices
2 Tbsp (30 mL) Dijon-style mustard
12 oz (360 mL) thinly sliced deli ham
1½ cups (375 mL) grated Gruyère cheese
8 whole eggs
2 cups (500 mL) whole or 2% milk
½ cup (125 mL) whipping cream
Pinch of nutmeg

SPECIAL EQUIPMENT
2 quart (2.2 L) casserole pan

*Leftover bread can be cut into cubes or pulsed
into crumbs in a food processor. Toss with a bit
of oil and dry in a low oven until crisp. Crumbs
or croutons can be stored in a plastic freezer bag
and frozen for up to 2 months.*

*Chop Swiss chard stems and add them to stocks
and soups, or blanch them in salted water and
toss them in salads.*

THIS IS my favourite brunch during the holidays. It's prepared the night before, feeds a crowd and always brings appreciative reviews. It makes for a relaxing no-fuss Christmas breakfast.

The strada is created by cutting bread lengthwise, layering the filling on top and then rolling the bread and filling jelly-roll fashion. Most bakers are happy to cut an unsliced loaf lengthwise for you. You can do so yourself, but if you're a stickler for uniformity, leave it to the pros.

■ Brush the casserole pan with butter and set aside.

Melt 1 Tbsp (15 mL) butter in a large saucepan over medium heat; add the onion and ½ tsp (2.5 mL) salt and cook for about 5 minutes or until the diced onions have softened.

Add the Swiss chard, another ½ tsp (2.5 mL) salt and stir to combine. Cook for about 2 minutes or until the chard has wilted. Add the lemon juice and stir to combine. Taste the chard and season with additional lemon or salt if desired. Set aside.

Trim the crusts from 6 slices of bread. Brush the length of one side of each slice with the mustard and remaining butter. Layer each slice with equal amounts of ham, Gruyère cheese and cooked chard.

Starting at the short end of the bread, roll each slice as you would a jelly roll, gathering any bits of stray filling and tucking them back in the bread as you roll.

Using a bread knife, cut each roll in half, spirals facing outward, then place the cut rolls in the prepared baking dish, cut sides up. (Bake any leftover trim separately in a suitably sized ramekin.)

Whisk together the eggs in a medium bowl and add the milk, cream, 1 tsp (5 mL) salt and a pinch of nutmeg. Stir to combine, then pour the custard evenly over the bread.

Cover the strada with plastic wrap, then place a small plate or cutting board on top, weighted with a couple of 14 oz (420 g) cans. Refrigerate overnight.

About an hour before you're ready to serve, place the strada on a baking sheet, remove the weights and bring to room temperature.

Remove the plastic wrap and bake in a 350°F (175°C) preheated oven for 60 minutes or until slightly puffed and golden on top, rotating the pan once during baking.

BAKED EGGS
makes 6 baked eggs

....

1 Tbsp (15 mL) melted unsalted butter

1–1½ cups (250–375 mL) savoury filling
   (see below)

3 Tbsp (45 mL) freshly grated
   Parmesan cheese

6 eggs

Kosher salt

Freshly ground black pepper

6 Tbsp (90 mL) whipping cream

SPECIAL EQUIPMENT

6 ramekins or ovenproof containers

Baking dish as deep as the containers and
   roomy enough for at least a 1-inch
   (2.5 cm) space between each

....

Whatever filling you use, first warm it through, taste and season it well with salt (and pepper if desired). Add a few drops of fresh lemon juice or vinegar, if it needs a little perking up. Fillings can be as firm or as creamy as you wish.

   Here are but a few filling suggestions, or have a peek into your fridge to come up with your own:

roasted tomatoes and garlic
sautéed chicken livers and onions
sautéed mushrooms and shallots
creamed spinach or chicken
diced baked ham with Gruyère cheese
cooked crumbled spicy sausage with tomatoes
poached shrimp or crabmeat
diced cooked bacon and spinach
blue cheese and sautéed leeks
smoked chicken with cooked diced asparagus
ratatouille
sautéed fennel and celery root

....

I ENJOYED many versions of baked eggs, or *oeufs en cocotte*, during a summer in France where they were often served for lunch or as an appetizer. I love them anytime—they're easy to prepare, cook quickly and transform everyday leftovers into French bistro fare.

   I've used a filling of sautéed kale and mushrooms, but any savoury filling will do. I often start with sautéed onion, then add whatever morsels my fridge has to offer.

   Consider this a template for making your own.

....

■ Preheat oven to 350°F (175°C) and bring a kettle or pot of water to a boil.

   Brush the inside of each ramekin with the melted butter. Place about ¼ cup (60 mL) seasoned filling into each ramekin and top with a spoonful of grated Parmesan cheese.

   Make a slight indentation in the filling with the back of a spoon in which to nestle the egg. Break an egg on top and season with salt and pepper. Drizzle with 1 Tbsp (15 mL) cream.

   Pour boiling water into the pan so that it comes halfway up the sides of the ramekins; be mindful not to spill water into the ramekins. Cover the pan with foil and carefully transfer into the oven.

   Bake just long enough to set the egg whites and firm the yolks to your liking, anywhere from 12 minutes for a runny egg to 18 minutes for a firm yolk. Timing varies depending on the size of containers and number of servings being baked at once. Rotating the pan halfway during baking helps the eggs cook evenly.

   If the eggs are slightly undercooked, allow the ramekins to rest for a couple of minutes outside the oven before serving; the residual heat will firm up the eggs.

POTATO RÖSTI

makes 1 rösti (2 servings)

2 large Yukon Gold or new potatoes,
    washed but not peeled
1 medium shallot, grated
½ tsp (2.5 mL) kosher salt
¼ cup (60 mL) vegetable oil, rendered
    bacon or duck fat
4 slices cooked bacon, diced
2 Tbsp (30 mL) goat cheese
Freshly ground black pepper

SPECIAL EQUIPMENT
8-inch (20 cm) heavy-bottomed
    nonstick pan

*There are about two dozen varieties of potatoes
in BC, generally classified into four categories:
red (or red skinned), yellow (or yellow fleshed),
white and brown-skinned Russet potatoes. Most
varieties can be used interchangeably, with the
exception of Russet which are best suited to
baking and mashing.*

RÖSTI (pronounced ROOSH-TEE) is simply grated potatoes pressed into a sizzling, well-oiled pan. They're traditionally served flat, but I've nudged mine into a little potato nest with a ring of chopped bacon and a coin of goat cheese. A poached egg works nicely too.

I precook my potatoes slightly to give them a head start. This ensures they're cooked on the inside when they're golden on the outside.

I use an 8-inch (20 cm) well-seasoned, cast iron skillet for this dish. Your pan should have a nonstick surface so the potatoes come out in one piece. Keep in mind, the smaller the pan, the easier it is to manage.

■ Preheat your oven to the lowest setting to keep the potatoes warm.

Fill a medium saucepan with the potatoes and enough water to cover them by 1 inch (2.5 cm). Bring to a gentle boil over medium heat for about 8 minutes until the potato is partially cooked and still firm when pierced with the tip of a knife. Plunge the potatoes into cool water to stop the cooking.

Grate the partially cooked potatoes into a bowl, using the largest hole of a box grater. Add the shallot and salt and stir to combine.

For each rösti, heat 2 Tbsp (30 mL) oil or fat in a nonstick pan over medium heat. Add half the grated potato mixture, leveling the potatoes with a spatula, and cook undisturbed for a few minutes, until the bottom is well browned. Regulate the heat as necessary to prevent burning. (If you move the potatoes about the pan, they won't stay in one solid piece when you turn them over.) Place a plate on top of the skillet then flip the pan over so that potatoes land on the plate, browned side up. Slide the potatoes back into the hot pan, browned side up.

Cook the potatoes until well browned on the bottom, then nudge the sides of the potato into a little nest with your spatula.

Slide the rösti onto a clean plate and season with a pinch of salt. Keep warm in a low temperature oven while preparing the next rösti.

Reheat the bacon and garnish each rösti with a slice of goat cheese, warm bacon and freshly ground black pepper.

ROOT VEGETABLE TERRINE

makes 1 terrine (8–10 servings)

½ cup (125 mL) melted unsalted butter +
  extra for the mold
6 new or Yukon Gold potatoes (about 3 lb
  [1.4 kg]), peeled, rinsed and held in water
1 large sweet potato (about 12 oz [360 g]),
  peeled and rinsed
½ cup (125 mL) whipping cream
½ cup (125 mL) finely grated
  Parmesan cheese
Kosher salt

SPECIAL EQUIPMENT
Ovensafe 11- × 3½-inch (28 × 9 cm) terrine
  mold or an 8- × 4-inch (21 × 11) loaf pan
Mandoline or hand-held vegetable slicer

I SERVE this beautiful layered terrine whenever the occasion calls for something special. It gets its distinctive shape from the mold, but a loaf pan does the job as well, if you don't mind a squatter, more rustic version.

The terrine is straightforward, but it takes time to assemble. A mandoline or hand-held vegetable slicer makes slicing a breeze.

Once the terrine is baked, it can be refrigerated for up to 3 days. It can be reheated in its container, or sliced as needed and heated in a hot skillet until the edges are crisp and the centre warm.

■ Preheat oven to 350°F (175°C).

Lightly butter the mold, then line it with parchment, leaving an overhang of a few inches on each side. (The butter keeps the parchment in place and the overhang is handy for releasing the potatoes from the mold.)

Slice the regular and sweet potatoes in uniform slices, about ¹⁄₁₆–⅛ inch (2–3 mm) thick; keep covered with water and pat dry before using.

To fit the potatoes snugly along the terrine's edges, cut some slices in half and place the straight sides against the terrine's edge.

As you assemble the terrine, press down on the potatoes occasionally to ensure the layers are even.

Layer the terrine as follows: begin with 3 layers of potato, brushing each layer lightly with melted butter. Drizzle every third layer with 1 Tbsp (15 mL) cream and sprinkle evenly with 1½ tsp (7.5 mL) Parmesan cheese. Add 1 layer of sweet potato and brush with a thin layer of melted butter, sprinkling evenly with a pinch of kosher salt. (Only the sweet potato layer will be seasoned with salt; you'll need no more than 2 tsp (10 mL) kosher salt in total, for a large terrine.) Repeat the layering until the terrine is filled.

Brush the final layer with 1 Tbsp (15 mL) cream and sprinkle with 1½ tsp (7.5 mL) Parmesan.

Place the terrine on a large foil-lined baking sheet (the cream may spill over) and bake, covered, for 1 hour. Remove the cover and continue baking for about 30 minutes, or until the potatoes are tender when you've tested them with a knife.

Allow to cool slightly before removing the potatoes from the mold. Carefully lift the parchment and potatoes from the mold, slide the terrine from the parchment and transfer to a platter.

If you don't plan to serve the terrine immediately, leave the potatoes in the mold and cool to room temperature before refrigerating. It lasts up to 3 days refrigerated.

DUCK CONFIT

makes 4 duck legs

....

2 Tbsp (30 mL) kosher salt

1 tsp (5 mL) freshly ground black pepper

3 garlic cloves, sliced thinly

2 large shallots, sliced thinly

2 tsp (10 mL) fennel seeds, lightly crushed

1 Tbsp (15 mL) freshly chopped parsley

3 sprigs fresh thyme

4 duck legs with thighs attached, (about 3 lb [1.4 kg])

2 lb (900 g) rendered duck fat

WHEN I tell people I'm preparing duck confit, they seem a little surprised. It's not a meat that often comes to mind but is readily available both frozen and, thanks to our Asian supermarkets, fresh.

If you enjoy duck confit, you'll know just how tender and flavourful the meat is (never mind the skin, which rivals crisp bacon).

Duck Confit is easy to prepare: season with salt and herbs for a day or two then poach in its own fat until fork-tender. While this may sound about as healthy as poutine, duck fat is actually high in cholesterol-fighting monounsaturated fat.

Serve Duck Confit with cooked lentils and diced carrots drizzled with Hazelnut Vinaigrette (page 29) or with a simple green salad.

....

■ In a small bowl, combine the salt, pepper, garlic, shallots, fennel seeds, parsley and thyme. Scatter half of the seasoned salt mixture in a dish large enough to hold the duck pieces in a single layer.

Pat the duck legs dry and place on top of the seasoned salt mixture, then cover with the remaining seasoned salt. Cover with plastic wrap and refrigerate for 24–48 hours.

When you're ready to poach the duck, preheat the oven to 300°F (150°C). Melt the duck fat in a medium saucepan over low heat.

Remove the duck from the salt mixture, rinse thoroughly and pat completely dry with paper towels. Arrange the duck pieces in a single layer in a shallow oven-safe saucepan, casserole or baking dish. Pour the melted fat over the duck. (The duck pieces must be completely covered by the fat.)

Transfer duck to the preheated oven and simmer, uncovered, for 2–3 hours or until the duck is tender enough to be easily pulled from the bone. Check the oven after 20 minutes and adjust the heat as necessary to ensure the fat is simmering very gently; confit can become tough if the temperature is too high.

Cool and store the duck in the fat; it can be refrigerated up to 1 month, provided it remains completely submerged in fat.

To serve, remove the duck from the fat, scraping off any excess fat, and place in a shallow ovenproof container. Warm in a 325°F (160°C) oven until heated through. To crisp the skin, place the reheated duck in a hot skillet and cook, skin side down, over medium heat until crisp. Cook in batches so as not to crowd the skillet.

Leftover duck fat can be melted over low heat, strained through a cheesecloth-lined strainer and stored in the fridge for up to 1 month.

Rendered duck fat is available at finer butchers and charcuteries. You'll enjoy having it on hand, if only to experience the culinary sensation of potatoes roasted in duck fat.

Storing the duck in fat provides an airtight sealant and an extended shelf life. It's an old preservation technique that's never gone out of style.

SLOW BRAISED LAMB *with* POLENTA

makes 4 servings

....

SPICE MIX

1 Tbsp (15 mL) mild sweet paprika

1 tsp (5 mL) freshly ground black pepper

2 tsp (10 mL) ground cumin

2 tsp (10 mL) ground coriander

1 tsp (5 mL) ground cinnamon

½ tsp (2.5 mL) ground cloves

½ tsp (2.5 mL) ground nutmeg

1 tsp (5 mL) kosher salt

MEAT

4 lamb shanks (about 2–3 lb [0.9–1.4 kg])

1 lb (450 g) oxtail, cut into 2-inch
(5 cm) pieces

BRAISE

2 Tbsp (30 mL) vegetable oil, divided

1 large onion, roughly chopped

½ tsp (2.5 mL) kosher salt

1 Tbsp (15 mL) whole coriander seeds

1 Tbsp (15 mL) whole cumin seeds

½ star anise

1 cinnamon stick (about 3 inches
[8 cm] long)

Three 1-inch (2.5 cm) pieces fresh,
peeled ginger

2 cloves garlic, roughly chopped

2 celery stalks, roughly chopped

2 large carrots, peeled and roughly chopped

2 Tbsp (30 mL) tomato paste

2 cups (500 mL) red wine

2 cups (500 mL) roasted beef stock
(page 257)

8 dried apricots, pitted

1 thumb-sized bundle of fresh cilantro stems

1 whole orange peel, bitter pith removed
and 1-inch (2.5 cm) piece reserved
for garnish

½ tsp (2.5 mL) hot sauce (such as Sriracha)

Polenta (recipe follows)

1 Tbsp (15 mL) freshly chopped mint

SPECIAL EQUIPMENT

5½ quart (5.2 L) casserole pot or dutch oven

THIS INTENSELY flavoured braised lamb recipe drew rave reviews from friends, even those who swore they didn't like lamb.

The fragrant braise, made with warm earthy spices, dried apricots and wine, yields a deeply flavoured meat and a sauce that's nothing short of intoxicating.

Although the ingredient list is lengthy, much of the cooking time is "hands-off." I've paired the lamb with polenta, but mashed potatoes or rice work beautifully too.

Plan to prepare the lamb a day or two before it's served; the flavours only get better after sitting in the fridge for a couple days.

....

■ Combine the spice mix ingredients in a small bowl.

Pat the lamb shanks dry with a paper towel and dust with the spice mixture at least 2 hours, or up to 24 hours, before cooking.

Bring the seasoned lamb and oxtail to room temperature about an hour before cooking. Pat the oxtail dry.

BRAISE Preheat the oven to 325°F (160°C).

Heat 1 Tbsp (15 mL) oil in a large skillet over medium-high heat and sear the seasoned lamb and oxtail in batches (so as not to crowd the pan) until well browned. Set aside.

Heat 1 Tbsp (15 mL) oil in a 5½ quart (5.2 L) casserole pot. Add the onion and salt and cook over medium heat, for about 5 minutes or until the onion is translucent.

Add the coriander, cumin, star anise and cinnamon stick and cook for about 2 minutes, until fragrant; stir frequently. Add the ginger and garlic and cook for another minute, being careful not to burn the garlic.

Add the celery, carrots and tomato paste, stirring to coat the vegetables. Add the wine, stock, apricots, cilantro stems and orange peel and stir to combine. Finally, add the seared meat.

Bring to a simmer, cover and transfer to the preheated oven for 2–2½ hours or until the lamb is completely tender. Check the meat after 20 minutes to ensure the braising liquids are at a slow, steady simmer; you may need to regulate the heat.

Using a pair of tongs, remove the lamb and oxtail from the casserole pot. Strain the braising liquid into a clean container, pressing the solids against the strainer to extract as much liquid as possible. Discard the solids. Reserve the oxtail for future use (the meat is delicious shredded in soups, stews or tossed with pasta or rice).

Add the lamb shanks to the strained braising liquid; cool to room temperature, then cover and refrigerate overnight.

. . . recipe continued

. . . Slow Braised Lamb with Polenta (cont.)

The next day, remove the solidified fat from the braising liquid. Warm the lamb and braising liquid (which will be gelatinous at this stage) in a medium saucepan over low heat. When the braise has returned to a liquid state, remove the lamb shanks to a plate, cover and keep warm in a low temperature oven while finishing the sauce.

Bring the braising liquid to a low boil until it has reduced and thickened enough to lightly coat the back of a spoon. Add the hot sauce and taste; season with additional salt or hot sauce if desired. (If the sauce becomes too thick, thin with water.)

Serve the reheated lamb over warm polenta with a ladle of sauce on top. Garnish with finely chopped orange zest and fresh mint.

POLENTA *makes about 6 cups (1.5 L)*

1 cup (250 mL) yellow cornmeal or polenta
4 cups (1 L) chicken stock (page 257)
½ tsp (2.5 mL) kosher salt
1 cup (250 mL) grated Parmesan cheese
1 Tbsp (15 mL) unsalted butter
Freshly ground black pepper (optional)

THE BEST technique I've found for making a creamy, lump-free polenta comes from *The Gourmet Cookbook*, edited by Ruth Reichl. It involves whisking, covering, then re-whisking the polenta at 10-minute intervals. Polenta sets quickly but the flavours take time to develop, so cook it for at least 30 minutes, even if it appears ready sooner. You'll have enough leftover polenta to enjoy it grilled or fried the next day (see sidebar).

Start the polenta about 35 minutes before serving.

Leftover polenta can be refrigerated until firm then fried or grilled. Pour warm leftover polenta in a lightly-oiled shallow container before the polenta sets. (The wider the container, the thinner the polenta.) Smooth with a spatula, cover and refrigerate. The next day, cut the chilled, firm polenta into wedges for frying or grilling, or into chunky "fries" for deep-frying.

▪ Pour the cornmeal in a spouted measuring cup.

Bring the stock to a boil in a heavy 2-quart (2 L) saucepan, add the salt and slowly pour in the cornmeal, whisking continuously as you do so. Continue to whisk for another 1–2 minutes, then reduce the heat to the lowest setting, cover, and set a timer for 10 minutes.

Stir the polenta with a wooden spoon for about a minute, cover, re-set the timer and repeat the process for at least 30 minutes, adding additional stock if the polenta becomes too thick.

Remove the pan from the heat, add the cheese and butter and stir to combine. Taste the polenta and add a pinch of salt if necessary, keeping in mind the Parmesan is salty. Add freshly ground black pepper, if desired.

Serve immediately. The polenta will thicken as it sits.

CHICKEN POT PIES

makes 6 – 8 pies

....

Flaky Pastry Dough (page 262)

SAUCE

⅓ cup (80 mL) unsalted butter + extra
   3 Tbsp (45 mL) for the vegetables

⅓ cup (80 mL) all-purpose flour

2¼ cups (560 mL) chicken stock (page 257)

1 cup (250 mL) whole or 2% milk

½ cup (125 mL) whipping cream

¼ cup (60 mL) lemon juice,
   freshly squeezed

½ cup (125 mL) freshly grated
   Parmesan cheese

1½ tsp (7.5 mL) kosher salt

½ tsp (2.5 mL) hot red pepper flakes

. . . ingredients continued

I REDISCOVERED these comforting pies shortly after I'd given birth to twins. A kindly neighbour I barely knew knocked on my door and I opened it balancing a wailing newborn in each arm. She presented me with a wooden tray of warm chicken pot pies and I nearly melted with relief.

Memories of those busy days are blurred, but every time I tuck into a chicken pie I'm reminded of my neighbour's kindness and the simple comfort of a savoury pie.

Those wailing babies? They're chatty, leggy teens now, who order up chicken pot pies whenever they're given the choice.

It's best to prepare the pastry in advance.

....

■ You'll need to first prepare the pastry dough according to the instructions on page 262.

Preheat oven to 375°F (190°C).

PASTRY Roll out the dough ⅛ inch (3 mm) thick onto a sheet of parchment dusted with flour. Cut the pastry into rounds ½ inch (1 cm) larger than your ramekins. Cut small holes or vents into each circle. Stack the pastry rounds, with a layer of parchment between each and refrigerate or freeze until ready to use.

SAUCE Prepare a roux (a thickener for your sauce) by melting ⅓ cup (80 mL) butter in a medium saucepan over medium-low heat. Whisk in the flour and cook for about 4–5 minutes, stirring constantly, until the flour and butter are golden in colour. Add the chicken stock, milk and cream to the roux and whisk until thickened and free of lumps, about 8–10 minutes. The sauce should be just thick enough to lightly coat the back of a spoon. Reduce the heat, add the lemon juice, Parmesan cheese, salt and the red pepper flakes. Taste the sauce and season with additional salt or pepper flakes if desired. If the sauce appears too thick, thin it with additional stock.

. . . recipe continued

. . . Chicken Pot Pies (cont.)

FILLING

1 medium onion, diced

2 celery stalks, peeled and diced ¼ inch (6 mm) thick

¼ tsp (1 mL) kosher salt, distributed in pinches

3 carrots, peeled and diced ¼ inch (6 mm) thick

⅔ cup (160 mL) frozen peas, thawed

2½ cups (625 mL) diced or shredded roasted or poached chicken (one small roasted chicken will give you more than enough meat)

3 Tbsp (45 mL) fresh herbs, finely minced (use a single variety or a combination of parsley, dill, chives and tarragon)

1 egg, lightly beaten or 2 Tbsp (30 mL) whipping cream for the pastry

SPECIAL EQUIPMENT

Six 8-oz (230 g) ramekins (or ovenproof containers) or eight 6 oz [175 g] ramekins (I opt for the smaller ramekins as the filling is rich)

FILLING Place a fine-mesh strainer over a bowl and set aside.

Heat 2 Tbsp (30 mL) butter in a large saucepan over medium heat. Add the onion, celery and a pinch of salt. Cook until the onion is tender, about 5 minutes, then transfer to the strainer to drain excess butter. In the same pan, melt 1 Tbsp (15 mL) butter and cook the carrots with a pinch of salt until just tender, taking care not to overcook them. Tip the carrots into the strainer with the onions and celery. The frozen peas do not need cooking.

Add the drained cooked vegetables, thawed peas, cooked chicken and herbs to the sauce and stir to combine. Taste and season with additional salt or lemon juice, if desired.

PUTTING IT ALL TOGETHER Place your ramekins on a baking sheet and fill with the creamed chicken and vegetable mixture.

Remove the pre-cut pastry from the fridge. Brush the rims of the ramekins with the beaten egg or cream. Place the pastry rounds on top of the ramekin and press the edges down with your fingers, crimping the pastry over the edge. Cut vents into the pastry, if you have not already done so. Brush the top of the dough with the remaining egg or cream.

Bake the pies for about 30–40 minutes until the pastry has browned and the filling bubbles from the pastry vents. Allow to cool for a few minutes as the filling is piping hot.

RUSTIC BEEF STEW

makes 4–6 servings

....

BRAISE

3½ lb (1.65 kg) chuck roast, trimmed of
    some (but not all) excess fat and cut into
    1½- to 2-inch (4–5 cm) cubes

2 tsp (10 mL) freshly ground cumin

2 tsp (10 mL) freshly ground coriander

1½ tsp (7 mL) kosher salt

1 tsp (5 mL) freshly ground black pepper

¼ cup (60 mL) vegetable oil + extra if needed

3 cups (750 mL) robust red wine (such
    as a BC Syrah), divided (reserve ¼ cup
    [60 mL] for the vegetables)

8–10 slices uncooked bacon, diced

1 medium onion, peeled and
    roughly chopped

2 medium carrots, peeled and
    roughly chopped

4 cloves garlic, peeled and roughly chopped

½ cup (125 mL) pitted prunes (about 14),
    roughly chopped

3 anchovies, rinsed and chopped

2 Tbsp (30 mL) tomato paste

2 red Thai chili peppers, cut lengthwise,
    seeds removed

Bouquet garni (handful of parsley stems,
    2 bay leaves and a few springs of fresh
    thyme, tied together with kitchen string)

2–3 cups (500–750 mL) Roasted Chicken or
    Beef Stock (page 257), divided (reserve
    ¼ cup [60 mL] for the vegetables)

. . . ingredients continued

THIS IS a remarkably flavourful take on a classic beef stew. The beef is seared with a coating of freshly ground cumin and coriander, then braised in wine and stock. A few unlikely ingredients—prunes, anchovies and Thai chili peppers—blend together to create a rich, deeply balanced sauce. I think you'll find this version a refreshing update.

There are three distinct parts to this recipe; you'll want to read the recipe and ingredient list through before you begin.

Stew is best made a day or two before it's served. The flavours only get better after sitting in the fridge for a couple days.

....

■ Preheat oven to 300°F (150°C).

Pat the beef dry with a paper towel and season with the cumin, coriander, salt and pepper.

Heat 1 Tbsp (15 mL) oil in a large skillet over medium-high heat, until it starts to shimmer. Sear the seasoned beef in batches until well browned, being mindful not to crowd the pan. Transfer the seared beef to a bowl (to accumulate the juices).

Drain the excess fat from the skillet, reheat the pan to medium-high and add ¼ cup (60 mL) red wine, scraping the bottom of the pan to dislodge any bits of meat; pour this liquid into the bowl of seared beef.

Heat 1 Tbsp (15 mL) oil in a 5½ quart (5.2 L) casserole pot, add the diced bacon, onion and carrots and cook on medium heat, stirring occasionally, about 8–10 minutes, or until the onion starts to brown. Add the garlic, prunes, anchovies and tomato paste, stirring constantly, until the ingredients are just coated in the tomato paste. Add a splash of wine if the mixture sticks to the bottom of the pot.

Add the seared beef, accumulated juices, chilies, bouquet garni, and all but ¼ cup (60 mL) of the remaining wine. Add enough stock to surround, but not completely cover, the meat.

. . . recipe continued

SAUCE

⅓ cup (80 mL) unsalted butter

⅓ cup (80 mL) all-purpose flour

1 tsp (5 mL) red wine vinegar (not Balsamic)

VEGETABLES AND GARNISHES

3 Tbsp (45 mL) unsalted butter, divided,
    plus more if necessary

3 Tbsp (45 mL) vegetable oil, divided, plus
    more if necessary

16-24 small button mushrooms, wiped
    clean and quartered

Kosher salt

2 dozen pearl onions, blanched, peeled and
    left whole

3 carrots, peeled and sliced into uniform,
    bite-sized pieces

4-5 slices cooked bacon, diced

½ cup (125 mL) freshly chopped parsley

SPECIAL EQUIPMENT

5½ quart (5.2 L) casserole pot or dutch
    oven

*To easily remove the skin from pearl onions,
score each with a small "X" at the root end with
a paring knife. Drop the onions into boiling
water for a minute or two, remove with a slotted
spoon and transfer to a bowl of ice cold water.
Gently squeeze each onion to release the skin.*

. . . Rustic Beef Stew (cont.)

Bring to a simmer, then cover and transfer to the preheated oven for about 2½ hours, or until the beef is tender enough to cut with a fork. Check the meat after 20 minutes to ensure the cooking liquids are bubbling at a slow, steady simmer; you may need to adjust the heat.

Using a pair of tongs, remove the cooked beef from the casserole pot. Strain the braising liquid into a clean container, pressing the solids against the strainer to extract as much liquid as possible; discard the solids. Combine the beef and strained braising liquid in a clean container and cool at room temperature; cover and refrigerate overnight.

The next day, remove the solidified fat from the braising liquid. Warm the beef and braising liquid (which will be gelatinous at this stage) in a medium saucepan over low heat. When the braise has returned to a liquid state, transfer the beef to an ovenproof container, cover and keep warm in a low-temperature oven while finishing the sauce.

SAUCE Melt butter in a small saucepan over medium heat; add the flour and stir constantly, about 6–8 minutes, or until golden and aromatic.

Whisk the flour mixture (a roux, in culinary-speak) into the saucepan of braising liquid, over medium heat, until the sauce thickens enough to lightly coat the back of a spoon. Add the vinegar. Taste and season with a pinch of salt or additional vinegar, if desired.

Pour the sauce over the beef and keep warm while preparing the vegetables.

VEGETABLES Heat 1 Tbsp (15 mL) each butter and oil in a large skillet and cook the mushrooms in batches until well browned, being mindful not to crowd the pan. Add a pinch of salt to each batch (about ½ tsp [2 mL] in total). After all the mushrooms have cooked, return them to the skillet with the remaining wine and cook on medium heat until the wine has all but evaporated. Add ¼ cup (60 mL) stock and continue to simmer until the liquid has evaporated and the mushrooms are glazed.

Heat 1 Tbsp (15 mL) each oil and butter in a small pan and cook the onions on medium heat until tender, watching carefully as they burn easily. Season with a pinch of salt.

Heat 1 Tbsp (15 mL) butter in a skillet with a tight fitting lid; add the carrots, a pinch of salt and barely enough water to cover the carrots halfway. Bring to a simmer, cover and cook on low heat for about 10 minutes or until the carrots are just tender when pierced with the tip of the knife.

PUTTING IT ALL TOGETHER Add the cooked mushrooms, onions and carrots to the beef and sauce and heat through; reserving a few carrots for the garnish, if desired.

Ladle the warm stew, into preheated bowls, over potatoes, rice or pasta. Garnish with bacon, freshly chopped parsley and a few reserved carrots.

SAUSAGE & PEPPERS
with KALE GNOCCHI
makes 4 servings

Kale Gnocchi (page 277)

1 Tbsp (15 mL) vegetable oil

1 lb (450 g) good quality sausage (about
    4 links)

2 onions, sliced

2 red bell peppers, cored and sliced

1 tsp (5 mL) hot red pepper flakes

½ tsp (2.5 mL) kosher salt

2 garlic cloves, peeled and sliced

2 Tbsp (30 mL) red wine vinegar

1 cup (250 mL) Roasted Chicken or Beef
    Stock (page 257)

Kale chip garnish (optional; recipe follows)

THIS IS a cozy-sweater kind of dish. The kale gnocchi is both light and comforting—just the sort of meal for a cold winter's day. Sausage makes this dish, so buy the best you can afford.

The recipe comes together fairly quickly once the kale gnocchi is ready. Gnocchi can be prepared in advance and refrigerated until needed.

■ You'll need to first prepare the kale gnocchi according to the instructions on page 277. You'll have more than you need for this recipe, so plan to freeze the rest.

Heat the oil in a large skillet over medium heat; add the sausages, pricking them in several places with the tip a knife to prevent bursting. Cook until evenly browned and cooked through. Slice into bite-sized portions, tent with foil and set aside.

Discard all but 1 Tbsp (15 mL) of the grease from the skillet (or reserve for later use, if desired) and add the onion; cook over medium heat until golden brown. Add the bell pepper, red pepper flakes and salt. When the red pepper starts to soften, add the garlic and cook for half a minute, stirring constantly until aromatic. Return the sliced sausages to the pan, add the vinegar and cook until no liquid remains. Add the chicken or beef stock and simmer until the liquid has reduced just enough to lightly glaze the sausages and vegetables. Taste and season with salt, if desired.

PUTTING IT ALL TOGETHER Heat the (precooked) gnocchi in a hot, lightly oiled nonstick skillet, over medium-high heat until heated through and golden around the edges.

Toss half the gnocchi, or more if desired, with the sausages and vegetables. Garnish with kale chips, if desired.

KALE CHIPS *makes plenty for garnish with extra chips on the side*

3–4 kale leaves

Vegetable oil

Kosher salt

■ Preheat oven to 350°F (175°C).

Tear kale leaves into roughly 4-inch (10 cm) pieces, and place them into a bowl. Lightly drizzle with vegetable oil, then rub the oil in the crevices of the kale with your hands. Spread onto a parchment-lined baking sheet with space between each. Season lightly with a pinch of salt. Bake until crisp, about 10–15 minutes, rotating the pan once.

STUFFED PORK LOIN
with BRAISED CABBAGE
makes 4 servings

....

2 pork tenderloins (about 1 lb [450 g] each)

2 tsp (10 mL) Dijon-style mustard, divided

2 slices of bacon

8 dried prunes, pitted

1 tsp (5 mL) kosher salt

1 tsp (5 mL) ground coriander

1 tsp (5 mL) freshly ground cumin

1 Tbsp (15 mL) vegetable oil

Braised Cabbage (recipe follows)

Pan Sauce (recipe follows)

SPECIAL EQUIPMENT

Kitchen string

Meat thermometer

PORK AND wine-braised cabbage are a classic combination and for good reason; the flavours are exceptional.

The pork can be seasoned, dressed and trussed up to 24 hours ahead of time, making this one of my favourite dinners for guests. The cabbage, too, can be prepared in advance, leaving only the searing and roasting, which takes about 30 minutes.

Pork is moist and flavourful when cooked to a pink blush.

....

■ Remove the silver skin, the thin pearlescent membrane that runs the length of the loin, from each tenderloin. Spread 1 tsp (5 mL) mustard along each tenderloin. Place the raw bacon strips along the length of 1 loin and lay the prunes in a single layer on top. Place the remaining loin on top of the prunes to create a prune and bacon "sandwich." Tuck in the narrow ends of the loins.

Tie the loins together with kitchen string at 1-inch (2.5 cm) intervals to fashion a uniform roast about 2½ inches (6 cm) thick. Rub the roast with salt, coriander and cumin; cover in plastic wrap and refrigerate for at least 2 hours or up to 24 hours. You'll want to prepare the cabbage before you cook the pork.

Bring the pork to room temperature for about an hour before cooking. Preheat the oven to 375°F (190°C).

Remove the plastic wrap from the room-temperature pork and trim, or cut the loin into 2 pieces, if necessary, to fit inside a large ovenproof skillet. Keep the string intact while searing the pork.

Heat 2 Tbsp (30 mL) oil in the skillet and sear the pork over medium-high heat until all sides are well-browned. Transfer the skillet to the preheated oven and roast for about 20 minutes, or until a meat thermometer registers 130°F (54°C), turning the pork once. (The temperature will continue to rise as the meat rests.)

Transfer the pork to a cutting board to rest and loosely tent with foil. If making a pan sauce, remove all but 1 Tbsp (15 mL) fat from the skillet the pork was cooked in. (Save excess fat for later use, if desired.)

. . . recipe continued

Fernie ski slopes

. . . Stuffed Pork Loin with Braised Cabbage (cont.)

PAN SAUCE (OPTIONAL)

1 Tbsp (15 mL) reserved fat

¼ cup (60 mL) chopped shallots or onions

½ cup (125) mL) white wine

1 cup (250 mL) chicken stock (page 257)

2 tsp (10 mL) Dijon-style mustard + extra
   if desired

Kosher salt

1 Tbsp (15 mL) unsalted butter

PAN SAUCE Heat the fat on medium heat in the pan the pork was cooked in. Toss the shallots or onions in the pan and cook until translucent, scraping up any bits from the bottom of the pan. Add the wine and bring to a boil until the liquid has all but evaporated. Add the chicken stock and boil this, too, until the sauce is reduced and just thick enough to lightly coat the back of a spoon. Whisk in the mustard and add any juices from the resting pork. Taste and season with a pinch salt, if desired. Just before serving, whisk in the butter.

PUTTING IT ALL TOGETHER When ready to serve, remove the string from the pork and slice pork into 1-inch (2.5 cm) thick portions. Serve on warmed plates with cabbage and drizzle with pan sauce if desired.

BRAISED CABBAGE *makes 4 servings*

2 Tbsp (30 mL) vegetable oil

1 onion, chopped

¼ tsp (1 mL) kosher salt

2 cloves garlic, chopped

½ head red cabbage, sliced

1 Granny Smith apple, peeled,
   cored and chopped

1 cup (250 mL) dry red wine

½ cup (125 mL) Roasted Chicken or Beef
   Stock (page 257)

¼ cup (60 mL) red wine vinegar

Pinch ground cloves

2 juniper berries (optional)

2 tsp (10 mL) sugar

2 Tbsp (30 mL) unsalted butter

■ Heat the oil in a 5½ quart (5.2 L) casserole pot over medium heat; add the onion and salt and cook, stirring occasionally, for about 5 minutes or until the onion is translucent. Add the garlic and stir until aromatic, about half a minute. Add the rest of the ingredients, except for the butter, and stir. Cover and cook over low heat for about 1 hour or until completely tender. Remove the lid and cook for another 15 minutes or until no liquid remains. Taste and season with salt, if desired. Just before serving, stir in the butter.

Hot Cranberry Apple Rum at Whistler

WINTER | *sweet*

....

BIG BATCH GRANOLA
makes 11 cups (2.75 L)

5½ cups (1.4 L) old fashioned rolled oats
(not the quick-cooking type)

1½ cups (375 mL) unsweetened coconut
(I like the large flake but any size will do)

1½ cups (375 mL) sliced almonds

¾ cup (185 mL) chopped walnuts

¾ cup (185 mL) flax seeds

1 cup (250 mL) peanut or almond butter
(or a combination of both)

¾ cup (185 mL) liquid honey

⅓ cup (80 mL) firmly packed light
brown sugar

1 tsp (5 mL) kosher salt

1 cup (250 mL) chopped dried fruit
(such as cranberries, raisins, apricots
and cherries)

I'VE ALWAYS loved granola but not the hefty price tag. I started experimenting with recipes at home and discovered just how simple and economical it is to make yourself.

The recipe has a lot of give, so feel free to tinker. This is my most recent version (the recipe seems to change with every batch). I like a dark, richly toasted granola but if you prefer yours lighter, simply take it out of the oven a few minutes earlier.

Granola doesn't last long in our home, so I always make a big batch. You can, of course, halve the recipe.

Serve with yogurt and honey, if desired.

■ Preheat oven to 350°F (175°C).

Mix together the oats, coconut, almonds, walnuts and flax seeds in a large bowl.

Spread the mixture evenly onto 2 baking sheets lined with parchment paper. Bake for about 15–20 minutes or until the oats and nuts are golden and aromatic. Turn the mixture 2 or 3 times during baking with a spatula, to encourage even browning. Remove the baking sheets and turn the oven off.

Heat the peanut or almond butter, honey, brown sugar and salt in a small saucepan over low heat, stirring until well blended.

Toss the toasted oats, nuts and warm nut-butter mixture together in a large bowl, stir with a large spoon or your hands (if the mixture is cool enough) and break up any large clumps. Return the granola to the baking trays and, providing you've turned off the oven, dry out the granola in the warm oven for about 30 minutes with the door slightly ajar.

Store cooled granola in a large jar with a tight fitting lid.

Add a spoonful of dried fruit to each helping just before serving.

NUTTY CARAMEL CREAM PUFFS (PROFITEROLES)
makes about twenty-four 2-inch (5 cm) cream puffs

24 Cheese Puffs (Gougères) (page 184)

CARAMEL TOPPING
½ cup (125 mL) sugar
¼ cup (60 mL) water
½ cup (125 mL) chopped hazelnuts
Pinch of cream of tartar

CREAM FILLING
1 cup (250 mL) whipping cream
1 Tbsp (15 mL) icing sugar + extra if desired

To clean any caramel stuck to the bottom of your pot, fill it with water and bring to a boil. The caramel will melt into the water. Repeat if necessary.

THESE INCREDIBLY light, bite-sized pastries are especially welcome during the holidays.

Traditionally, cream puffs are made using the exact recipe for Cheese Puffs (Gougères) (page 184), minus the cheese. I discovered by lucky accident that leaving the cheese in the dough adds a faint but delightfully savoury note to these classic pastries.

The baked pastries are dipped in hot caramel, studded with hazelnuts, and filled with whipped cream. You could also fill them with Coffee Ice Cream (page 51) or Pastry Cream Lightened with Whipping Cream (page 293).

As for the topping, cooking caramel is easy but requires your full attention—sugar changes from dry crystals to clear liquid in minutes, and from golden amber to smoking black in a heartbeat. Before you start, have your ingredients and tools ready and read the instructions to the end. Twice.

■ First, prepare and bake the Cheese Puffs (Gougères). (They can be made ahead of time.)

You'll need a medium heavy-bottomed saucepan to cook the sugar and a larger skillet filled with ice cold water to quickly cool the base of the saucepan and prevent the sugar from further cooking. You'll also need a pastry brush and a cup of water near your stove. As the sugar cooks the pastry brush will be used to brush any sugar that sputters to the sides of the saucepan. This helps prevent the sugar from crystallizing, which can seize and ruin your caramel.

Line a baking sheet with parchment or a nonstick baking mat before you start.

CARAMEL TOPPING Combine the sugar, water, nuts and a pinch of cream of tartar in a medium saucepan and mix to combine. Cook the mixture over medium heat for about 4–5 minutes or until the sugar melts and turns amber; brush down any bits of sugar that splatter onto the sides of the pan with your moistened pastry brush.

When the sugar turns amber, plunge the base of the saucepan into the skillet of water to prevent further cooking.

Working quickly, use a pair of tongs to carefully dip the top half of each pastry into the caramel, then place the pastries onto the prepared tray, sugar side down. Set aside to firm.

. . . recipe continued

. . . Nutty Caramel Cream Puffs (cont.)

CREAM FILLING Whisk the whipping cream and icing sugar together in a medium bowl until the mixture forms a firm peak. Taste the cream and add more sugar, if desired.

Cut the cream puffs horizontally and fill with a generous dollop of whipped cream. Alternatively, fill a pastry bag (fitted with a narrow piping tip) with the whipped cream. Poke a hole in the base of each cream puff with a skewer and pipe the cream into the opening.

POACHED PEARS IN PORT
makes 4 pears

3 cups (750 mL) ruby port
½ cup (125 mL) sugar
4 small ripe but firm pears, peeled with
    stems intact
¾ cup (185 mL) balsamic vinegar

THESE ELEGANT pears are about as easy as it gets. They are poached in port and refrigerated for up to 2 days, while they deepen in colour.

The port is later reduced with balsamic vinegar, which makes a luxurious sauce. The sauce also makes a fantastic topping for ice cream and is lovely drizzled over pork and duck.

If you're looking for a more substantial dessert, serve the pears alongside Raspberry Truffle Cakes (page 108).

The reduced port sauce alone makes for an extravagant and decadent gift.

■ Pour the port and sugar in a saucepan large enough to fit the pears snugly. Bring to a simmer over medium heat, stirring until the sugar dissolves. Submerge the pears in the port, cover with a lid and simmer on the lowest setting for 30 minutes. Cool the pears in the port and place in the refrigerator for up to 48 hours.

On the day you plan to serve the dessert, remove the pears from the port, cover and set aside. Strain the port through a fine-mesh strainer into a clean saucepan. Add the balsamic vinegar and simmer uncovered over medium-low heat until the liquid has reduced and reaches a syrup-like consistency. This can take up to 1 hour, depending on the size of your saucepan (the larger the pot, the faster the reduction). You should be left with about ¾ cup (185 mL) sauce.

If the sauce becomes too thick, thin with a bit of water.

Serve the pears drizzled with a bit of sauce, with extra sauce on the side.

SPICED HAZELNUT LOAF

makes 2 small or 1 medium-sized loaf

....

1 cup (250 mL) shelled hazelnuts

½ cup (125 mL) unsalted butter at room
   temperature + extra for loaf pans

1 cup (250 mL) firmly packed light
   brown sugar

1½ tsp (7.5 mL) ground coriander

1 tsp (5 mL) ground cinnamon

1½ tsp (7.5 mL) ground ginger

½ tsp (2.5 mL) ground nutmeg

¼ tsp (1 mL) salt

4 eggs + 1 extra yolk (at room temperature)

¾ cup + 2 tsp (195 mL) all-purpose flour +
   extra for loaf pans

SPECIAL EQUIPMENT

2 small loaf pans (about 6 × 3 inches
   [15 × 8 cm] each)

Food processor

Electric mixer

....

*To remove the bitter skins from unpeeled
whole hazelnuts, roast the nuts on a baking sheet
until the nuts are fragrant, about 10 minutes.
Tip the warm nuts onto a tea towel and gather
the fabric to enclose them. Rub the hazelnuts,
through the tea towel, to loosen and peel their
skins. Some skins will remain but not enough to
leave an aftertaste.*

THIS IS a simple, classic pound cake made with freshly ground hazelnuts and flavoured with coriander, cinnamon, ginger and nutmeg. Serve warm or at room temperature with last summer's Rumpot, as pictured, (page 100) or Baked Apples (page 171) and a dollop of whipped cream.

The loaf freezes exceptionally well.

....

■ Preheat the oven to 350°F (175°C).

Grease the loaf pans with butter, dust with flour and set aside.

Pulse the hazelnuts in a food processor, about 15–20 seconds or until most of the mixture is fine-textured, with some irregular coarse pieces.

Mix the butter in a large bowl or the bowl of a standup mixer fitted with a paddle attachment, until completely smooth. Add the brown sugar, spices and salt and mix until well combined.

Add the whole eggs and yolk, 1 at a time, beating after each addition until well combined; scrape down the sides of the bowl as necessary with a spatula. Add the flour and ground hazelnuts and mix until well combined.

Transfer the batter to the prepared loaf pans, smoothing the top with a spatula. Bake in a preheated oven, rotating the pans once during baking, about 30–35 minutes (or until a toothpick inserted in the centre of the loaf comes out clean). The loaf should be puffed in the centre and the top may crack.

Remove the loaves from the pans and cool on a wire rack.

CHOCOLATE HAZELNUT TARTS

makes twenty-four 2-inch (5 cm) tarts

Sweet Tart Dough (page 265)

HAZELNUT FILLING
½ cup (125 mL) skinned hazelnuts*, whole
   or halved
¼ cup (60 mL) unsalted butter
   (room temperature)
⅓ cup (80 mL) light brown sugar
½ tsp (2.5 mL) vanilla
⅛ tsp (0.5 mL) table salt
2 large eggs + 1 room temperature yolk

CHOCOLATE TOPPING
½ cup (125 mL) finely chopped, good
   quality semi-sweet chocolate
¼ cup (60 mL) whipping cream

SPECIAL EQUIPMENT
Twenty-four 2-inch (5 cm) tart molds or
   4 dozen 1-inch (2.5 cm) tart molds
Food processor

If your hazelnuts still have skins refer to sidebar on page 229.

I'M TEMPTED to call these splendid little tarts "cookies" because the pastry has a firm cookie-like texture. They are filled with sweetened ground hazelnuts and topped with a little pool of chocolate ganache.

You'll want to make these tarts bite-sized because they're so rich. You can make larger ones, of course, but you'll need to adjust the baking time accordingly.

Best served on a blustery afternoon with a mug of hot cocoa.

■ Preheat the oven to 350°F (175°C).

Prepare the sweet tart dough following the instructions on page 265 and line the tart molds with the dough. Cover with plastic wrap and refrigerate for at least an hour before filling.

HAZELNUT FILLING Toast the hazelnuts in a dry skillet over medium heat until aromatic, about 2–3 minutes. Transfer the hazelnuts to a plate to cool, then pulse in a food processor until most of the mixture is fine-textured with some irregular coarse pieces.

In a medium bowl, combine the butter, sugar, vanilla and salt and mix until smooth. Add the eggs and yolk, one at a time, mixing after each addition. Stir in the ground hazelnuts.

Fill each tart with the hazelnut filling. Bake on a baking sheet for 15–20 minutes, rotating the pan once during baking. Cool on a baking rack.

CHOCOLATE TOPPING Place the chopped chocolate in a bowl and set aside. Pour the cream into a small saucepan and bring to a simmer over medium heat. Pour the hot cream over the chocolate and stir until the chocolate has melted and no streaks remain.

Cool the chocolate until it thickens just enough to form a small puddle that holds its shape, about 15 minutes. Transfer the chocolate to a plastic freezer bag with a small hole snipped from 1 corner (or a pastry bag, if you have one) and drizzle the chocolate onto the tarts.

CRANBERRY MERINGUE
makes 10–12 meringues

4 large egg whites with no traces of yolk
  (room temperature)
1 cup (250 mL) superfine or berry sugar
1½ tsp (7.5 mL) cornstarch
½ tsp (2.5 mL) white vinegar
¼ cup (60 mL) cranberry purée (recipe
  follows) or strawberry jam

SPECIAL EQUIPMENT
Electric mixer
Food processor or blender
  (for the cranberry purée)

*To make your own superfine or berry sugar,
place granulated sugar in a food processor and
process until the crystals are extra fine.*

*If you lose count while separating eggs, it's easy
to get back on track if you own a kitchen scale.
Egg whites weigh about 1 oz (30 grams) each.
Good enough reason to invest in a scale.*

I FIRST took notice of meringue on a trip to France. Every bakery seemed to have one version or another—large, small, some brightly coloured—piled high in their window. It wasn't until I tasted one that I understood their popularity.

Crisp on the outside and marshmallowy-soft on the inside, meringue makes a festive treat for the holidays, especially when laced with a tart cranberry purée.

Meringue can be made days in advance and sealed in an airtight container.

■ Preheat oven to 250°F (120°C).

To keep the meringue uniform, draw circles onto the parchment, using a teacup as a template. (See the Apricot Pavlovas on page 98 for a depiction of this method). Leave a 2-inch (5 cm) space between each circle. Turn the parchment over (ink or pencil can mar the meringue) and use as a guide when spooning or piping the meringue onto your tray.

Whisk the egg whites in a meticulously clean bowl at medium speed for about 1 minute or until a network of tiny bubbles have formed. Gradually add the sugar and increase the speed to high and whip until the whites have expanded and formed billowy, firm, glossy peaks. Be mindful not to over-whip, otherwise the whites will turn grainy and lose their shape. Reduce the speed to low and add the cornstarch and vinegar until just blended.

If using a pastry bag, spoon the meringue into a pastry bag fitted with a ¾-inch (2 cm) tip. Pipe or spoon the meringue onto your prepared tray, using the template as a guide. Dip a butter knife into a bit of cranberry purée or jam and gently drag the purée around the unbaked meringues to create a marbled effect.

Bake for about 1 hour on a rack in the lower third of your oven or until the meringues are dry. Turn the heat off and leave the meringues in the oven until cooled. The meringues will crack slightly. Store in an airtight container in a cool dry place.

CRANBERRY PURÉE *makes ¾ cup (185 ml)*

1½ cups (375 mL) fresh or frozen
  and thawed cranberries
  (about ½ standard package)
6 Tbsp (90 mL) sugar

■ Purée the cranberries in a food processor or blender until smooth. Pour the purée through a fine-mesh strainer into a small saucepan, using the back of a ladle or a large spoon to press the solids against the strainer and extracting as much liquid as possible. Heat the purée over medium heat with the sugar and reduce until the mixture is thick enough to coat the back of a spoon. Set aside ¼ cup (60 mL) for the meringue and use leftover purée as a topping for ice cream or swirled into puddings, muffins, loaves, pancakes or cookies.

FROSTED CRANBERRY JELLIES

makes 16 oz (475 g), enough to fill eight 2-oz (60 g) sherry or shot glasses

....

2 cups (500 mL) sweetened
   cranberry juice, divided
1 Tbsp (15 mL) unflavoured gelatin
   (1 package)
2 Tbsp (30 mL) Grand Marnier + extra
   for cranberry garnish
¼ cup (60 mL) sugar
8 whole cranberries

THESE HOLIDAY jellies, laced with a touch of Grand Marnier, are perfect for entertaining. I always considered them an elegant treat until my daughter called them Jell-O shots.

"Noooo, these are not shots dear, they're very special …"

"They've got Jell-O and booze—they're shots."

Whatever you call them, please enjoy them in a sherry glass with a tiny spoon, not upended from a plastic cup.

....

■ Heat 1 cup (250 mL) cranberry juice in a small saucepan over medium heat. When the juice starts to simmer, remove the pan from the heat and add the gelatin, stirring until dissolved. Pour the hot liquid into a large spouted measuring cup; add the remaining cranberry juice and the Grand Marnier, stirring to combine. Set aside to cool.

Pour the sugar onto a small plate. Dip the rim of your glassware into a bit of water, then into the sugar, so that the sugar sticks to the edge of the glass, as pictured.

Fill your glassware with the cooled fortified juice and refrigerate until the jelly sets.

Place the whole cranberries in small cup and cover with Grand Marnier. Soak the cranberries in the liquor for an hour or up to 24 hours. Just before serving, roll the berries in sugar.

Serve the jellies chilled, topped with frosted cranberries.

Port can be substituted for Grand Marnier if you don't mind an opaque, rather than clear, jelly.

HOT CRANBERRY APPLE RUM

makes 9 cups (2.25 L)

....

4 cups (1 L) cranberry juice

4 cups (1 L) unsweetened apple juice

3 cinnamon sticks (about 3 inches [8 cm] each)

1 cup (250 mL) dark rum (or more as desired)

TAKE THE chill off with a steaming mug of cinnamon-scented apple and cranberry juice laced with rum.

....

Warm the cranberry and apple juice in a medium saucepan over medium heat. Add the cinnamon sticks and rum to taste. Serve warm.

FUNDAMENTALS

IF YOU want to become a better cook, start from scratch.
Master the fundamentals and your cooking skills will soar.

FUNDAMENTALS

....

a QUESTION *of* TASTE

AT CULINARY school we were required to present our food to our Chef Instructor in front of our classmates. Our food was evaluated and graded on flavour and presentation. I remember the pride I felt offering up a fillet of snapper, seared to perfection and garnished with a trendy heap of micro greens. My Chef took one bite of the fish and spit it out with such force I jumped—I had seasoned my fish with a liberal coating of extra hot paprika, mistaking it for sweet paprika. I slunked back to my workstation, dumped my fish and ran from the kitchen not realizing I had just learned the most valuable lesson about cooking (at my Chef's expense): taste your food—before anyone else does.

You might wonder why it's necessary to taste your food if you're following a recipe to the letter.

Well, if we all used the same tomatoes from the same vine, for example, we might not have to adjust recipes. But your tomatoes may be sweeter than mine, or more tart, or as bland as cardboard.

Food can be fickle. Sometimes shallots and garlic offer just the right amount of kick; sometimes they're shockingly potent with a bitter edge.

I once demonstrated a spicy jalapeño mayonnaise to a cooking class, only to discover my jalapeños were as tame as green peppers. I had to quadruple the peppers just to eke out the slightest bit of heat, then add a generous splash of hot sauce.

There are many factors that influence the final outcome of a dish (temperature, timing, the size of your cooking vessel and such) but tasting your food is the most effective way to ensure your dish lives up to your expectations.

Start a recipe by tasting your raw ingredients, taste as you cook and taste the final dish before you serve.

A SALTY NOTE

One of my friends admitted to ignoring the all-important catch phrase at the end of most recipes: Taste and season with additional salt, if desired. "I just put my salt shaker on the table. If my guests want more salt, they'll add it themselves." I recognize this is customary for many cooks, but sprinkling salt on a finished dish isn't the best way to season food. You'll likely add too much (salt shakers offer little control) and you'll only affect the top layer, which will taste of salt rather than the food you wish to enhance. Salt heightens the intrinsic flavours of food and, used judiciously, makes the difference between good and great food.

The savoury recipes in this book are made with kosher salt. It has larger granules than table salt, making it easier to pick up with your fingers and sprinkle evenly over food.

I use a pinch here and there throughout the cooking process, for perfectly seasoned food. How much, exactly, is a pinch? In my thick fingers, a pinch is a generous ⅛ tsp (0.5 mL). Some cooks find small fractions too fussy (I don't even own a spoon that small) so I've opted to season my recipes with salty "pinches." Over time your fingers will calibrate to just the right amount. (If you're not sure how much is correct, pinch some kosher salt into a small bowl and measure it.)

Keep a jar of tasting spoons and a small bowl of kosher salt next to your stove and, before you know it, tasting and seasoning will become second nature.

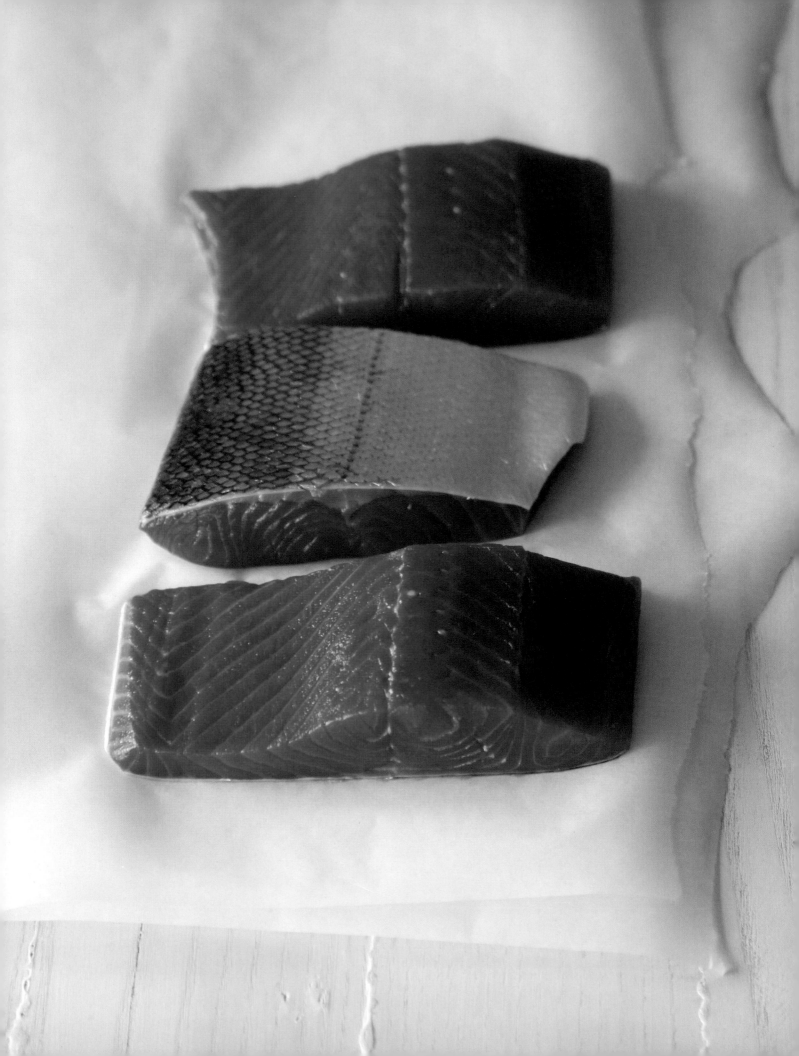

KEEP *it* FRESH

....

I LEARNED to get up close and personal with seafood at culinary school. I was taught to bring fish to my nose to inhale its mild—not fishy—sea-breeze aroma, and to test its body with my fingertips for a firm, springy resistance and tightly knit scales. I learned to lift the flaps on both sides of the head to examine the colour of the gills (they should be pinkish-red, rather than grey) and to look the fish in the eye to establish its worth (clear is fresh, cloudy is not).

But how do you determine freshness when you're staring into a sanitized glass case filled with pre-filleted, headless fish and plastic lemons? Forget about asking to smell or touch the fish—the staff will eye you suspiciously, as will any customers within hearing range (I speak from experience). Best to buy fish from a store with high turnover. Ask plenty of questions; the staff should know where the fish is from and when it arrived. Learn to be flexible; you can easily substitute one variety of fish for another in these recipes. The dish will have a subtle flavour difference but will be just as tasty. Fresh always trumps.

Seafood, one of our tastiest natural resources, is governed by strict sustainability practices. British Columbia's commercial fishing industry and its customers, particularly its passionate chefs, take fish conservation seriously. Fortunately, it's never been easier to shop for well-managed seafood. Select fish with labels like Ocean Wise or SeaChoice, or download their smartphone apps for sustainability guides. New technologies, like Vancouver's ThisFish, can trace a fish's journey from sea to store. If the fish has a tracking label, you can enter its code into a smartphone app to discover where, when and how your dinner was caught.

A FROSTY NOTE

It may seem preferable to opt for fresh fish over frozen, but fish frozen at sea, minutes after being caught, is a tastier option than "fresh" fish transported a great distance and left lingering for days in a refrigerated display case.

HOW *to* COOK BEANS

THERE ARE many ways to prepare beans and cooking them can be confusing if you've never done it before.

Some suggest dried beans be soaked up to 24 hours before cooking, others opt for a brief boil, while, some argue beans need no soaking at all.

Fortunately, beans are obliging seeds and they'll happily yield to all three methods. Pre-soaking simply gives beans a head-start, although some tender varieties, like lentils, need no such advantage.

One cup (250 mL) dried beans yields about 2½ cups (125 mL) cooked. Cooked beans only last for 3–4 days in the fridge, so if I'm not able to use them quickly I'll freeze them in manageable 2- to 3-cup (500–750 mL) portions.

Before you cook beans, sort through and discard any errant stones or beans that are shrivelled past their prime. Beans can be sorted quickly when spread onto a baking tray. After they're sorted, tip the beans into a strainer and rinse with water.

Beans cook at different rates depending on their age, variety and whether or not they've been soaked. If you're, cooking more than one variety at a time, do so in separate saucepans.

If you're opting to soak your beans, cover them with at least 2 inches (5 cm) cold water and leave anywhere from 1 hour to overnight. Be sure to drain the soaking water and rinse the beans before cooking.

To cook the beans, place them in a saucepan with enough water to cover them by at least 2 inches (5 cm). Season the water with whatever aromatic vegetables and herbs you have on hand: chopped onion, garlic, carrots, parsley stems, bay leaves, celery fronds and such.

Bring the beans to a gentle boil (vigorous boiling can burst them), then reduce to a slow even simmer; cook uncovered until tender, anywhere from 30 minutes to 2 hours depending on the variety. Midway through cooking add a few generous pinches of salt. The best way to test for doneness is to taste them. They should be tender but retain their shape.

Cool the beans in their seasoned water. Drain and reserve the liquid; it makes an excellent, nutritious soup base.

GARBANZO BEANS
(ALSO CALLED CHICKPEAS)

LENTILS

BLACK BEANS

WHITE BEANS (ALSO CALLED
GREAT NORTHERN OR NAVY BEANS)

the HUMBLE EGG

Brown eggs or white, which is best? There's no nutritional or taste difference. The colour of the shell is determined by the breed of hen. The colour of the yolk is determined by the hen's diet.

If you've refrigerated boiled eggs alongside raw eggs you can easily tell the difference by spinning an egg on a flat surface. Cooked eggs spin rapidly while raw eggs are sluggish.

THE KEY to good eggs is to start with eggs that are perfectly fresh. My children are so used to eggs fresh from a farm, they're not fooled by anything else. If I run out of "good" eggs and try to slip them a generic one, they'll call me on it.

Even if you don't buy eggs directly from a farm, it's easy to tell if your eggs are fresh. A fresh egg (in its shell) will lie flat in a bowl of cold water. As the egg ages, its blunt end lifts towards the water's surface due to an expanding air cell. This is okay, but if the egg floats, it should be discarded.

Another way to determine an egg's freshness is to crack it open. The albumen (the white) is plump and gelatinous in fresh eggs, particularly near the yolk; if it spreads like water, it's past its prime. The chalaze (the little white cord that anchors the yolk in the centre of the albumen) is more prominent in a fresh egg.

Eggs are porous, so keep them in their carton to prevent them from absorbing odours in your fridge, and remember to check the sell-by date on the carton, discarding any eggs that are cracked. Refrigerated eggs will keep for several weeks past their sell-by date.

BOILED EGGS

MY FRIEND Karri taught me this simple method for timing perfectly boiled eggs.

Place 4 large eggs (straight from the fridge) into a saucepan and fill with enough room-temperature water to cover the eggs by 1 inch (2.5 cm).

Heat the water over high heat just until it reaches a full boil (this can take a while). Immediately set your timer to your preferred doneness and reduce the heat to medium.

■ Remove the eggs with a slotted spoon and serve immediately with salt and freshly ground black pepper.

Timing will vary slightly depending on the size of saucepan and the number of eggs in the pan.

SOFT: 3 MINUTES   **MEDIUM: 5 MINUTES**

FIRM: 7 MINUTES   HARD: 8 MINUTES

POACHED EGGS

WHETHER YOU enjoy eggs oozing with molten yolk or solid throughout, there's nothing quite as comforting or satisfying as a simple poached egg.

If you're planning to serve a crowd, eggs can be poached in advance, and held in water in the refrigerator, until you're ready to re-warm them in simmering water. I add a spoonful of vinegar to my poaching water when I remember to (I was taught it holds the white together) but I find an easy gentle simmer, rather than a vigorous boil, keeps the white from dispersing just as well. Adding a generous pinch of kosher salt to the water seasons the eggs more evenly than a last-minute smattering.

■ You'll need a slotted spoon, a paper towel and a kitchen timer. With practice, you won't need the timer—a seasoned index finger pressed against a warm yolk is a more reliable gage. A soft yielding yolk is runny, and a firm one is, well, firm.

Fill a skillet with at least 3 inches (8 cm) generously salted water and bring to a steady, gentle simmer. Crack an egg into a teacup or a small bowl. Holding the cup at the water's level, tip the egg into the water and don't disturb it. It takes about 4 minutes to firm an egg white—after that, it's a question of how you enjoy your yolk:

SOFT (LOOSE, RUNNY YOLK): 4 minutes
MEDIUM (CREAMY YOLK): 5–6 minutes
FIRM (SOLID YOLK): 8 minutes

Remove the egg with a slotted spoon and transfer to a paper towel to blot dry. Trim the ragged edges with a knife for a neater egg, if desired. Serve immediately with hot buttered toast and freshly cracked pepper.

CLASSIC OMELETTE
makes 1 omelette

3 eggs

1 Tbsp (15 mL) Clarified Butter (page 289)
or half unsalted butter/half vegetable oil

Kosher salt

1 Tbsp (15 mL) finely chopped mixed herbs
such as parsley, tarragon and chives

SPECIAL EQUIPMENT

7–8 inch (18–20 cm) nonstick skillet
(a well-seasoned cast iron works well)

Spatula that won't damage the finish of your
skillet (plastic, wood or silicone)

DESCRIBING HOW to make an omelette is like explaining how to swim. You need to dive in to understand the process.

Preparing an omelette isn't difficult, but it does require a bit of dexterity. Grab the skillet handle with one hand to shake the pan to and fro, while you stir the eggs using your other hand. It's a bit like patting your head and rubbing your tummy at the same time. The continuous motion prevents curds from forming, resulting in a tender and pleasantly light omelette. Fortunately, the entire process takes only a minute. With patience, practice and a decent nonstick pan, you'll be on your way.

I coat the skillet in Clarified Butter (page 289), because it withstands higher temperatures without burning. You can use half oil, half butter, but clarified butter is easy to make, lasts for ages, and you'll be grateful to have it on hand.

■ Heat the skillet over medium-high heat and add the clarified butter or butter/oil mixture.

While the pan is heating, whisk the eggs and herbs in a small bowl and season with a pinch of kosher salt.

Pour the eggs into the hot skillet and stir continuously as if making scrambled eggs; at the same time, grab the pan's handle with your free hand and shake it to and fro. When the eggs are almost but not completely set, remove the pan from the heat and smooth the surface of the eggs with a spatula. Loosen the omelette from the pan by running a spatula around the sides of the skillet. Tip the omelette to slide the eggs to one side of the pan and, using the spatula, gently fold one-third of the omelette onto itself. Hold the pan over a plate, slide and roll the omelette onto the plate so that it is now folded in three (like a letter) and lands seam-side down.

Brush the omelette with butter and give yourself a pat on the back.

ROASTED CHICKEN *or* BEEF STOCK
makes 12–15 cups (3–3.75 L)

....

5 lb (2.2 kg) meaty bones, cut into 2- to
 3-inch (5–8 cm) chunks (in the case of
 beef, ask your butcher to do this for you)
Bouquet garni (handful of parsley stems,
 bay leaves and fresh thyme, tied together
 with kitchen string)
2 bay leaves
½ tsp (2.5 mL) whole peppercorns
2 small onions, peeled and quartered
3 carrots, peeled and coarsely chopped
1 celery rib, coarsely chopped

ONE OF the most important lessons I learned at culinary school was how to make a good stock. It's a simple task but one that makes the difference between mediocre and fabulous soups, stews and sauces.

Tossing a roasted chicken or turkey carcass into a pot of water makes a perfectly good stock but you'll have more flavourful results if you start with raw, meaty bones. Take it a step further and roast the bones, and you'll have the richest stock imaginable.

A good cleaver will serve for chopping chicken bones into manageable pieces but some butchers, if you ask nicely, will chop them for you. I use chicken stock most often, even in recipes like beef stew, because it's more economical and tastier than anything you'll find in a box or cube.

This recipe is for a traditional stock but it's not a rigid formula. If I have a ham bone, I may add it to the chicken bones. If I'm pressed for time, I'll skip the roasting part and leave the bones raw or use half-raw and half-roasted. Sometimes I'll roast the vegetables, other times I'll omit them altogether. It's all very flexible.

Once the stock is made, it can be reduced and concentrated until it reaches a syrup-like consistency, then poured into molds, as pictured on the following page. It freezes well and can be added to anything that needs a flavour boost. Just don't salt your stock, or it will be over-salted when it's reduced.

....

■ The following instructions are for a rich roasted stock. For a lighter stock, simply omit the roasting instructions.

Preheat oven to 350° F (175°C).

Scatter the meaty bones in a single layer on a baking sheet. (Note: do not line the tray with parchment or foil for easy clean-up. There's a lot of flavour in the roasted bits of meat that stick to the bottom of the pan, and they're key to a rich tasting stock.) Roast until browned, turning the bones as necessary to colour them evenly. This can take up to 1 hour.

When the bones are golden, transfer them to a stockpot. Drain the fat from the roasting pan and place the pan directly on the stove, over medium-high heat, straddling 2 burners if necessary. Add just enough water, about ⅓cup (80 mL), to loosen any bits of meat stuck to the bottom of the pan, then scrape the pan clean with a flat-edged wooden spoon or spatula. Pour the liquid into the stockpot, bits and all.

. . . recipe continued

. . . Roasted Chicken or Beef Stock (cont.)

Add the bouquet garni and enough cold water to cover the bones by 1 inch (2.5 cm).

Bring the stock to a simmer, uncovered, for 3–4 hours (6–8 hours for beef stock), adjusting the heat as necessary to maintain a bare simmer. Using a ladle or large spoon, skim and discard any foam that rises to the surface of the pot. Add additional water as necessary to keep the bones covered. The stock should not boil, as this tends to cloud the stock.

While the stock is simmering, spread the vegetables on a lightly greased roasting pan in a single layer and roast until golden, turning the vegetables as necessary to colour them evenly. Add the roasted vegetables to the stock towards the last 40 minutes of simmering.

To test the stock, ladle a ¼ cup (60 mL) stock into a cup and season with a light pinch of salt. Taste, and if the stock needs more flavour, continue to simmer.

When you are satisfied with the flavour, strain the stock through a colander and discard the bones and vegetables. Pass the liquid again through a strainer lined with cheesecloth into a clean container.

Cool the stock quickly by placing the container of stock into a larger bowl filled with ice water. Once cooled, place in the refrigerator overnight or long enough for the fat to solidify and form a layer on top. Remove the solidified fat with a spoon and discard.

The stock, now somewhat gelatinous, can be used immediately or portioned into freezer bags and frozen until ready to use.

If you wish to reduce the stock, transfer it to a large, wide saucepan, and boil until it reaches a syrup-like consistency. Pour into flexible muffin molds or ice cube trays and freeze until ready to use.

HALIBUT STOCK

makes about 8 cups (2 L)

....

3 Tbsp (45 mL) vegetable oil

2 onions, roughly chopped

2 stalks celery, roughly chopped

2 leeks, white part only, roughly chopped

1 fennel bulb, roughly chopped

4 whole garlic cloves, peeled and bruised
   with the side of a knife

1 cup (250 mL) dry white wine

2½–3 lb (6–8 cm) fresh halibut trim, collar
   and bones, chopped into 2- to 3-inch
   (5–8 cm) chunks, rinsed in cold water

Bouquet garni (a few sprigs of fresh thyme,
   a generous handful of fresh parsley
   [including stems] and a couple bay leaves
   bundled together with kitchen string)

1 tsp (5 mL) whole peppercorns

Cold water

YOU CAN make a good stock from most any fish, with the exception of oily fish like salmon, but I prefer the clean taste of halibut. Most fish sellers receive a steady supply of fresh halibut during spring and summer and they don't mind saving the trim, meaty collar and bones, if you ask for them. The cost is minimal and everyone is happy to put the bones to good use.

Halibut bones are large and difficult to cut through, so ask your supplier to chop the bones into 2- to 3-inch (5–8 cm) chunks.

....

◾ Heat the oil in a large stockpot over medium heat. Gently cook the onions, celery, leeks, fennel and garlic until the vegetables soften slightly, without browning. Add the wine and continue to cook until the wine has evaporated by about half. Add the fish bones and cook gently for a few minutes until the meat on the fish bones starts to turns opaque. Add the bouquet garni, peppercorns and enough cold water to just cover the ingredients.

Bring the stock to a gentle simmer and continue to simmer for 30 minutes, removing any foam that rises to the surface with a spoon or ladle. The stock should not boil.

Strain the stock and discard the solids. Use immediately or refrigerate for up to 3 days. The stock can also be stored in plastic freezer bags and kept frozen for up to 4 months.

Before using, skim any semi-solid fat that rises to the surface.

FLAKY PASTRY DOUGH

makes enough pastry for 1 double-crust pie

2¾ cups (685 mL) all-purpose flour

1 tsp (5 mL) table salt

½ lb (250 g) lard or solid vegetable
   shortening, cut into 1-inch
   (2.5 cm) pieces

1 egg, room temperature

1 Tbsp (15 mL) white vinegar

Ice cold water

SPECIAL EQUIPMENT
Pastry blender (optional)

THE KEY to flaky pastry is a light touch and the minimal use of flour.

If you roll the dough between a sheet of lightly floured parchment paper and plastic wrap (plastic on top to see the dough) you won't need additional flour to prevent the dough from sticking to your work surface or rolling pin. This also prevents excessive handling of the dough.

You can easily double this recipe, but if you're not accustomed to making pastry then it's best to start with this smaller, more manageable amount.

Flaky pastry is featured in Ratatouille Pie (page 90), Chicken Pot Pies (page 207), Deep Dish Ham and Vegetable Quiche (page 72) and Rhubarb Pie with Apple and Ginger (page 55).

■ Place the flour and salt in a large bowl and mix to combine. Add the lard or shortening and cut the fat into the flour with a pastry blender or 2 knives until the mixture is crumbly—there should be some larger pieces of fat among the (mostly) finer particles.

In a spouted measuring jug, combine the egg, vinegar and enough ice water to equal 1 cup (250 mL); mix with a fork. Gradually pour about half the liquid into the flour and mix with a fork, adding only enough additional water to make the dough cling together in an untidy mass. You won't use all the water—you'll have anywhere from ¼–½ cup (60–125 mL) leftover.

When the dough becomes too difficult to mix with a fork, transfer it to a lightly floured work surface and shape into a disc about 1 inch (2.5 cm) thick. Cover with plastic wrap and refrigerate for at least 1 hour.

The dough is now ready to roll out and use in your favourite recipe. Pastry dough can be stored in the fridge for 2 days or in the freezer for up to 6 weeks.

SWEET TART DOUGH

makes enough dough for two 10-inch (25 cm) tarts or forty-eight 2-inch (5 cm) tarts

1 cup + 2 Tbsp (280 mL) unsalted butter
   (room temperature)
1 cup (250 mL) sugar
¼ tsp (1 mL) table salt
2 large eggs, room temperature
3½ cups (875 mL) all-purpose flour

SPECIAL EQUIPMENT
Electric mixer (optional)

SWEET TART dough comes together easily and provides a firm and buttery base for your favourite tart filling. Using butter rather than shortening makes a delicious but delicate pastry with a crisp cookie-like texture.

Roll the dough between parchment paper and plastic wrap (plastic on top to see the dough) to prevent the dough from sticking to your work surface and rolling pin. If the dough becomes too soft, chill in the refrigerator to firm, then start again.

Sweet tart dough is featured in the Fall Apple Tart (page 158) and Chocolate Hazelnut Tart (page 230) recipes.

■ Combine the softened butter, sugar and salt in the bowl of a standup mixer fitted with a paddle attachment, or a large bowl if mixing by hand.

Add the eggs, one at a time, mixing after each addition. Add the flour all at once and mix until the dough just comes together.

Transfer the dough to a lightly floured work surface and shape it into a disc about 1 inch (2.5 cm) thick. Cover with plastic wrap and refrigerate for at least 1 hour.

The dough is now ready to roll out and use in your favourite recipe. Pastry dough can be stored in the fridge for 2 days or in the freezer for up to 6 weeks.

HANDCRAFTED PUFF PASTRY

makes about 3½ lb (1.6 Kg)

....

BUTTER

1 lb (454 g) unsalted butter
(room temperature)

1½ oz (45 g) all-purpose flour

DOUGH

21 oz (600 g) all-purpose flour + extra
as needed

2½ oz (75 g) unsalted butter
(room temperature)

2½ tsp (12.5 mL) table salt

13–14 oz (375–400 g) cool water + extra
as needed

SPECIAL EQUIPMENT

Electric mixer (optional)

Kitchen scale

PUFF PASTRY is a recipe you might not consider making from scratch, but it's so much better than store bought that you'll be glad you did. It's like comparing margarine to butter—the two are not the same.

Puff pastry takes time but it's not difficult once you understand the ingenuity of laminated dough. Simply put, one slab of butter is sandwiched, or laminated, between two layers of dough. The "sandwich" is then rolled into a rectangle and folded in three, as you might fold a letter. This process is repeated a total of six times, with a resting period between folds.

This technique creates a multi-layered pastry separated by butter. In a hot oven, the butter creates steam that pushes up the individual layers to create the pastry's magical puff.

The secret to working with the dough is managing the butter's temperature: too warm and it will squish out the sides when you roll it, too cold and the pastry will tear. If you think of your fridge as the means for firming up your butter and your countertop as the butter softener, you can move the dough between the two to manage it at its most pliable. It takes a bit of practice but you'll get comfortable after the first fold.

I've offered instructions for mixing the dough with a standup mixer but it can be made just as easily by hand.

The ingredients are listed in weights, rather than conventional measurements because a scale yields the best results. I've reasoned that anyone keen enough to attempt this recipe will have, or not mind purchasing, a kitchen scale.

Plan to make puff pastry over a day or two.

Puff pastry is featured throughout the book in Pastry Straws (page 48), Patchwork Tart (page 104), Peach Tarts with Honey Rum Mascarpone (page 111), Mushroom Lover's Tart (page 145) and Vegetable Pot Pies (page 83).

....

▢ BUTTER Blend together the butter and flour in the bowl of a standup mixer fitted with a paddle attachment. Scrape the butter mixture onto to a sheet of plastic wrap or parchment paper and smooth into a rectangle about 6 × 8 inches (15 × 20 cm) in size. Wrap and refrigerate.

DOUGH Using the same bowl in which the butter was mixed, combine the flour, butter and salt until the butter forms small nuggets in the flour.

Replace the paddle with the dough hook and add 13 oz (390 g) water, mixing on low speed for about 3 minutes. If the dough is not holding together, add additional water by the spoonful. If the dough sticks to the hook or the sides of the bowl, add additional flour by the spoonful.

When the dough comes off the sides of the bowl easily, transfer the dough (still rough at this stage) to a sheet of parchment paper dusted with flour.

. . . recipe continued

. . . Handcrafted Puff Pastry (cont.)

Roll the dough into a 12- × 16-inch (30 × 40 cm) rectangle (or the size of your baking sheet). Add additional flour as necessary to prevent the dough from sticking to the rolling pin. Brush off any excess flour, place on a baking sheet, cover with plastic wrap and refrigerate for at least 30 minutes.

After the dough has rested, transfer it to a lightly floured sheet of parchment paper. Use the parchment paper, as pictured, to keep the rectangle's edges straight and the corners square.

Remove the butter from the fridge and, when it's malleable, place it on half of the dough; fold the remaining dough over the butter, like a butter sandwich.

Seal the edges by pinching them together and roll the dough into a rectangle about 12 × 16 inches (30 × 40 cm) or the size of your baking sheet, dusting with flour as necessary and aiming for straight edges and square corners. Brush off any excess flour. If it's difficult to roll the dough, the butter may be too firm. Cover and leave at room temperature until the butter is more manageable.

After you've rolled the dough into a rectangle, place on a baking sheet, cover with plastic and refrigerate for at least 40 minutes.

After the dough has rested, transfer it to a lightly floured sheet of parchment. Brush off any excess flour and fold the dough into thirds, as you would a letter; cover with plastic and refrigerate. This is your first completed "turn" (in pastry-speak). You'll need a total of six turns.

If you're still with me, the rest is rote: roll out the folded dough and shape into a rectangle about 12 × 16 inches (30 × 40 cm), fold in thirds again (as you would a letter), refrigerate at least 40 minutes and repeat the entire process a total of 6 times.

To help remember which turn it is, make an indentation in the dough with your fingerprint before resting the dough in the fridge: one fingerprint for each completed turn.

Each time the dough is rolled out, keep the folded seam on the same side. This technique helps your pastry rise evenly by stretching the gluten in the flour in equal directions.

Make sure the dough is well covered with plastic wrap, in the fridge, otherwise it will dry and crack. You can leave the dough refrigerated between intervals anywhere from 40 minutes to 12 hours, so don't worry about finishing the dough in 1 day.

When you've completed 6 turns, cover and refrigerate up to 2 days or freeze for later use.

Use as you would with standard pastry dough.

FRESH PASTA

makes about 1 lb (450 g), enough for 4–6 servings

2 cups (500 mL) all-purpose flour + extra
  for kneading
1 tsp (5 mL) table salt
2 eggs
¼ cup (60 mL) water + extra as needed

SPECIAL EQUIPMENT
Rolling pin or pasta roller (manual
  or electric)

IN CULINARY school we had to roll fresh pasta dough with a rolling pin until our arms ached. Later, I marvelled at the ease of using a hand-cranked machine. These days, I feed pasta dough through a pasta attachment on my standup mixer that presses out paper-thin dough with astonishing speed. Whatever you use to roll out pasta, there's something very gratifying about making your own.

Fresh pasta is featured in Ravioli with Pea Shoot Pesto (page 26), mushroom ragù (page 150) and Creamy Tomato Sauce (page 38).

◼ Combine the flour and salt in a large wide bowl, or directly on a countertop, and mix with a fork. Make a shallow well into the middle of the flour and crack the eggs directly into it. Add the water and mix with a fork, gathering more flour as you mix. When the dough becomes too unwieldy to mix with a fork, use your hands to work the dough and gather any loose bits of flour. Add an additional 1–3 Tbsp (15–45 mL) water by the spoonful, as necessary, just until the dough comes together in a ragged ball. If using a bowl, turn the dough onto a clean, flour-dusted work surface.

Knead the dough until smooth, about 3–5 minutes. Gather the dough into a ball, cover with plastic wrap and rest for an hour at room temperature.

If using a rolling pin, cut off a manageable-sized piece of dough and roll it onto a flour-dusted work surface as thinly and evenly as possible. Cover the ball of dough with plastic wrap or a tea towel to prevent it from drying out.

If using a pasta machine, cut off a manageable-sized portion of dough, dust it with flour, and feed it through the machine's rollers at its widest setting (#1). Fold the pasta in half, dust with more flour and repeat. Gradually narrow the rollers after each feed, flouring as necessary to prevent sticking, until the pasta is smooth and thin (about #6 on the roller's setting).

Repeat with the balance of the dough, covering the dough to prevent it from drying out. Cut the dough into desired shapes.

If serving immediately, toss the fresh pasta into a large pot of rapidly boiling, generously salted water for 1–2 minutes. Drain and serve.

If not using immediately, let the pasta dry for 1 hour or more on parchment paper dusted with flour, or draped over racks or chair rungs that have been protected with parchment paper. Fettuccine-sized pasta can be fashioned into little nests and dusted with flour to prevent sticking. Store pasta between sheets of parchment in plastic freezer bags. Refrigerate for up to 2 days or freeze up to 2 weeks.

Frozen pasta needs no thawing, but it will take about 1 or 2 minutes longer to cook.

WHOLE WHEAT PIZZA DOUGH

makes two 9-inch (23 cm) pizzas

....

½ tsp (2.5 mL) quick-rise (instant) yeast

1 cup (250 mL) lukewarm water

1½ cups (375 mL) white flour

½ cup (125 mL) whole wheat flour

1 tsp (5 mL) sugar

1½ tsp (7.5 mL) salt

2 Tbsp (30 mL) vegetable oil

2 Tbsp (30 mL) plain yogurt

SPECIAL EQUIPMENT

Pizza stone

Wooden paddle

THIS DOUGH comes together very quickly and makes a nice change from a traditional white flour pizza dough. The dough tastes even better after a day in the fridge, so plan to make it the night before you serve it.

If you enjoy pizza, a pizza stone and wooden paddle are a good investment; the stone provides a crisp crust and the paddle makes it easy to get your pizza in and out of the oven without any mishaps.

Pizza dough is featured in the Roasted Cauliflower and Broccoli Pesto Pizza recipe (page 153).

....

◼ Dissolve the yeast in the water in a spouted cup and stir to combine.

Mix the dry ingredients together in a large bowl.

Add the oil and yogurt to the yeast and water, mix well, then pour over the dry ingredients and stir together with a fork. When the mixture becomes too unwieldy, use your hands to gather the dough into a ball, swiping the sides of the bowl with the dough to gather any stray bits of flour.

Turn the dough onto a lightly floured surface and knead for 1–2 minutes until the dough becomes soft and pliable.

Place the dough into a lightly oiled bowl and cover and rest in a warm draft-free area, such as the top of the stove, or in an oven with only the light bulb on, for about 1 hour.

After the dough has rested, knead for about 1 minute, re-shape and return it to the bowl. Cover and refrigerate at least 4 hours, preferably overnight before using.

DINNER BUNS
makes 36–40 buns

2 Tbsp (30 mL) quick-rise (instant) yeast

3 cups (750 mL) lukewarm water

½ cup (125 mL) sugar

6 Tbsp (90 mL) vegetable oil

2 tsp (10 mL) table salt

2 eggs (room temperature)

7 cups (1.75 mL) all-purpose flour + extra
   as needed

½ cup (125 mL) unsalted melted butter,
   to brush the buns, just before baking

SPECIAL EQUIPMENT

Electric mixer (optional)

Kitchen scale (optional)

To check yeast for freshness (yeast can lose its leavening power over time), mix together 1 tsp (5 mL) yeast with a pinch of sugar in a small cup of lukewarm water. Set-aside for 5 minutes. If foam appears on the surface of the water, your yeast is active, if not, start with a fresh package.

I FIRST enjoyed these light and airy dinner buns when my good friend, Noreen, made them for me. I loved them so much I convinced her to teach a bread-making course at my former cooking school, French Mint. This recipe has been in Noreen's family for years and was generously passed along by their family friend, Jackie Price.

This dough is also used for the Sticky Buns recipe (page 164).

■ Arrange the oven racks into the middle and lower positions and preheat oven to 360°F (180°C)

In the bowl of a standup mixer, or a deep mixing bowl if mixing by hand, combine the yeast with the water, sugar, oil, salt and eggs; whisk together until there are no traces of yeast. Using the dough hook attachment (or a sturdy wooden spoon if mixing by hand) start with about 4 cups (1 L) flour and gradually add a total of 7 cups (1.75 L), or more as necessary, allowing the dough to come together and pull away from the edge of the bowl, about 3–4 minutes. The dough will be very sticky.

Whether you're using a machine or not, finish kneading the dough by hand. Turn the dough out onto a lightly floured surface, incorporating more flour as needed until the dough is smooth, about 5–7 minutes. The dough will be slightly sticky.

Shape the dough into a ball and place into a lightly oiled bowl; rotate the dough to cover it with a light film of oil. Loosely cover with a damp towel and allow the dough to rise in a warm draft-free area.

When the dough has doubled in size, after about 20 minutes, gently punch the dough down a few times to deflate it. Reshape the dough into a ball, cover and allow it to rise until it has doubled again, about 20 minutes. Gently punch the dough again then shape into balls about 1½ inches (4 cm) in diameter. If you're a stickler for uniformity, and own a kitchen scale, divide the dough into 2-oz (60 g) portions.

There are many methods to shaping buns and this is the one that works for me: make a circle with your index finger and thumb (like an okay sign) and push a 2-oz (60 g) portion of dough up and through the circle using the thumb of your free hand. Remove your thumb and squeeze the hand holding the dough to shape it into a ball. To prevent the dough from sticking, moisten your hands with water as necessary.

Arrange the buns on two parchment-lined baking sheets, leaving about 1 inch (2.5 cm) between each bun. Brush the entire surface of each bun with melted butter.

Allow the dough to rise again just until the buns start to touch each other.

Place each baking sheet on separate oven racks and bake for about 20–25 minutes or until browned. At the halfway point, switch the positions of the baking sheets (lower baking sheet moves to middle rack) to promote even browning.

POTATO GNOCCHI

makes 8 servings

....

5 large Russet potatoes (about 2½–3 lb
    [1.2–1.4 kg]), washed but not peeled
1 egg, lightly beaten
2 tsp (10 mL) kosher salt
1¾ cups (435 mL) all-purpose flour
    (approx.), divided

SPECIAL EQUIPMENT
Potato ricer or a food mill
Food processor (for the Kale Gnocchi)

HAND-CRAFTED gnocchi is light and tender and nothing like the dense vacuum-sealed gnocchi found at the grocer.

The trick to keeping gnocchi light is to work the dough briefly and with little flour. Once you get a feel for this base recipe you can tinker with additions like kale (see below).

Gnocchi can be prepared in advance and reheated just before serving.

....

■ Preheat the oven to 350°F (175°C).

Pierce the whole potatoes with a fork and bake until tender, about 1 hour. (Alternatively, peel, chop and boil the potatoes until tender).

While the potatoes are still warm, peel and press them through a ricer or food mill into a large bowl. Add the egg, salt and about half the flour. Mix with a fork until a soft dough starts to come together.

Turn the dough onto a flour-dusted work surface and gradually incorporate just enough flour to form a soft, pliable dough. You may not need all the flour. Knead briefly, just until the dough comes together.

Divide into 8 equal parts and, using the palms of your hands, roll each portion into a rope about ¾ inch (2 cm) thick × 12 inches (30 cm) long. Line up the "ropes" and cut them into ¾-inch (2 cm) pieces. You can either leave the pieces smooth or etch grooves in them by pressing each portion against the tines of a fork or a gnocchi paddle. (The groves help the sauce cling to the dumpling.) Spread the gnocchi on a flour-dusted baking sheet.

Bring a large pot of salted water to a boil and drop small batches of gnocchi into the water, being mindful not to overcrowd the pot. As soon as they float to the surface, remove immediately with a slotted spoon. If left too long, they'll disintegrate.

Toss with your favourite sauce and serve. Pre-cooked gnocchi can be pan-fried, if desired.

If not serving immediately, plunge the just-cooked gnocchi into a bowl of ice-cold water and drain well. Toss with a bit of vegetable oil, cover and refrigerate.

If freezing, place the gnocchi on a baking sheet until firm, then transfer to a plastic freezer bag. Gnocchi does not require thawing before reheating.

KALE GNOCCHI

1 bunch kale, rinsed, with stems
    and core removed
1 recipe Potato Gnocchi (above)

■ Plunge the greens into in a large pot of rapidly boiling, salted water for about 3 minutes, then transfer to a bowl of cold water. Drain and squeeze dry. Compressed, you should have a green clump about the size of a tennis ball. Process the greens in a food processor or chop very finely by hand.

Stir the greens into the warm, just-processed potatoes at the same time as the egg, salt and flour. Mix with a fork until a soft dough starts to come together and continue with the recipe.

FLOUR TORTILLAS

makes 8 tortillas

....

9 oz (270 g) all-purpose flour or 5 oz
    (150 g) all-purpose flour combined with
    4 oz (120 g) whole wheat flour
1 tsp (5 mL) kosher salt
¼ tsp (1 mL) baking powder
2 oz (60 g) lard or vegetable shortening,
    or 1 oz (30 g) olive oil
4½ oz (135 g) warm water (they're difficult
    to roll if the water is cool)

SPECIAL EQUIPMENT
Pastry blender (optional)

I NEVER considered making tortillas until my friend, Gail White, offered me a batch she had freshly baked, along with this recipe. Since then, I've made them about once a month—they're handy for lunches and snacks and freeze beautifully. You don't need any special equipment, just a rolling pin, a hot dry skillet and a bit of practice.

I make tortillas with lard, but switch to olive oil or vegetable shortening when cooking for vegetarian friends. Sometimes I use just white flour, other times I'll add whole wheat flour to the mix. However you make them, there's no comparison to the mass-produced variety. Authentic hand-rolled tortillas are in a class of their own.

The ingredients are listed by weight for better accuracy and better results.

....

■ Whisk together the flour, salt and baking powder in a large bowl. If using lard, cut the lard into the flour mixture using a pastry blender or fork, until the mixture resembles a coarse meal; if using oil, drizzle it into the flour mixture and mix with a fork until fine clumps are formed. Stir in the warm water with a fork until a shaggy dough forms. If the mixture is too dry, add additional water, 1 tsp (5 mL) at a time.

Turn the dough onto a lightly floured surface and knead until smooth and soft, about 2–3 minutes. Shape the dough into a ball, cover with plastic wrap and rest at room temperature for at least 30 minutes.

Divide the dough into 8 equal portions and form into balls. Using a rolling pin, roll each ball of dough onto a lightly floured surface and shape into thin circles about 8 inches (20 cm) in diameter each. It takes a bit of practice to roll the dough evenly. If you're a stickler for uniformity, place an 8-inch (20 cm) lid over the dough and trim to a perfect circle. Re-roll any excess trim.

Heat a large nonstick skillet over medium heat. Place a tortilla in the hot dry skillet until it bubbles and puffs, about 30 seconds. (The tortilla will shrink.) Pierce any large bubbles that form with the tip of a knife. Flip the tortilla over, with tongs, and cook for another half minute or so until brown spots appear on the bottom. Be careful not to overcook them otherwise they'll become stiff and difficult to fold. Transfer to a plate and cover with a clean tea towel. Repeat with the remaining dough.

Leftovers can be frozen. Separate tortillas between layers of parchment paper and store in freezer bags in your freezer.

MARINATED & QUICK-PICKLED VEGETABLES

MY FONDNESS for marinated and quick-pickled vegetables was rekindled by David Mincey, one of the most imaginative and energetic chefs I had the pleasure of hosting at my cooking school. Chef Mincey included a pickled component in most every dish he demonstrated, creating food as vibrant and colourful as his personality.

Poached, pickled or marinated, you'll appreciate having a head start in the kitchen. Imagine the convenience of having garlic, peeled and poached in oil, ready to use anytime you need it!

MARINATED OLIVES

HOT PICKLED CHERRY PEPPERS

BOOZY DRIED FRUIT

GARLIC POACHED IN OIL

CURRIED PICKLED
VEGETABLES

PICKLED PURPLE CABBAGE

PICKLED
MUSHROOMS

HOT PICKLED CHERRY PEPPERS *makes 2 cups (500 mL)*

2 lb (900 g) small hot cherry
   or Fresno peppers
6 Tbsp (90 mL) vegetable oil
12 larges cloves garlic,
   peeled and left whole
6–8 sprigs thyme
1 cup (250 mL) red wine vinegar
2 Tbsp (30 mL) honey
1 tsp (5 mL) kosher salt

DELICIOUS IN sandwiches, pasta sauce, served with cheese or with an antipasto platter.

■ You'll want to wear food-grade kitchen gloves to handle the peppers. Cut the tops from the peppers and scoop out the seeds using a small spoon.

Heat the oil in a medium skillet over medium-high heat. Add the peppers and cook until their skins start to blister, about 5–10 minutes; shake the pan to prevent burning. Lower the heat and add the garlic and thyme. Cook, partially covered, until the peppers soften and their skin loosens, about 20 minutes depending on their size. Shake the pan occasionally to prevent the garlic from burning.

Transfer the peppers and garlic to a bowl, cover tightly with foil and set aside. Discard the thyme.

Add the vinegar, honey and salt to the skillet and mix well; transfer to a clean jar.

When the peppers have cooled, peel them as you would bell peppers. They're finicky but worth the effort. Place the peeled peppers and garlic into the jar with the vinegar/honey mixture.

Refrigerate for up to 2 weeks.

MARINATED OLIVES *makes 2 cups (500 mL)*

2 cups (500 mL) assorted olives
2 cups (500 mL) extra virgin olive oil
2 sprigs rosemary
2 sprigs thyme
2 fresh Thai chilies or 4 Serrano chilies
4 cloves garlic, peeled and bruised
2 bay leaves
1 tsp (5 mL) whole coriander seeds
1 tsp (5 mL) whole cumin seeds
2 large pieces lemon peel from a clean,
   organic lemon

EXCELLENT PARTY nosh; serve warm with soft goat cheese and crackers or with an antipasto platter.

■ Place all the ingredients in a medium saucepan and warm over low heat until aromatic, about 20 minutes. Strain the olives, reserving the oil, garlic and herbs; serve warm.

Store leftover olives in the oil (with the garlic and herbs) in the refrigerator up to 10 days.

PICKLED MUSHROOMS *makes 2½ cups (625 mL)*

2 Tbsp (30 mL) soy sauce
2 Tbsp (30 mL) fish sauce
3 Tbsp (45 mL) sugar
1 Tbsp (15 mL) hot sauce (such as Sriracha)
½ cup (125 mL) vegetable oil
2 tsp (10 mL) whole cumin seeds
2 tsp (10 mL) whole coriander seeds
2 lb (900 g) button mushrooms, as uniform
   as possible, wiped clean
¾ cup (185 mL) white wine vinegar

IDEAL AS an appetizer, tossed in a pasta sauce or with an antipasto platter.

■ In a small bowl, combine the soy sauce, fish sauce, sugar and hot sauce. Set aside.

Heat ¼ cup (60 mL) oil in a large skillet over medium heat. Add the cumin and coriander seeds; when the spices release their fragrance, about 1–2 minutes, add enough mushrooms to fit the pan in a single layer. Cook the mushrooms in batches, until softened, about 6–8 minutes, adding the additional oil as necessary to prevent them from sticking to the pan. When all the mushrooms have been cooked, return them to the pan, add the hot sauce mixture and continue cooking over medium-high heat until the liquid has almost evaporated and the mushrooms appear lacquered. Turn off the heat, add the vinegar and stir to combine.

When the mushrooms have cooled, transfer them and the liquid to a clean jar. Store in the refrigerator for up to 2 weeks.

GARLIC POACHED IN OIL *makes about 1 cup (250 mL)*

1 cup (250 mL) peeled garlic (about
   35 cloves or 3 bulbs)
1 cup (250 mL) vegetable or olive oil

JUMP-START your cooking with this mellow but flavourful garlic. Use as you would raw garlic in soups, stews, omelettes, sauces, dressings and stir-frys. The oil is great for salad dressings, bruschetta and anywhere you'd like a hint of mellow garlic.

■ Place whole garlic cloves and oil in a small saucepan. Gently poach on very low heat, uncovered, until the garlic is soft enough to easily pierce with a knife, about 30 minutes. When the garlic and oil have cooled, transfer to a clean jar and store in the refrigerator. Use within a week.

PICKLED PURPLE CABBAGE *makes 8–10 cups (2–2.5 L)*

1 cup (250 mL) white wine vinegar

¼ cup (60 mL) sugar

2 tsp (10 mL) kosher salt

Pinch of dried chili flakes + extra if you
    enjoy spice

½ red cabbage, thinly sliced

1 medium red onion, thinly sliced

PERKS UP salads, sandwiches and wraps. Delicious finely chopped and tossed with lentils, nuts and goat cheese.

◼ Heat the vinegar, sugar, salt and chili flakes in a small saucepan over medium heat, just until the sugar dissolves.

Toss the cabbage and onion in a large bowl. Pour the warm vinegar mixture over the vegetables and toss to coat. Transfer the vegetables, and the liquid, to a clean jar. Store in the refrigerator for up to 2 weeks.

To serve, strain the cabbage and onions, reserving the liquid for another use, and toss the strained cabbage with a bit of oil. Taste and season with additional salt, if desired.

The liquid can be used to start a new batch of vegetables or as a dressing base.

BOOZY DRIED FRUIT *makes 1 cup (250 mL)*

1 cup (250 mL) raisins, currants, dried
    apricots or dried figs (or a combination
    of each)

¾–1 cup (185–250 mL) rum or brandy

GIVE ICE cream and baked goods a potent kick with plump spiked fruit. Especially good in muffins, pound cakes, bread puddings, scones and savoury stuffings.

◼ Place your choice of fruit in a glass container and fill with rum or brandy. The fruit can be used immediately but gets better over time. Lasts up to 4 months in the refrigerator.

CURRIED PICKLED VEGETABLES
makes 8–10 cups (2–2.5 L)

¼ cup (60 mL) vegetable oil

1 shallot, chopped

1 heaping Tbsp (about 15 mL) curry powder

6 cloves garlic, sliced

6 small carrots (about 1 lb [450 g]), sliced
    or halved lengthwise

2 chilies (serrano or jalapeño, halved
    lengthwise with seeds removed, or Thai
    chilies left whole)

1 medium cauliflower (about 2 lb [900 g]),
    separated into bite-sized pieces

¾ cup (185 mL) white wine vinegar

1 tsp (5 mL) kosher salt

DELICIOUS PAIRED with cheese, chopped and tossed in salads, with lentils, or as part of an antipasto platter.

■ Heat the vegetable oil in a small saucepan over medium heat and add the shallot and curry powder. Continue to cook until the oil is fragrant with curry, taking care not to scorch the spice. Cool the mixture.

Place the garlic, carrots and chili peppers in a large bowl.

Bring a large pot of heavily salted water to a boil. Add the cauliflower and blanch for a few minutes until the cauliflower has softened slightly but still has a bit of crunch. Drain the cauliflower and, while hot, transfer to the bowl containing the garlic, carrots and peppers. Pour the vinegar over the vegetables, add the salt and toss until well coated. Pour the curry oil through a small strainer onto the pickled vegetables. (The residual curry powder, left in the strainer, can be scraped into a jar, topped with more oil and refrigerated for later use.)

When the vegetables have cooled, transfer them, and the liquid, to a clean container. Store in the refrigerator for up to 2 weeks.

To serve, strain the vegetables, reserving the liquid for another use. Add a pinch of salt and drizzle with additional curry oil if desired.

HOT PICKLED CHERRY
PEPPERS (PAGE 282)

MARINATED OLIVES
(PAGE 282)

PICKLED MUSHROOMS
(PAGE 283)

PICKLED CURRIED VEGETABLES
(PAGE 285)

ANTIPASTO

THE PICKLED vegetables on the forgoing pages make for great antipasto offerings. With everything prepared in advance and served at room temperature, it makes for great party fare.

I serve antipasto buffet-style, with platters of pickled and marinated vegetables, thinly sliced meats, artisan cheeses, bread sticks and a selection of seasonal fruit. It's an all-inclusive meal with enough variety to satisfy dieters, vegans, meat lovers and your gluten-free pals too.

For a more substantial meal, serve antipasto alongside a slow-cooker of Minestrone (page 188), Roasted Squash Soup (page 132) or spicy Clam Chowder (page 134).

CLARIFIED BUTTER

makes ¾ cup (185 mL)

1 lb (450 g) unsalted butter

IF YOU'VE ever burned butter, you'll appreciate having clarified butter on hand. It allows you to fry foods at temperatures that would normally burn butter. It's a simple process of melting the butter and removing the quick-burning milk solids.

Clarified butter also acts as a handy airtight seal for pâtés and Potted Meat (page 127).

◼ Slowly melt the butter in a heavy-bottomed saucepan over low heat until a froth appears on the surface. Remove and discard the froth with a spoon. Slowly pour the clear fat through a strainer lined with cheesecloth into a clean container, being mindful not to include the thin milky residue at the bottom of the saucepan.

Clarified butter keeps for several weeks covered in the refrigerator.

COMPOUND BUTTER
makes about 1 cup (250 mL)

KEEPING A stash of flavoured butters in the freezer is a reliable chefs' trick, and a simple one at that. Mix together softened butter with lemon or vinegar and a few other seasonings and you've got compound butter.

Slice a disc ¼–½ inch (6–10 mm) thick from the butter log and melt it over warm fish, steaks, vegetables, soups and sauces to brighten their flavours and lend a mellow richness.

I've included a few of my favourite flavour combinations, but feel free to play around with the recipe. You can't go wrong—butter goes with everything.

■ In the bowl of a food processor, combine all the ingredients except the butter. When the mixture is finely chopped, add the softened butter and mix well. Alternatively, chop the ingredients finely, place into a bowl, add the softened butter and mix well. Taste with bread or a cracker and season with additional salt, if desired.

To roll the butter into a neat log, place the butter in the centre of a sheet of parchment paper, fold the parchment over the butter then, using a pastry scraper or ruler (or anything with a straight edge) nudge the butter into a neat tight cylinder. Roll the butter in the parchment and twist the edges to secure.

Fresh butter, properly wrapped, lasts up to 1 month in the refrigerator or several months in the freezer.

CILANTRO & JALAPEÑO BUTTER
featured in Chunky Seafood Stew page 76

1½ cups (375 mL) fresh cilantro leaves

¼ cup (60 mL) fresh mint leaves

2 cloves garlic, chopped

2–3 jalapeño peppers, seeds removed and chopped

½ tsp (2.5 mL) sugar

1 tsp (5 mL) kosher salt

¼ cup (60 mL) freshly squeezed lemon juice (about 1 lemon)

1 cup (250 mL) unsalted butter (room temperature)

OLIVE & CAPER BUTTER
featured in Halibut Cooked in Parchment page 37

½ cup (125 mL) deli-style whole olives, black and green varieties

3 anchovy fillets, mashed with a fork

2 Tbsp (30 mL) rinsed capers

1½ tsp (7.5 mL) hot smoked paprika

1 tsp (5 mL) hot sauce (such as Sriracha)

½ tsp (2.5 mL) sugar

1 tsp (5 mL) kosher salt

¼ cup (60 mL) freshly squeezed lemon juice (about 1 lemon)

1 cup (250 mL) unsalted butter (room temperature)

SUN-DRIED TOMATO BUTTER
featured in Poached Salmon in a Tomato Wine Broth page 87

2 Tbsp (30 mL) chopped sun-dried tomatoes

2 cloves garlic, chopped

½ tsp (2.5 mL) granulated sugar

1 tsp (5 mL) kosher salt

1 Tbsp (15 mL) red wine vinegar

1 cup (250 mL) unsalted butter (room temperature)

HORSERADISH BUTTER
delicious on grilled steak

3 Tbsp + 1 tsp (50 mL) creamed horseradish

1 tsp (5 mL) Dijon-style mustard

1 tsp (5 mL) kosher salt

1 tsp (5 mL) freshly squeezed lemon juice

Pinch of chopped thyme leaves

1 cup (250 mL) unsalted butter (room temperature)

LEMON & HERB BUTTER
featured in Spot Prawns page 17

½ cup (125 mL) fresh herbs (tarragon, dill, parsley, cilantro)

½ clove garlic, finely minced

1 tsp (5 mL) kosher salt

¼ tsp (1 mL) sugar

¼ cup (60 mL) freshly squeezed lemon juice (about 1 lemon)

1 cup (250 mL) unsalted butter (room temperature)

SPECIAL EQUIPMENT
Food processor (optional)

CILANTRO AND
JALAPEÑO BUTTER

OLIVE AND
CAPER BUTTER

HORSERADISH
BUTTER

SUN-DRIED
TOMATO BUTTER

LEMON AND
HERB BUTTER

CRÈME ANGLAISE

PASTRY CREAM
LIGHTENED WITH WHIPPING CREAM

CRÈME ANGLAISE & PASTRY CREAM LIGHTENED *with* WHIPPING CREAM

CRÈME ANGLAIS and Pastry Cream are staples in professional pastry kitchens because they're easy to make, can be refrigerated for days, and flavoured with just about anything—lemon, chocolate, fruit purees, spices and coffee to name a few possibilities. Their cooking methods are similar but Pastry Cream is thickened with flour, making it firm enough to fill pastries and tarts, and Crème Anglais is light enough to pour.

I prefer Pastry Cream "lightened" with whipped cream as only the French can say with a straight face. It transforms a thick custard into a light and creamy one and is well worth the extra calories.

CRÈME ANGLAISE *makes 1 cup (250 mL)*

1 cup (250 mL) whole milk
5 Tbsp (75 mL) sugar
3 large egg yolks

■ Before you start, place a fine-mesh strainer over a spouted jug, to strain the warm cream.

Heat the milk with half the sugar in a small saucepan over medium heat. Bring to a boil, then remove from the heat.

Whisk the yolks with the balance of the sugar in a small bowl until smooth. Add about half the warm milk, mix well and return the mixture to the saucepan of milk.

Cook over medium heat without boiling, stirring constantly, until the cream thickens and lightly coats the back of a spoon. Pour the sauce through the strainer, into the jug.

If not serving immediately, nestle the jug of cream in a bowl of ice water. When the cream has cooled, cover and refrigerate up to 3 days. Serve chilled or gently reheated (without boiling).

PASTRY CREAM LIGHTENED *with* WHIPPING CREAM *makes 3 cups (750 mL)*

1½ cups (375 mL) whole or 2% milk
⅓ cup (80 mL) sugar, divided
3 egg yolks
3 Tbsp (45 mL) all-purpose flour
1 cup (250 mL) whipping cream

■ Heat the milk in a medium saucepan and stir in about half the sugar. Bring to a simmer, then remove the pan from the heat.

Combine the yolks in a small bowl with the remaining sugar and whisk until smooth. Add the flour and mix until well incorporated (the mixture will be very thick at this stage). Thin with half the warm milk, mix well and pour the mixture back into the saucepan.

Stir constantly over medium heat with a small whisk or a wooden spoon—the mixture will thicken as it cooks. When the custard comes to a boil, stir for 1 continuous minute, then remove from heat and transfer to a bowl to cool. Cover and refrigerate up to 3 days.

When ready to serve, re-whip the custard to loosen it (it will be very thick). Whip the cream to a soft peak and fold it into the custard, in 2 or 3 batches, until well combined.

MAYONNAISE

makes ½ cup (125 mL) with the small batch method or
1½ cups (375 mL) with the blender method

HOMEMADE MAYONNAISE is one of the most underrated and versatile sauces imaginable. Think of it as a creamy canvas for everything from minced garlic to fiery chipotle peppers.

Because real mayonnaise contains raw eggs, make only enough to use within a day or two.

If you can get through a big batch, say 1½ cups (375 mL), within 48 hours, you can prepare it in a blender or food processor. Otherwise you'll need to whisk it by hand, the old-fashioned way. The blender or food processor method provides a slightly thicker version, but both taste the same. However you make your mayonnaise, the eggs and oil must be at room temperature.

Note: If you have a compromised immune system or are concerned with the risks associated with raw egg consumption, do not make mayonnaise.

SMALL BATCH METHOD

2 large egg yolks, room temperature
2 tsp (10 mL) Dijon-style mustard
½ cup (125 mL) vegetable oil
1½ tsp (7.5 mL) white wine vinegar
¼ tsp (1 mL) kosher salt

■ To secure your bowl in place while you whisk the eggs, create a "nest" with a damp tea towel and nestle your bowl in it. Alternatively, place your bowl in a saucepan snug enough to hold it in place—put a tea towel between the bowl and saucepan to prevent them from sticking together.

Whisk together the egg yolks and mustard, in the secured bowl, until absolutely smooth.

Starting with just a few drops, add the oil whilst continuously whisking, adding more oil drop by drop. Gradually drizzle the oil in a narrow stream, whisking all the while. It takes a few minutes of continuous whisking to incorporate all of the oil—you may need to give your arm a rest now and then. By the time you add all of the oil, you should have a smooth thickened mixture, but not quite as thick as the store-bought varieties.

Add vinegar and salt. Taste and season with additional salt, if desired. Store covered in the fridge and consume within 48 hours.

BLENDER *or* FOOD PROCESSOR METHOD

3 large fresh egg yolks (room temperature)
1 Tbsp (15 mL) Dijon-style mustard
1½ cups (375 mL) vegetable oil
1 Tbsp + 1½ tsp (22.5 mL) white wine vinegar
¼ tsp (1 mL) kosher salt

SPECIAL EQUIPMENT
Food processor or blender (optional)

■ Place the egg yolks and mustard into the food processor or blender and mix until smooth. With the motor running, add the oil in a slow narrow stream, the mixture will thicken as more oil is added.

Add vinegar and salt. Taste and season with additional salt, if desired. Store covered in the fridge and consume within 48 hours.

dollop

smidgen

dash

MAYONNAISE CAN be flavoured with just about anything:
Roasted or raw garlic, toasted cumin, capers, mustard, wasabi, horseradish, honey and mustard, minced shallots,
chipotle peppers, fresh ginger, pickled beets, chili sauce, lemon or lime juice, roasted bell peppers, miso paste,
tomato paste, chopped herbs, chopped olives, avocados, anchovies, grated Parmesan, curry paste, pickled ginger,
apple cider, sun-dried tomatoes, coriander . . .

BEST DRESSED

IT ALWAYS strikes me as funny when I see someone dress a large salad in a small bowl, a near impossible feat.

Just before serving, place your rinsed and dried salad greens in a ridiculously large bowl. Add just enough dressing to lightly coat the salad greens, then grasp the bowl with both hands and give it a few sharp jerks so that the salad tosses into the air and coats itself with dressing. If you're not feeling adventurous, use tongs instead.

Transfer the tossed salad to a salad bowl or platter and serve additional dressing on the side.

If you wish to serve your salad chilled, place your serving bowl and salad plates in the refrigerator before serving.

Don't forget to whisk or shake the dressing and taste-test it with a lettuce leaf before using.

When you're staring blankly into the fridge wondering what to make for dinner, a good dressing can spark your imagination.

The following dressings, pestos and vinaigrettes appear throughout the book. We've brought them together so you can pick and choose your favourite to use however you like.

HOUSE DRESSING

White wine vinegar and Dijon-style mustard is a classic dressing and a staple in our house. Great with mixed greens and blanched or roasted vegetables. See page 21 for recipe.

CAPER GARLIC DRESSING

Pickled capers and garlic go beautifully with hearty mixed greens, blanched vegetables, fish, chicken, lentils and pasta. See page 31 for recipe.

SESAME DRESSING

Fresh ginger, garlic and soy sauce make this Asian-inspired dressing the perfect complement for raw vegetables, fish, quinoa, orzo, rice and noodles. See page 191 for recipe.

GARLICKY MISO DRESSING

This earthy and garlicky dressing is fantastic with blanched vegetables or drizzled over fish and chicken. See page 71 for recipe.

BROCCOLI PESTO

A hearty, garlicky and nutty pesto packed with flavour; great slathered on sandwiches, pizza and tortillas or mixed with chickpeas. See page 154 for recipe.

PEA SHOOT PESTO

Nuts, lemon and pea shoots give this pesto a fresh, satisfying crunch. Fantastic with crostini and goat cheese or mixed with pasta, rice, orzo or polenta. See page 27 for recipe.

TOMATO CILANTRO PISTOU
Serrano peppers, fresh tomatoes and raw shallots
make for a piquant sauce with enough kick to
liven up soups, fish, chicken and steaks.
See page 189 for recipe.

HAZELNUT VINAIGRETTE
Nutty, earthy hazelnut oil and sherry vinegar
work beautifully in this mellow dressing.
Delicious drizzled on salads, soft cheeses, grains
and beans. See page 29 for recipe.

CILANTRO MINT SAUCE
Fresh ginger, lime and yogurt make this refreshing
sauce ideal for potato croquettes, seafood, chicken and
grilled vegetables. See page 17 for recipe.

PEAR DRESSING
Caramelized pears give this dressing just
the right touch of sweetness for bitter
and hearty greens, duck and roasted pork.
See page 138 for recipe.

PARSLEY DRESSING
Plenty of fresh parsley and lime juice give this tangy
sauce loads of flavour. Brightens beans, fish, chicken and
blanched vegetables. See page 33 for recipe.

MICROPLANE

TONGS

SMALL WHISK

FINE-MESH STRAINER

KITCHEN STRING

MEASURING CUP WITH A SPOUT

CHEESECLOTH

KITCHEN SCALE

VEGETABLE
PEELER

LOW TECH TOOLS

You don't need a lot of fancy gadgets to cook well,
but these practical kitchen tools are invaluable.

SMALL WHISK—for whisking dressings or sauces in small containers

MEASURING CUP WITH A SPOUT—indispensable for sauces

VEGETABLE PEELER—no kitchen is complete without one

MICROPLANE—ideal for zesting citrus fruits and finely grating garlic and ginger

TONGS—makes tossing and turning foods easy (scratch-resistant for nonstick pans)

FINE-MESH STRAINER—for straining soups, sauces and custards

KITCHEN STRING—handy for bundling herbs or trussing meat

CHEESECLOTH—for lining strainers for super clear liquids

KITCHEN SCALE—great for weighing pastry, when precise measurements are required

PARCHMENT PAPER—a nonstick liner for baked or roasted foods

NONSTICK BAKING MAT—sturdy, re-usable and great for easy clean-ups

MORTAR AND PESTLE—for grinding whole spices, smashing garlic and making pesto

ROLLING PIN—tapered-style pins offer more control when rolling dough

PASTRY BLENDER—ideal for blending fat into flour as with pie or tortilla dough

BENCH SCRAPER—handy for baking or whenever flour is used

MORTAR AND PESTLE

ROLLING PIN

NONSTICK
BAKING MAT

PASTRY BLENDER

PARCHMENT
PAPER

BENCH SCRAPER

ACKNOWLEDGEMENTS

WRITING THIS cookbook has not been a solo journey. Behind the scenes were generous volunteers who tested recipes, reviewed text, hosted travel adventures, provided information and cheered us onward with raised whisks and wooden spoons.

Here's to our stellar team of steadfast recipe testers, near and far, who shopped, chopped and made a mess of their kitchens in support of this venture. This book is all the better for your hard work, honest feedback, thoughtful suggestions and dishpan hands.

Thank you doesn't even begin to cover our appreciation for your efforts.

AKEMI AKUTSU

PATRICIA BARBETIA

TAMMY BROWN

DAVE COATES

NOREEN DENNIS

NANCY FROST

DIANA AND MARK GILLIS

BRENDA HAMMOND

CAROLYN HENSON

KARRI HEYWOOD-SMITH

DIANE KALLAL

JEAN LAYLAND

ELISE MARCHESSAULT

LUCIE MARCHESSAULT

NICOLE MARCHESSAULT

PHIL MCEVOY

JANICE MILLER

NANCY PEARSON

SUE AND EMMA PEARSON

MARINA ROGGEVEEN

KIM TURNER

GRACE VAN DEN BRINK

GAIL WHITE

SPECIAL THANKS

MY COOKBOOK partner, Caroline West, whose exceptional photography skills made this project possible. Caroline's eye for detail, sense of style and calm professionalism made every photo session a special event, even when the sun (or stove) was uncooperative. Caroline's outrageous wit often made me laugh until I cried and I can't imagine working with a more generous collaborator. Thank you my friend, it's been a delicious and joyful journey.

Caroline and I would like to jointly thank our publisher, Nick Rundall, Whitecap Books, for believing in our vision and giving us the opportunity to create the book we had envisaged. To Jesse Marchand, Associate Publisher, for her unwavering dedication to this project and to Andrew Bagatella, Designer, for bringing it to life in vivid colour. To Jordie Yow, for his initial direction, and our editor Patrick Geraghty, for giving the manuscript such thoughtful consideration. Patrick's fastidious edits and considerate suggestions brought clarity to my recipes and words. We are grateful.

My husband, Claude, and twin daughters, Lucie and Elise—lifelong recipe testers—who endured weeks of repetitive meals while I endeavoured to get each recipe just right. Thanks for your patience while I focused on the cookbook, and little else, and especially for checking with me first before devouring any work-in-progress. And special thanks to Stephanie, Claudia and Michael, my earliest taste testers, for never complaining about my food, even when it missed the mark.

Marco Khalil, Caroline's husband, for all the heavily lifting, literally and figuratively. Thanks for scouring the countryside to help Caroline find just the right crockery, and for stepping in whenever needed; more than we could have possibly imagined.

Nancy Pearson for her steadfast support from day one, when the cookbook was but a delicious dream. Nancy rallied a group of recipe testers across the country, first for the initial proposal and later for the real thing. Nancy collected feedback, edited countless recipes and tested more than her fair share, all while holding down a full time job and whipping up wedding cakes in her spare time.

Michelle Barker, writing mentor, cheerleader and fearless 'bounty-hunter' (who wrestled excessive 'bounty' references from my text). Thanks for the heartwarming counsel, text polishing and true grit, especially when life took such an unexpected turn. You are wonderful. Can't wait for you to get to Vancouver!

Terra Murdoch, AKA Eagle Eyes, for pouring over countless recipes and tending to persnickety details, all while keeping me entertained with amusing notes and endless debates about ye old salt. Thanks also for years of cooking school assistance and for raising the bar to lofty heights for all the volunteers that followed.

Noreen Dennis, dear friend, long-time cooking school side-kick and go-to-gal for everything from recipe analysis to pasta yield debates. Noreen's witty emails, and photos of plates licked clean, kept me bolstered, especially when things didn't turn out picture perfect.

Kathy McAree, for bringing Caroline into my kitchen and into my life. Your friendship, rollicking support and gift for linking like-minded people was never more appreciated.

Don & Karri Smith, for the memorable adventures on Mudge Island and for touring us around like princesses in a parade, riding high in lawn chairs in the back of your pick-up truck. Thanks to Karri for her first-rate recipe testing, lip-smacking crispy oyster recipe, and steady support, dating back to the days when we sported towering paper toques.

Amber Sessions, stellar snowman-builder and impromptu model, for generously sharing your cozy cottage in Whistler complete with roaring fire and snow falling on cue. There's no better place to photograph a heartwarming bowl of beef stew.

Inge and John Sieger, lifelong friends, for graciously hosting us in Kelowna without a moment's hesitation. Thanks for the delicious meals and for pointing us in the right direction for our Great Okanagan Adventure. More importantly, for the culinary inspiration way back when you first welcomed me to your table and into your generous lives.

Chef Castro Boateng and Chef Janusz Urban for the memorable mushroom outing. Thanks to Castro for sharing your secrets for the best smoked duck imaginable and for all your inspirational cooking lessons. A special nod to Charlotte and Castro for allowing us to photograph your beautiful son Kaeden with the rock star hair.

Bob Hopcott and Hopcott Farms, for allowing us to jump on your cranberry equipment during harvest, take photos and ask endless questions at the most inconvenient of times.

Skipper James Simpson of the Nordic Rand, for being a stellar model along with his feisty spot prawn co-stars.

Catherine and Jim Gowans of Omnivore Acres, for spoiling us with farm fresh eggs and setting the record straight with timely information.

Dianne Driessen of the BC Cranberry Growers Association, for lively cranberry discussions at the outset and for such enthusiastic support.

Cheryl Rule, talented writer and generous friend, for your ongoing support and wise counsel. Thank you for spoiling me in the most thoughtful ways and for turning a tricky header into a scrumptious one.

Mike McDermid and Robert Clark, sustainable seafood gurus and co-owners of Vancouver's The Fish Counter, for sharing their wealth of seafood knowledge.

Pamela Tarlow-Calder for the impromptu invitation, among the chirping birds, to join her writing group. That serendipitous meeting in the park resulted in an avalanche of support for this project, especially towards the finish line. A bouquet of puff pasty straws to Pamela and fellow writers Phillipa Sherill, Courtney Waverick, Jane Miller, Karen Sawatzky and Sylvia Taylor. Special thanks to Sylvia, author of *The Fisher Queen,* whose reverence for British Columbia and its coastal waters shaped this book's preface.

Thank you, dear mermaid, for the timely lessons and great push forward when I was at my wit's end.

Elisa Wirsching, lifelong BFF and steadfast champion, whose unwavering support keeps me focused. Special thanks for the lucky wishbone that saw me through culinary school and still works like a charm.

Sweet sibs, Brenda Pirani, Brian and Robert Bourdages, Louise Anker and Lorette Shea whose love steadies me through all life's ups and downs, inside and outside the kitchen.

Mother-in-law, Mary, for years of long-distance cheerleading and sister-in-law Nicky for following recipe instructions to the letter even when it's not in her nature to do so.

Dear friends, Sue Pearson, Jenni Bass, Carolyn Henson, Akemi Akutsu, Tricia Barbetta, Janice Miller, Mariel Robson and Judy Morris—for their steadfast support in all my culinary adventures; acting alternatively as cooking school assistants, students, enthusiastic promoters, child minders and recipe testers—cheering me forward even when when a move landed me in a wretched kitchen far from theirs.

Caroline's steadfast friends near and far, Libby Sanderson, Christine Kerrigan, Matthew Lipscombe, Jacqueline Foord, Lucy Culliton, Carolyn Lockhart, Louise Wilson, Richard Corman and Stephen Mazonowicz.

Caroline's dear friend, Gina Tyler, for her unwavering support and genuine interest in this project. Thank you for being there for both of us.

Finally, our heartfelt thanks to Andrea Healy, the most elegant of angels, for soaring in at the end and wrapping up the book in the most beautiful of bows.

Lions Gate suspension bridge, Vancouver

INDEX

Oysters at
Mudge Island

Cranberries at
Hopcott Farm

Blueberries at
Westham Island

Denise lives here

Halibut at
Port Renfrew

mushroom hunt

Caroline lives here